To Jon,
I hope the
in this book INSPIRE
you to achieve all your
goals and desires! All the
best with the Novels!
NKB

INSPIRED

Inspired

by

Neo Kalungu-Banda

First published 2021 by

ISBN: 978-1-914002-08-3

Further copies of this book, as well as details of other publications and services, are available from:

www.wordsbydesign.co.uk

All images are the property of the author.

Cover image by Tudor Photography

Email | neokalungubanda@gmail.com

Instagram | neo.kb

Twitter | neo_kb1

Dedication

I dedicate this book to the Kalungu family,
the Banda family
and in memory of my grandfather,
Moses Chanda Kangwa Kalungu.

Contents

Foreword xiii
Editor's Note xv

Prologue 1

Section One: People Who Have Inspired Me

1 Dave 9
2 Mr Bell 16
3 Stormzy 20
4 Drake 23
5 Kevin Hart 35
6 Will Smith 39
7 Mr Atkinson 45
8 The Nazarene 49
9 My Mother 57
10 My Father 59
11 Mr Proudfoot 63
12 Michael Jordan 67
13 LeBron James 79
14 Barack Obama 87
15 The Mandem 95

Section Two: Sharing Inspiration I Have Found within Myself

16	Perception is Key	111
17	My Locked-Down Expedition Adventure	119
18	Stop Caring	131
19	GCSEs	142
20	BGN: The Transition	146
21	My Relationship with Fashion	160
22	Run Before You Walk	177
23	Reflections on Social Media	182
24	My Relationship with Social Media	186
25	Shakespeare for Schools	196
26	Starting University	207

Section Three: Places Which Have Inspired Me

27	Africa	225
28	The Pitch	237
29	Lourdes	263

Section Four: How Time in Lockdown Has Inspired Me

30 My First Week of Lockdown 279
31 The Highlights of Lockdown 290
32 A Ride with Gilbert 294

Section Five: Events that Have Inspired Me

33 My Upbringing 307
34 Small Things Matter 316
35 What's in a Name? 320
36 The Gap 325
37 My Duke of Edinburgh Awards 332
38 The Coronavirus Pandemic: Neo's Take 348
39 It's in the DNA 361
40 Album Mode 367
41 Reflections from Neo: It's Not About Me 379

Afterword 382
References 387
Acknowledgements 390

Foreword

When I met Neo Kalungu-Banda a few years ago, a few minutes into our conversation, I could tell that there was something special about him. There was a sparkle in his eyes as he respectfully bombarded me with one question after another. He wanted to know the behind-the-scenes story that made me into the footballer that I became. He would ask a piercing question and then mobilise every ounce of energy in him to listen to my story.

I am always fascinated by and interested in engaging in dialogue with young people, because I am convinced that we all increase chances of blossoming into what life has in promise for us if there are people who show interest in our story. Although I had never seen Neo on the football pitch, his keen interest in finding out what made someone successful in their field allowed me to see that there was something special that Neo was going to crack in his young life. At the time Neo requested to have a chat with me, he was playing football in England for a local Sunday league team.

I gave Neo as many tips as I could to become a successful footballer. Four years have passed since I have spoken to Neo, and I was pleasantly surprised when I received a request from Neo to write a foreword for his book. That is when I realised that this young man had managed to transfer the lessons and skills I had been trying to share with him during our meeting. I remember sharing with him six key lessons: (1) practice, practice – become a master of the ball; (2) keep extremely physically fit; (3) stay focused; (4) be a team player; (5) be successful with others; (6) failure is part of the deal.

Clearly reading through this book I couldn't help but feel so proud that Neo was able to transfer lessons from football to other aspects. The many stories he captures in the book exemplify both focus and team playing. Focus because he was able to see something special in the likes of Dave and Michael Jordan; team player, because you can see he has circles of friendship that have inspired him. Like I used to do in football, you must see possibility where no one is seeing possibility. Those free-kicks that made me successful, nationally and internationally, were a case of seeing the goal post nearer and wider than the average eye was able to see. It seems for Neo, ordinary friends have much more to offer than just friendship, and that is what makes him see a barber as a source of wisdom and the Banbury Irish football coach as an inspiring leader.

Through this book, Neo has helped me to communicate what I have always wanted to say to young people. If you are focused, disciplined, determined and try to keep as much good health as life allows you to, nothing is impossible. This includes writing a book that captures the depth and breadth of insights that can help one live a fulfilled and responsible life.

Kalusha Bwalya,
African Footballer of the Year 1988

Editor's Note

This first book from up-and-coming new author, Neo Kalungu-Banda, is one of the most insightful, intelligent, thought-provoking and, at times, hilariously funny manuscripts I have ever worked on in my long career as an editor. It is a very impressive work indeed – especially so as Neo completed this brilliant book before his 19th birthday. In addition to his engaging writing style, this young gentleman has wisdom beyond his years and shockingly impressive levels of discipline, focus, and life ethics which we can all learn from.

INSPIRED is a delightful journey through the inspirations Neo has found in his life, through other people, experiences, places, within himself and, indeed, through the time of a global pandemic when the majority of the world was in lockdown due to COVID-19. Within the chapters of this book, Neo tells us a series of both funny and moving stories which allow us to get to know him, so he may share with us the lessons he has learned and the inspirations he has found. Neo handles all subjects with the perfect balance of respect and wit, seriousness and playfulness, self-confidence and the ability to laugh at oneself. He also shares with us some enjoyable and enlightening reader exercises, asking us questions to ponder on within our own lives. I have experienced many "Aha!" moments whilst working on this book, I have cheered, I have laughed, and... I have most certainly felt inspired!

INSPIRED is definitely a book which will grace my own bookshelves and which I shall be recommending to my own friends and family.

Without further ado... we welcome you to discover your own inspiration!

Jules J. Foreman, Editor

Prologue

During my later years of school life – so from year 10 onwards until the end of year 13 – due to the way that I behaved, thought and spoke around certain issues, a few of my classmates would tell me that I came across as quite a motivated person and had quite a motivational persona. A few of them would tell me, "You should become a motivational speaker or something." I was flattered by their words and allowed these types of comments to sit with me as I continued with my life. Here and there, people would tell me, at times, that certain things I did in my own life, or things I said to them, would both inspire them and motivate them. This book is based around inspiration, as opposed to being focused on the theme of motivation.

The reason I decided to base this book around inspiration instead of motivation is because inspiration is a long-term factor whereas motivation is a short-term factor. Inspiration is a driving force that comes from within someone, or is instilled in an individual through multiple means. A person may be inspired due to the way a certain individual lives, or by a place they have visited. Motivation, on the other hand, is an external force and is more of a pulling force for someone wanting to achieve something.

A student may be motivated to do their homework one evening because they know the consequences of not doing their homework will be a detention from their teacher. That same student who was motivated to do their homework that one evening, to avoid a punishment from their teacher, might not be motivated to do their homework weeks from that same point. Say, for instance, that same student was set geography homework to create a poster around the area they live in and that assignment is due in four weeks from the point that it was set. The same person may have been motivated one evening to do their homework to avoid punishment the following day, but they may not be motivated to do their four-week geography assignment over a prolonged period of time – and therein lies the issue. The motivation to do the homework is only temporary, depending on the specific situation the student is in. Now, picture this same student, who only gets motivated to avoid detentions from their teachers when they complete their homework, using inspiration from a professional athlete who said in an interview that they always did their homework when they were younger because they wanted to teach themselves the principle of accountability. After seeing the same interview with the professional athlete, that same student who found it hard to do their homework properly over time and instead only did it the night before its due date to avoid detentions, may be inspired by this elite athlete who they look up to due to their status and the fact that they are being interviewed about their life.

This interview and athlete may be the inspiration the student needed to complete their homework on time, every time they were given an assignment, and it may make the student want to teach themselves the principle of accountability through handing in their homework by the specific deadline. This inspiration from the interview with the athlete has the potential to remain with the student for the rest of their life, as opposed to just one evening. It can be used day after day to give the student the drive and energy required to complete their homework on time and to a good standard – every time.

Inspiration is a far more long-term source of energy and drive than motivation. An inspiring moment, story or person can remain with an individual for decades. This is the reason I have decided to base this book solely around inspiration as opposed to motivation. By the way, that same student who was only motivated to do their homework the night before it was due, to avoid a detention, was me during my early years in secondary school. I was the student who was given a four-week geography project to find out information about the area that I lived and I decided to leave it three weeks and six days before I started working on the project. The motivation I had and used to avoid a detention for not completing my homework may have helped me in not being punished by my geography teacher, but it sure did not help me in scoring a high grade on my poster.

These factors and events mentioned earlier have influenced and persuaded me to attempt writing a book, but there was one specific event that started this entire process. During the early months of 2020, the coronavirus pandemic had hit the world and had become a global pandemic by March. Due to the fact that my A-level exams had been cancelled because of the pandemic, I had a lot of time on my hands while the UK was under lockdown. One day, during the first days of the UK lockdown, I was talking to my good friend Gilbert Healey on a Facetime call. We were discussing the lockdown, the virus, and everything that was going on around the world at the time. One of the things that Gilbert knew about me as an A-level student was that I had plenty of time on my hands now I no longer had to revise and prepare for my exams which were intended to take place in the summer of 2020. Gilbert and I usually like to push each other in whatever it is we are doing in life, so that we can see each other reach our potential. I used to push Gilbert a lot and try to give him advice, as he was an aspiring musician at the time and remains so. Gilbert would always check that all was well with me and my studies throughout the time I was preparing to sit the most important exams for my future.

So, after learning that this process of revising and preparing for exams was no longer possible due to COVID-19 and, therefore, I had a full 24 hours free, Gilbert suddenly bellowed over the phone to me while we were chatting: "You should write a book!" Once he abruptly said this to me, I just sat there and thought: "This guy is crazy. I'm 17 years old and I have barely even lived. What am I going to write a book about?". I soon replied to Gilbert, asking him the same question, "Write a book...what would I even write about?". He hesitantly replied, "Write about your life, maybe". We then left the idea of writing a book and went on to talk about other things. I allowed Gilbert's idea of writing a book to sit with me for some time. I thought about what I would write and include in the book, why I was writing the book, who I was writing the book for, and the entire concept and journey that Gilbert had challenged me to embark upon.

So, on Wednesday 25th March 2020, just after the first lockdown started in the UK, I woke up one morning at 6am, grabbed my laptop from my desk and, remaining in bed, began to simply write my thoughts down about an event that had occurred in my life. The event that I wrote about was my experience of taking my GCSE exams, how I prepared for them, and the implications of my actions on my life and my friendships during this period of time. I managed to write around 1,000 words in 30 minutes and soon realised that I was actually quite fast at typing my thoughts down on a computer. I truly enjoyed the feeling of writing my first chapter of this book, and soon continued with my writing after feeling positive from the process of it. Unfortunately, my laptop broke early in my writing stages and I had to resort to using my iPhone for writing the remaining content of the book. I had to use my phone because it was only my parents and me at home and both my mother and father used their laptops often for work. I used the 'Notes' app on my phone to write different sections of this book between March and late September. In September, my parents kindly bought me a laptop as I was starting university in October. By then, however, I had written just under half of the book and had written up to 45,000 words using my phone alone. I got my laptop in September 2020 but didn't do any writing at university, I only proofread the contents I had written over the past couple of months. Once January 2021 came around, however, a new burst of ideas came to mind and I finished writing the remaining contents of this book over the whole of January and the first week of February.

So, 11 months later, in February 2021, I had managed to write my first ever full book by the age of 18. I guess my original thoughts about being too young to write a book, or not having lived long enough, were just my own ways of finding excuses for not really knowing what the entire process of writing a book was going to be like and, more or less, being slightly overwhelmed by this challenge that Gilbert had set for me. Despite this, my open mindedness and ability to rise to a challenge rose victorious above the ambiguity and overwhelming feeling of writing a book and I managed to conquer Gilbert's challenge through simply giving it a go.

SECTION ONE

PEOPLE WHO HAVE INSPIRED ME

1. Dave

David Orobosa Omoregie is a British rapper, singer, songwriter, record producer and actor, who is commonly known by his stage names, Dave or Santan Dave. Dave grew up in Streatham which is a district in South London. Dave didn't have the easiest of upbringings. His father was deported to Nigeria when he was just a few months old. Both of his older brothers were charged for crimes and both spent time in prison, one of them receiving a life sentence before Dave managed to turn 18. Dave also didn't grow up in the best of environments; certain parts of Streatham were associated highly with gangs, drugs and violence among young people. Dave even mentions, in one of his songs called 'Streatham', that at the same time his teachers in secondary school were giving him test papers, he was also receiving drugs from his friends to try out. Dave managed to overcome his tough upbringing and difficult environment through the specific choices he made to forge a career out of music. He made tough decisions and sacrificed a lot to make his way up within the music industry in Britain and be recognised as one of the best musicians in Britain as well as worldwide. It is these choices that Dave specifically made for himself, his life and his family, which caused me to be so inspired by him.

I never really used to listen to any of Dave's music as he only began releasing music in 2015. Dave was still quite young at the time that he was growing as a musician. He was born in 1998, so was only four years older than me. A lot of my friends would listen to Dave but I never was really drawn to his music. Between the ages of 13 and 17, I mostly used to listen to music purely for the sound. I rarely used to hear what musicians were actually saying in their songs. At the time, Dave was quite a lyrical artist and most of his songs were filled with meaning and messages, so at those ages I wasn't really enticed by such a genre of music. I much preferred to listen to artists such as Future, Kodak Black and Drake. With musicians such as Kodak Black and Future, it can be slightly difficult to hear every word that they say and, at times, some of the things they rap or sing about are very questionable. However, the sound which is sent to my ears feels heavenly so I happily listen to them, song after song, whenever I am just enjoying the sound or melody of a song.

It was as recently as 2020 that I decided to finally start listening to a bit more of Dave's music. After the British Phonographic Industry's BAFTA music awards in February 2020, I had seen that my friend Champhe, Champ for short, had posted on his Snapchat story the YouTube video of Dave's performance of his song 'Black' at the award ceremony. The post was accompanied by a quite heavy reaction, with a caption saying, "Dave man!" and an emoji that showed a shocked facial expression. I had not watched the BAFTA awards and was curious as to what Dave had done to make Champhe react the way he did. Soon after, I watched the YouTube video of Dave's performance of 'Black' and I was also astonished. Dave had put on one of the greatest performances I had seen by a musician and I'm guessing that many other people who watched his performance live had seen how good it was. He managed to play the piano alongside another pianist, Fraser Smith, who has helped produce some of Dave's songs. Mr Smith continued playing the instrumental of the song 'Black', while Dave stood up and performed in front of the audience. Dave even finished his performance by calling out the Prime Minister, Boris Johnson, for being a racist and not doing enough for people, especially people of colour, in regard to providing accommodation after the Grenfell fire in London in June 2017, resulting in many people dying and survivors becoming homeless.

Now, many people had mixed feelings about what Dave did in regard to calling the Prime Minister a racist on national television. Some people were happy about how he confronted Mr Johnson, and others thought he could have dealt with the situation a lot better and maybe could have arranged to have a meeting with Mr Johnson to address the issues he felt needed to be raised. When I showed it to both of my parents, my mother, on the one hand, was proud of Dave and was happy about what he said at the end of his performance, whereas my father was completely shocked at what Dave did and felt he could have dealt with the situation a lot better. Even Champhe thought the same, that Dave could have dealt with the situation a lot better than he did. Personally, I was unsure how I felt about what Dave did and the manner of his approach. On the one hand, I saw a young man with passion stand up for his people, but on the other hand, after hearing the views of other people, I do believe he could have dealt with the situation slightly better. Nonetheless, just like everyone else, Dave is entitled to make mistakes.

After I watched Dave's performance on stage, I decided to go downstairs into my living room and watch the 2020 BAFTA awards from the beginning on catch-up TV. I watched the awards ceremony and, during it, Dave actually happened to be given one of the best awards of the evening. He was awarded Album of the Year after he released his first studio album called 'Psychodrama' in 2019. 'Psychodrama' tells Dave's story of his life thus far: his upbringing, his depression, and struggles from his life that led him to seek help through psychodrama, which is a form of therapy. The album also reveals the changes Dave made to his life to make it in music, and to get where he was in that moment during the BAFTA awards ceremony. It is an album which I very much enjoyed listening to and continue to enjoy. During Dave's acceptance speech, he was initially shocked and you could tell, while he stood there giving acknowledgements and thanks to the people who had helped him with his career so far. He even found it difficult to gather any words together and articulate to the audience. That moment that he received Album of the Year simply caught him off guard slightly, in the sense that his first studio album had achieved such success so early on in his career.

However, it was what he said during his acceptance speech that really made me think. Dave went on to thank his team who helped him to create the album and who had been with him up to that point in time during his journey as a musician. He also addressed the younger generations of today, including myself and people slightly younger than me, to go on to achieve our dreams and goals and make things happen for ourselves. Dave humbly told the younger generations that he was no different to us, that he was "just a guy". Dave told the younger generations that it was possible for us to achieve anything we wanted to if we put our minds to it. The part of Dave's acceptance speech which really caught my attention was when he mentioned that, at one point during his life, he was just like any other ordinary kid. In that moment, I looked at Dave and saw him not as Dave the superstar and rapper, but as David the human being. I saw him similarly to the way I see myself each time I look in the mirror and simply saw him as another ordinary person who had managed to make his dreams a reality. It was after this event that I decided I wanted to learn more about Dave, his mindset when he was my age, and the decisions and choices he made in order to be standing where he was, winning the British Album of the Year by age 21. The easiest way that I was going to learn these things about Dave was to stick some headphones into my ears and begin streaming all of his music, from the first song he ever released to the last one on 'Psychodrama.'

This time, while listening to Dave's songs, I decided to truly listen to the messages the songs portrayed, as opposed to just listening to the sound. I managed to learn quite a few things about Dave. I learned that he decided to start pursuing music from quite a young age, around 13–14 years old. I also learned that, by the time he was 15, he had a very different mindset to most 15-year-olds and was grafting as hard as he could to make music his career in life. By then, Dave knew that music was the thing he was most passionate about and was probably the best and strongest gift he had. Being lyrically gifted, Dave didn't do too badly in English at school, usually scoring high in his assessments. However, as mentioned earlier, throughout his journey to becoming a musician, Dave grew up in quite a tough environment where few people, including his friends, were ambitious about what they wanted to do with their lives and their futures, and were more or less happy just living in the present. This makes sense for a 15-year-old mindset; usually, people don't really know what they want to be, maybe until they turn 18 or get close to their early twenties. On the other hand, some people may know exactly what it is they want to do or be by the age of ten. Dave happened to be one of those people who had managed to discover his calling in life, and was prepared to sacrifice everything he could to pursue a career in music.

He mentions in his songs how he had to make certain sacrifices, such as not attending as many parties and distancing himself from certain friends who had different aims to him at the time. During the time that Dave was being recognised as a musician through his songs, music videos and social media platforms, he was still at school and was yet to complete his secondary education. Therefore, many of his friends and the people he grew up with were just ordinary schoolchildren, while Dave was trying to chase his dream of becoming a musician and, in this, he was becoming well known around his area and the UK. Somewhere along the way he had to distance himself from those who only chose to experience and view life through a tunnel of fun and games, while he was trying make his dreams happen for himself, his future, and his family who were struggling at the time and quite poor. Soon, Dave began to get even more attention for his music and received cheques for some of the views and streams he was beginning to count up on his songs. By then, Dave had completed secondary education and was currently preparing to study law at De Montfort University in Leicester, having securing a place there. Dave wasn't completely keen on his academic life and much preferred to devote the next three years of his life and time pursuing a music career rather than attend university. This was especially due to the fact that his songs were getting just under one million views. Dave had a conversation with his mother that involved him letting her know his true desires and passion in life for music, and he informed her that he wouldn't be attending university. After this, and choosing his career path, Dave continued to write lyrics and produce more songs and soon became an established musician after working with other musicians, such as AJ Tracey, in 2016. In the same year, another event occurred for Dave which truly boosted his career as a musician; one of the best musicians on the planet decided to feature, on a remix, on one of Dave's songs that he released when he was 18 years old. Global music mogul Drake decided to remix Dave's song called 'Wanna Know'. This pretty much made it certified that Dave was going to be a big star. It boosted his reach regarding how many people knew him around the world and listened to his music. This remixed song by Drake was truly a big moment for Dave and a pinnacle moment in his career so far.

We can see that, from his music and the way he talks and carries himself, Dave is a person who carries an old person's head on a young person's shoulders. He was very wise in the decisions he made, which led to him becoming a global music superstar, achieving his dreams of becoming an established musician. The sacrifices Dave made very early on in his life are what led to so much success very early on in his life. His work ethic and mindset, simultaneously, worked hand-in-hand to help his career as a musician take flight. There is so much to learn from this young man and the choices he made to become so successful. Dave vividly shows and preaches about how important the decisions you make in life truly are. Through his actions, he demonstrates where life can take you if you make the correct choices and decisions that lie in your best interests. Some of these decisions may be tough and some of them will make you question whether they really are the correct decisions. It is down to you to make similar decisions in your own life and choose which path you believe is correct for you. This path should lead you to discover your own greatness and establishment as an individual.

Reader Exercises:

Reader exercises are optional, however, throughout this book you will find sections where I invite you to ask yourself questions based on the chapter you have just read and meditate on the answers which come up. I also invite you to take action on these, in order to realise your highest potential.

- What sacrifices are you prepared to make in your own life to reach your highest potential?
- What choices do you make on a daily basis – are they choices which benefit you and your future self?
- Is there something in your life that you are eager to start, but you don't have the courage to embark on this journey because you are scared of what other people might think? What might help you to be brave and take this leap of faith?

2. Mr Bell

The barber shop is a place where the community gathers. It is where conversations about television series, sports, women, and many other subjects take place. Two of my best friends and I rarely shared our honest thoughts on any given topic. We simply nodded and agreed with things that were not very controversial. At least once a month, we sat on the one long bench in the barber shop, waiting to be called to Mr Orwa's chair to have our latest hair styles and patterns made in our hair.

The day we met Mr Delmaine O'Neil Bell for the first time was one of the biggest blessings my 12-year-old self was ever going to receive. The story of how Mr Bell and I came to know each other is truly an amusing one. My friends and I never wanted to sit in his chair when we saw him for the first time as a new barber in Mr Orwa's shop in October 2014. We prejudged him and completely underestimated Mr Bell's ability to cut hair. We even used to choose who was going sit in his chair next, instead of sitting in Mr Orwa's chair. In hindsight, it does make logical sense that we preferred Mr Orwa over Mr Bell, simply because we were more familiar with Mr Orwa. However, we viewed having our hair cut by Mr Bell as a punishment rather than just missing out on a 'good haircut' by Mr Orwa. Now that I am a couple of years older and have had more life experiences, I can see how the attitudes and prejudgments my friends and I made about Mr Bell were completely foolish. As young as we were, we thought we had it all worked out regarding who was the better barber, without even having had a haircut by Mr Bell.

My memory of how my own relationship with Mr Bell built up over the years is very poor. Nevertheless, I know that it must have taken one sitting in his chair and a conversation that sparked something that my life was not expecting. Ever since I allowed myself to be more open to the idea of Mr Bell cutting my hair, I discovered that he was actually an exceptionally excellent barber. It came to a point in time where we, as we always could, chose which chair we wanted to sit in and, funnily enough, over time I switched seats and selected Mr Bell's chair while I stared over at Mr Orwa. Mr Bell and I used to have good conversations about all sorts of things. Unfortunately, as time moved onwards, Mr Bell decided to leave and make his own barber shop in his garden. At the time, my friends and I were shocked at his move because it had come to the point where each and every one of us would wait until we had the opportunity to sit in Mr Bell's chair each time we were in the barber shop. Mr Bell had made a big move in the barbering industry of my local town. He even created his own website for bookings and enquires. This looked very trendy and helpful to us.

Furthermore, Mr Bell has had such an influence on my life. From the time he arrived in this country, he has continuously showed great acts of service to people of my generation and the generation above. I remember vividly, one day, while I sat in his chair at Mr Orwa's shop, telling him that I was playing football for one of the local teams, Banbury Irish, and the conversation continued on to the point where he told me he would come and watch me play on the following Sunday of that same week. I was slightly shocked by his interest in taking time out of his Sunday to come and watch me play football. So, when it came to kick-off time on the Sunday, Mr Bell and his son were walking towards the area where the crowd stood and I was thinking, Well you better perform kid. When it came to the end of the match, I cannot recall how my performance was, but I do remember being given some advice from Mr Bell on different areas of my game that I could improve and I think this was my first time encountering such a conversation with him. As time moved forward, Mr Bell had got to know a lot of the youth in the town, mostly the boys who played football. He decided to set up his own Sunday evening football, which the majority of attendees refer to as 'O'Neil's'. It has been up and running for seven years now and has truly evolved into a place of community. A place where one can catch up with a friend who they haven't seen all week, and somewhere where one can intensively compete in sport. During the early stages of O'Neil's, it was mostly Mr Bell who would give coaching points to different players and he especially did this for the boys he knew were currently playing football locally or even wanted to take their game to a higher level. However, over time the actions of Mr Bell have encouraged other people to step up and play a similar role to him. Now, other players tend to give coaching points whenever they see necessary.

It was only recently that I discovered why Mr Bell decided to set up Sunday football those seven years ago. As I sat in his new chair, he told me that he set it up in order for kids of Banbury to have an area where they can participate in sport with no costs. He said that he also wanted to build communities and bridges between the people who attended his Sunday football and create a space for males of all ages to have a recreational area to attend on a Sunday evening. This act from Mr Bell inspired me, in that he did not owe anything to the people who attended his football, nor did he want to earn money from their pockets. He set up O'Neil's in order to give back to the community of Banbury and strengthen it. He set it up so people could look forward to playing sport rather than lazing around at home on a Sunday evening. He created it for the people, and it has ended up strengthening and creating relations between the people who attend. Guys that I used to look up to and saw as the 'cool guys' during my upbringing attend this same football, and it has finally given me an opportunity to know them better and create friendships with them. This act of service by Mr Bell to different young people and people around the area, is one that I think everyone can learn from.

Reader Exercises:

- How do you think you can best serve the communities that you are part of?
- Is there anything that you have thought about starting up in your local area or town and have just had doubts about? What are these doubts and what action can you take to overcome them?

3. Stormzy

Mr Michael Owuo Jr, also known as Stormzy, is a British rapper, singer and songwriter. It is only recently that I have chosen to listen to more of his music and try to really listen to the message of his songs and, at times, the suffering he has revealed that he has experienced in his life. Mr Owuo Jr has inspired me in multiple ways now that I have chosen to learn and know more about him, his past and his personality.

Stormzy had a tough upbringing. However, he did not allow this to break him as a person or kill his spirit. Instead, he would either smoke away the pain with marijuana or write songs to express his repressed and sad feelings. This is something which I already see as admirable about this young man, his ability to take something painful and upsetting and turn it into goodness and something people want to hear and learn from. I think this is a tough skill to acquire but, over the years, with committed hard work, Mr Owuo Jr has now become one of the biggest names in British music and is currently a household name. Despite his large fame, he seems to be the type of person who enjoys letting other people have their time on stage and tends to give a lot to young adults and children from an Afro-Caribbean background. I realised that Stormzy was a man of culture who enjoys embracing the talents of others when I witnessed him do something quite special at the 2020 BRIT Awards.

Stormzy was given the opportunity to perform at the BRIT Awards and he produced a truly amazing performance for the audience. The performance began with Stormzy singing a solo at the start of one of his songs from his 'Heavy is the Head' album. Stormzy also had Miss Tiana Major, a fellow musician, on stage with him, helping him with the song. Less than a minute into the performance, a choir which was singing part of the backing track of the song was shown on a stage behind him. Now, Stormzy would have more than likely needed help during this performance at the BRIT Awards, but I have a slight suspicion that he involved as many young adults as he possibly could to give them their chance to shine on stage – thus the choir. Stormzy's performance continued with a medley of songs from his album, but the part which surprised me most about this young gentleman's performance was when he invited Mr Damini Ogulu, also known as Burna Boy, onto stage to help him with a song they had written and released together called 'Own It'.

Before Stormzy even walked on stage when it was announced that he was going to perform at the Awards in a few moments, no one was expecting this wholesome performance and the mass involvement of people, especially Burna Boy, coming on to help Stormzy. Yet, Stormzy still had a surprise waiting for the audience while his and now Burna Boy's performance continued. He actually gave Burna Boy one minute of his performance time to perform one of his popular Afrobeat songs, 'Anybody'. What got me really excited about this performance was when Burna Boy sang 'Anybody' and there were dancers and different performers. This showed a whole other side to the music – the African side. I was simply stunned by the events I was watching at a British awards ceremony. I believe that the audience, both present and those at home, were equally stunned. Stormzy then closed the performance by having rain fall on stage as he performed his and Miss Major's last song, 'Rainfall', with over 100 other youngsters on stage with him.

This entire performance showed many values and qualities of Stormzy. It showed how selfless he is, how cultured he is, and demonstrated his overall generosity by letting so many young people have the opportunity to shine on one of the biggest stages. The reason I found this performance very touching and moving was because, on a much lower level, I used to work with teachers and classmates helping younger children in my school to come up through the system. At the time I was doing this, I had hoped to carry out similar acts to Stormzy, such as to embrace the young children of my generation and give them their opportunities and chances to shine too.

In my last year of sixth form, many of my classmates and I played a big part in being role models to the younger children. However, I refused to believe that we were superior or better than the young ones we were mentoring. I was against thinking that we knew more than any of the other children in the years below us. If we had seen things that way, we would have never been able to embrace and give space to anyone else who was not among our year group to demonstrate their talents and capabilities. It was equally important that we were given the chance to express and show our talents, as were the children in any other year groups. So, if there is one thing that I have definitely taken from Stormzy and his incredible performance at the BRIT Awards it is that when you become a star or a household name, always remember that there are also many other stars around you. They may not be as bright as you at that moment, but they are still present. So, at times, instead of always wanting to shine as a lone star you need to have the courage and generosity to turn down your own brightness so that the stars around you have their chance to shine too.

4. Drake

Aubrey Drake Graham is a Canadian rapper, singer, songwriter, actor, producer and entrepreneur. He is mostly known for his status as a musician and is commonly known by his middle name, which also happens to be his stage name, Drake. I first experienced Drake and his music at a friend's birthday party while I was between the ages of eight and ten years old. One of the party songs that had come on was Drake's song called 'Over'. The music video of this song was shown on my friend's television and I was soon drawn to the type of music I was hearing, as well as the cool visuals from Drake's music video. It was after this that I began to add a lot more Drake songs to my playlists whenever I listened to music, and I have put him above any other artists when it comes to my favourite music artists and songs.

Drake had an extraordinary run and was dominant between 2010 and 2020. He had started his music career slightly earlier than this, and began releasing music publicly in 2006 when he released his first mixtape, 'Room for Improvement'. Before Drake actually started to write songs, he was an actor on the Canadian TV programme 'Degrassi', where he played the character 'Jimmy Brooks'. It was towards the end of Drake's career as an actor that his true love for music began to unravel and become more apparent. Drake had always been into music and grew up around it, as his father, Dennis Graham, was also a musician. While Drake was still an actor in Toronto, his home city, and was also aspiring to be a musician aged 17, he had a very difficult work schedule. Drake was having to be on set for 'Degrassi' from 9am and then, after finishing work, he would go to the music studio to write and make music. He would stay at the studio until late the following morning and would actually just return to his actors dressing room around 5am and get four hours or so of sleep before getting up and ready for another day on set. It soon became apparent to Drake, his work colleagues and his employers at 'Degrassi', that this type of lifestyle simply wasn't sustainable. So, Drake had to make a choice between a music career and an acting career, and he chose music.

He mentioned in an interview with Jian Ghomeshi that the reason he chose music over acting and much prefers it, is because he was able to be more in control of doing what he enjoyed, loved, and wanted to do. Drake mentioned how, as an actor, you are required to get an agent, rely on your agent to be good and help you get auditions, attend auditions and be cast for parts which, altogether, was a long process. Music, on the other hand, was something Drake viewed as a profession that he had far more control over and all it (mostly) required of him was to pick up a pen and paper and put in the time and hours required to make music, and get his songs recorded and produced. It seems that Drake made the correct career decision by choosing music, as he went on to become a globally recognised musician and person in history. He has achieved many record-breaking feats, changed and set trends, and paved a new way for how musicians from the city of Toronto, and Canada as a whole, are viewed. He essentially revolutionised the industry of music in his own way. Drake did not do this alone, however, he had a team of people who helped make his career what it is. It is the way that Drake decided to write his own legacy through his music career that makes me admire him so much. The calculated, strategic and wise decisions he made were crucial aspects in his unprecedented successes, and this is what I am going to focus on within his chapter of this book.

Drake was not always a talented musician who had it in his blood and was destined for success. He worked hard for it and made many correct decisions which led him to become a global star. When he started off as a musician, he was just known in Toronto as the kid who was an actor who decided to now become a rapper. Drake was not as confident as he may seem today through his social media platforms and countless music videos. In the beginning, Drake became something we all should try to be from time to time, and that was a 'sponge'. When Drake was being introduced to big names and established people in the music industry, such as American rapper Trey Songz and other big producers, he soaked up all of the information he could from them while he was an aspiring musician. He was even seen as the kid who sat in the corner of the studio, minded his own business, and observed those who had much higher music statuses than he had at the time. He allowed himself to learn more about the music industry. There soon became no question whether Drake was a good musician, or was destined to be a good musician, once he began to release more music and write more songs.

People, both those in the music industry and listeners, began to see that what Drake brought to the music table was different, it was new and something which many had not witnessed before. His sound, ability to sing as well as rap, and his lyrical technicality and skill is what set him aside from the average musician. After making quite a few hit songs and releasing some of his first studio albums, Drake began to grow as a musician and was pretty much established and well-known. He was signed to a big music production company, Young Money Entertainment, and was working with and for big music stars such as Lil Wayne. Despite the environment that Drake was in at that time, and the connections he had, people were still heavily focused on who Drake was growing to become, both as a musician and an individual.

One of Drake's wisest decisions in music was to expand his sound. Drake already had an incredible degree of versatility with his singing and rapping capacity, but what he did with this and how he spread this to other fields and regions of music is what played a big role in the making of his legacy. Drake mostly portrayed a typical American type of musician in the music genres of hip hop, R&B and rap. However, he had a uniqueness due to his Canadian sound. Drake did not limit himself in the type of music that he made, as he decided to try out his sound on different genres of music. He began to write lyrics and songs to Caribbean and Afrobeat types of beats and instrumentals. He attempted to do more songs where he rapped rather than sang – singing was mostly how he started his career. He changed his sound. Doing this demonstrated how versatile he was as a musician and the different types of songs he was able to make. It also showed that he was still able to sound good on different genres of music. This is what led his music to spread globally, as opposed to just remaining in American and Canadian ears.

Towards the end of Drake's run, he was criticised for being a 'culture vulture', which is someone who adopts something from a different community and makes it their own. However, it is also argued that there is no law in music against embracing other cultures through song writing and that it should be embraced, as opposed to looked down upon. Personally, I do not view Drake's decision of spreading his sound to other cultures as bad, because the music he made was still extremely good. In fact, it was even better and enticing to play because it was a new side of Drake that I had not heard before. Drake's versatility in changing his sound led to Caribbean-style songs, such as 'One Dance' and 'Controlla' from his album 'Views', becoming such big hits and remaining in the charts for weeks on end. Drake knew that, as much as you may be a big fan of his, you cannot always listen to his music as it will just get repetitive. He knew that to keep listeners engaged, he would have to change his sound and I think that most people who know of Drake would say that it worked. Drake used his versatility to his advantage throughout his music career, and this is something each one of us can learn from. Being a versatile person in any field of work is quite crucial, as it allows you to be utilised, moulded and shaped in any way possible. It increases the likeliness of you being chosen to carry out a specific task at work, or being asked to play a certain position that needs filling on the day of a sports match. It simply allows you to be used for more than one thing, one specific domain or area and, ultimately, increases your value as a person. Versatility is an attribute that, if acquired and practised, can lead to others seeking your advice and help on various things, frequently.

One other aspect of Drake's career that is difficult to go without noticing is, not only his rise to the top of the music food chain, but the dominant nature that he made it there, as well as the dominance that he maintained at the top during his generation and time as a musician. Towards the end of his decade that began in 2010, Drake was undoubtedly seen as one of the greatest musicians on the planet. He was and still remains the most streamed artist on Spotify ever, and he has broken multiple industry world records. He didn't have enough arms to hold and pose with all 13 of his Billboard Awards and would have had to use either a wheelbarrow or something similar to take his awards home that evening. Lastly, he was the first artist ever to get one billion streams on the first week of an album release when he released his fifth studio album, 'Scorpion'. Many people have argued that 'Scorpion' was not Drake's best work compared to his previous albums, but this didn't matter to the billions of listeners who streamed 'Scorpion' that week. Once Drake reached that achievement in his number of streams, it didn't matter whether what he released was good or not, people just wanted to hear his voice and what he had to say. To get to this point, however, Drake took many steps, made plenty of sacrifices and, once again, was extremely strategic in every move he decided to make. During Drake's ten-year run, he was very calculative on which other artists he was going to make music with and write verses for to feature in songs. This helped him gain dominance as a musician and own the charts. Drake's dominance as a musician during the 2010s was confirmed after he was awarded the Artist of the Decade award in 2021 by Billboard.

Among all the strategic plays that Drake made to reach the top, there was one crucial aspect that played a big role in

Drake's reign – the internet. During the early 2010s, social media platforms such as Instagram, Snapchat and TikTok were not around meaning the way that musicians could spread their music was a lot more limited. However, once these platforms were invented and came around, it became a lot easier for musicians to share their music as they had a high following on their accounts. On the internet, early in his career, Drake was seen as a meme – a person used in photographs, with captions that bring laughter to others, and shared between people. When your photograph, face or brand is used as a meme, it can have positive or negative connotations in life. Drake became a meme because of his status as an artist, but also due to the way that he decided to live his life, carry himself and express himself. Drake soon saw how the internet viewed him and, instead of feeling upset about his face being on most memes, good or bad, or GIFs –short, looped video forms of memes – he decided to use this as a way to grow and spread his music. Drake knew that almost anything he did, from reacting to a comment during an interview to drinking some water, could be turned into a meme and shared across the internet rapidly. Therefore, in making his music video for his song 'Hotline Bling', Drake decided to dress in some simple clothes, have a design and backdrop in his video that changed colour, and dance freely throughout the entire music video. Now, Drake isn't known for being a dancer and does not identify as a dancer, so when people watched the video, all they saw was this famous musician dancing in his music video, almost goofing around in a way, and simply having fun while recording his music video. Drake made specific dance moves that he knew would have very high meme potential and, soon after watching it and analysing it before it was released to the public, he knew what was possible for the number of views it would get and how much it would spread across the internet. The music video for 'Hotline Bling' was soon released and, within the first week of release, Twitter was full of Drake memes from the same music video. The fact that people were making memes from the video, laughing and joking about it, must have meant they went onto YouTube and searched for the music video. This was all Drake needed and wanted, as it meant more views and streams for his song and more growth for him in the charts. 'Hotline Bling' even went on to win two Grammy awards in 2017 for Best Rap Song and Best Rap/Sung Performance.

The way that Drake used and saw the internet and various social platforms to grow his music career is a marketing technique and methodology that every individual can use. Whichever field of work you specialise in, using techniques such as Drake did will enable you to grow and market whatever it is that you want people to consume from you more effectively. Most people probably won't be standing in the same shoes as Drake throughout their lifetime, where anything they do can be turned into a meme or is of great interest to other people, on which they can capitalise and use to their advantage. Nonetheless, the idea of being this strategic and clever in the moves that you decide to make can be extremely beneficial to oneself if used correctly. It may not even be the case that you wish to sell and market products or have a line of work that involves this; the idea that you can make the best out of a situation involving yourself, in a manner that Drake did, can always lead to good things.

Lastly, there is one aspect of Drake's strategic ways that I think plays a pinnacle role in his successes and that is his ability to know when the time is right. Drake's work involves making products and songs, and releasing them to the entire world in exchange for profits through consumption via streams, views and concerts. Throughout Drake's run during the 2010s, it seems that he was able to tell exactly when the time was right to release a particular song, mixtape or album. His release of music changed over time as, at the start of his career, his aim was to make as much music as he could and get out the best songs and albums he had, in order to prove to the rest of the world, as well as himself, how good a musician he was. After he had managed to get the world's attention and was established and recognised as a big musician, he was in control of how he distributed his music to the world. Once Drake had released his second and third studio albums, people wanted him to be releasing more music because they were interested in his story, what he had to say, and the mannerism that he would deliver this in a song.

Drake doesn't just release his music for the sake of it, or give it out for people to listen to, learn from and enjoy casually. He does it in a controlled way and almost acts like a supplier who knows his product is truly loved and in high demand, but chooses when to supply it. The tables turned. Before, people were waiting for Drake to release good music so their ears could be pleased and that, in turn, pleased Drake, because the people enjoyed his music. Now that Drake has pleased the people and showed them what he is capable of, it is a blessing whenever he decides to release music to the public. Drake would have figured this out early on, from the reactions he got from his fans at concerts and over the internet. Drake, as a musician, knows that we are not waiting for him to release music for us to see how good he is, as we were during the early days of his career. Now, we simply long for him to make songs and share them with us. We no longer want to wait for them. This change in relationship puts Drake in control of when he releases music and the manner that he does so.

Drake used this knowledge to its best advantage for his music career through his songs and release of albums. On his 'More Life' mixtape, in one of the songs, 'Do Not Disturb', he states that he would be back next summer to give his listeners the summary of the contents he was discussing in that mixtape. He released 'More Life' in March 2017 and went on to release his fifth studio album 'Scorpion' in June 2018, where he gave his listeners the summary. There are not many musicians who can tell their listeners that, in a year's time, they will tell them the rest of a story that had begun on one of their projects. He made his listeners wait an entire year to see what else he had to say in regard to certain matters on his upcoming studio album. The type of influence and power that he held over his listeners was truly astonishing. During the period that people waited for 'Scorpion' to be released, people were excited that they were going to be gifted another album by Drake in a year's time. They couldn't wait for what he had to say and what type of beats he would have used to portray his message, his punchlines or his play on words in his lyrics. It was during this excitement that you could see Drake had developed the skill of knowing when to sell and release his product in order to get people ready and excited to consume it. He told his listeners a year in advance that he had another product coming their way and the year between the release of 'More Life' and 'Scorpion' gave them a lot of time to talk about, discuss, and write about what was going to be coming their way. He used time to his advantage.

Another time that Drake showed his genius in knowing when the time is right, was in 2019, when he decided to have a quiet year and barely released any songs at all. Despite this, 'Scorpion' was still being streamed worldwide and was enough to keep people entertained and satisfied. Even though 'Scorpion' was still being streamed by many throughout 2019, soon that became repetitive and fans sought new Drake sounds. With him not releasing much music in 2019, listeners, including myself, were limited to what they could consume when it came to Drake's music. Once 2020 came around, after the quiet 2019, Drake got the ball rolling through releasing his first song, 'Life is Good', with another well-known artist called Future. There were speculations that Drake was going to release his sixth studio album in 2020, due to Instagram posts that he had made in late 2019. Drake also released another song and music video in April 2020, called 'Toosie Slide', which was shot in his mansion in Toronto and ended up being a simple TikTok challenge shared over all social media platforms, through Drake doing a simple dance in the music video and quoting the dance in his lyrics. Part of the chorus of the song goes, 'right foot up left foot slide, left foot up right foot slide'. This was also another strategic move by Drake, as it led to more streams of his song due to its popularity on TikTok as well as the fact that he was clever enough to make a basic music video in his home, as the coronavirus pandemic limited the number of people who he could be in contact with to shoot music videos. The Toosie Slide dance was inspired by Micheal Jackson's famous moonwalk, Micheal was a musician that Drake heavily looked up to and still does. As the year continued, Drake released more songs and, in one of them called 'Popstar', released in June, he stated how in 2019 he kept his head down and had a quiet year, but in 2020 he came to make noise and once again make his mark on the music scene. In May 2020, he released another mixtape called 'Dark Lane Demo Tapes', which led him to becoming the tied record holder with Madonna for the most top ten hits on the Billboard Hot 100, with 38 hits. Drake's mixtape grossed streams once again, putting his name and songs at the top of multiple charts across several countries. He was extremely fortunate to have released this mixtape during the coronavirus pandemic, as most people were in their homes and didn't have many things to keep them entertained, so music and television consumption would have increased.

Drake didn't actually end up releasing his sixth studio album in 2020 and, instead, kept people on the edge, believing that he was going to do so for most of 2020, until his birthday in October when he announced that he was going to release the album called 'Certified Lover Boy (CLB)' in January 2021, which he also deferred for personal reasons and ended up releasing CLB on September 3rd 2021. Despite this, it was still seen that Drake owned 2020 with his release of new music and new sounds. For Drake to release the amount of music that he did in 2020, he must have already produced it in 2019, or maybe even before then, for it to be released in such quantity as it was in 2020. So, Drake could have probably released the same 2020 music in 2019, but simply decided not to. He strategically planned that 2020 was the year when he wanted to dominate as a musician once again, and decided that 2019 could be a quiet year that would get people hungry and ready for more of his music. This strategic plan of his once again worked. Through Drake's cunningness and knowledge of when the time was right, he managed to once again make an entire year his own. It is most likely true that he didn't even work as much as people thought he was working throughout 2020, apart from on his upcoming album, as he had already recorded the music that people were listening to and was just choosing the right time to release it. It is this knowledge and ability that Drake has had throughout his career as a musician that has given him his throne at the top of the charts. It is something that can be discovered and used to the best of its ability for musicians, especially, but even those who have their own personal businesses, authors who write and sell books, and almost anything that involves marketing and selling a product. Knowing when the time is right is crucial and can seriously work to one's advantage if capitalised upon correctly.

Overall, I have a huge amount of love and admiration for Drake. From the way that he is able to write catchy lyrics to a beat or instrumental, to the way that he inspires me through his words and the way he goes about his own life. There are many things to learn from Mr Graham, from his songs to his words during interviews, but there is also a lot to learn in the way that he decided to dominate music, globally, during his long and fulfilling ten-year reign. There is a lot to learn from him from his work ethic, his metaphors and riddles, but there's also a lot to learn from the steps he took and the decisions he made to ensure that his run was as successful as it was. Using some of the strategic methods that Drake used throughout his growth as a musician are methods which I truly see as heading one towards greatness if used and administered correctly. If you do decide to use some of the strategies and tactics that Drake used throughout his reign, I can only see it leading to one thing for an individual – complete domination.

Reader Exercises:

- How often do you allow yourself to become a sponge and learn as much information as you possibly can about something you are passionate about?

- How versatile are you as a person? Are you a person who can be moulded and sculptured into different roles and given several responsibilities, or is your skillset only applicable to one role – if so, how do you think you can change this?
- Do you regularly reflect and think about whatever it may be that you are doing in your life, working on, or trying to put into the world, and whether the timing is right and is in your best interest?

5. Kevin Hart

Kevin Darnell Hart is an American stand-up comedian, actor and producer. He started off as a comedian in Philadelphia, the place he was born, and made moves to different areas of America in order to pursue his dream of becoming a comedian. It is only recently that I learned more about Mr Hart and it was through this learning that I gained a lot of inspiration from him. Many of you will know of Mr Hart either through his stand-up comedy shows on Netflix and other platforms, or you will have seen him star in a movie. Wherever he may have crossed your path, it is most likely true that he managed to make you laugh greatly.

On 21st May 2020, Mr Hart released his audiobook 'The Decision' on Audible. The book only comes in audible format as opposed to hard copy. I had the opportunity to listen to the book after it was released on YouTube, allowing anyone to listen to it for free. I was fortunate that my friend Champhe had shared it on social media. I had seen many promotions by Hart on his Snapchat social media platform, for his upcoming book. From the promotions it seemed like my type of book. It is focused on the livelihoods of individuals and how the decisions people make on a daily basis affect their lives and the lives of those around them. It also includes strategies and mechanisms people can use to improve their own lives and the decisions that they make on a daily basis.

At the time I began listening to 'The Decision' I was in my first year of university. The first time I pressed 'play' was while I went running. I rarely listen to music and only tend to listen to it during exercise, so substituting 'The Decision' for music was not too much of a loss. I noticed early on that Mr Hart involved his methodology of including humour in the narrative of his book. For me, this is what gives him the edge to reach out to many more people and have mass consumption for the material he produces. The humour that he includes in his storytelling gives the listener more opportunities to see themselves in the same situation, despite Mr Hart's high status. Kevin Hart also tends to be quite raw and explicit when it comes to explaining situations and the theories he has, and I believe this gives 'The Decision' more authenticity, as opposed to listeners feeling distanced from what is being explained. Mr Hart's ability to take a story, period or moment in his life and transform this into a lesson is a skill which I think each person would benefit from. He does it in such a way that you don't just see Kevin Hart the movie star and multimillionaire comedian, but you see Kevin Hart the individual who makes mistakes just like the rest of us, the Kevin Hart who doesn't get every decision correct, and the Kevin Hart who is also just another human being.

I soon made a habit of going running and listening to 'The Decision'. I also usually listened to it if I was either walking somewhere or travelling on the bus. The space of being outdoors, in nature and away from school work, gave me the opportunity to tap into a deeper level of thinking and reflection which truly allowed the words Mr Hart spoke to enter into my mind and life. Each time, either while I was listening or after I had come to a stop in listening, I would reflect on some of the lessons being spoken about and how they could be applied in my own life, especially while I now was in a new environment. This entire process of learning more about Mr Hart and his life stories, and being able to apply the lessons he has learned from his past to my own life and future, was truly special and I am grateful that I had the opportunity to do that.

One thing that Kevin Hart touches upon in 'The Decision' is his work ethic and how he managed to develop this. His mother played a big role in developing his work ethic, especially since she spent a lot of time raising Kevin and his older brother, Robert Hart, by herself. Mr Hart came from a working-class family. His mother worked two jobs in order to provide for him and his brother. Kevin mentions how seeing this developed the work ethic he has. Mr Hart's ideology around work and working hard is thoroughly based around the question, "Can you do more?". He focuses solely on whether he can do more in current situations that he is in. When he had finally managed to make it as a comedian and became established, he had no intention of doing movies. The opportunity came and he seized it, through continuously asking himself, "Kevin, can you do more?". Seemingly he could, as he was still able to work his main craft of being a comedian, but now he was also on movie sets shooting movies.

Mr Hart has developed this type of work ethic through not being completely satisfied and content with what he has achieved or is in the process of achieving. He feels as if this will lead to complacency and, therefore, a decrease in performance. Mr Hart recognises when he has done well and gives himself the credit he is due, but he doesn't like focusing on the greatness of his achievements, as this may lead to him feeling he has already reached his full potential and thus prevent any more personal growth. Incorporating this strategic quality into one's life can be of such use, as it prevents oneself from believing that they have reached their optimum potential. Each person's optimum potential is unknown and forever remains unknown, so continuously pushing towards it, no matter the circumstances or how greatly or badly one is doing in life, is simply a push in the right direction towards greatness.

On social media, I see that Mr Hart always has products and content to sell on Snapchat or YouTube. I have noticed recently that these products are increasing in quantity. He has his 'Cold as Balls' series, where he has informal interviews with famous people while he and the person he is interviewing sit in ice baths; and he also has a new series called 'Coach Kev', which involves motivational and inspirational life lessons that he has learned in his own life and shares with the rest of the world. On top of all this, he is still managing to shoot movies and do stand-up comedy shows, as well as raise his four children. It was only after listening to 'The Decision' that I was able to learn so much more about Mr Hart, what he has been through to get where he is today, and the steps he took to get there. I found it inspirational as well as motivational to listen to how he has transformed his life through the multiple decisions he has made, and the decisions he still continues to make. Learning a few life lessons and more about the people you look up to can have a profound effect on your own performance throughout life and the crucial decisions that you make on a daily basis.

Reader Exercises:

- Do you take time out of your day to contemplate on some of the decisions you made throughout it and how those same decisions will affect your life in the long run?
- Do you take time to reflect upon your life and think whether you can be doing more on top of the multiple activities that you are already doing?
- Are you a person that is known to have a work ethic that is considered substantially above the norm?

6. Will Smith

Will Smith is a person I did not even know played a big role in my life. I have mostly been interested in and inspired by people such as Drake, Kevin Hart, and many other people who have made it to the top in different industries. Unconsciously, however, Will has always been in my life and has played a big role. This ranges from his ability to keep me entertained while I watched and continue to watch television shows such as 'The Fresh Prince of Bel-Air', or any one of his many amazing movies. I would put 'I am Legend', 'Men in Black 3' and 'I, Robot' as my top three favourite movies that he has starred in. It is so difficult to choose with him though, his ability, talent and sheer hard work to produce entertainment for people, make them laugh and engaged in him as a person, is simply admirable. Mr Smith's ability to take up any role or character and play it with maximum energy is a skill that I would also like to develop and grow. Above all of his great achievements and life lessons, I think it is important that we retreat to where it all began for Will Smith on his journey to great success.

Before 'The Fresh Prince of Bel-Air' was born, Will was into music and made a lot of music with a friend of his from 'The Fresh Prince' show, Mr Jeff Townes, though some of you may know him as 'Jazz'. The story of how Will became 'The Fresh Prince' is an interesting but also relatable and inspiring one too. While unemployed, Will attended a party with other big celebrities, musicians and politicians, at record and TV producer Quincy Jones' home. Will had ended up at Quincy's home as his girlfriend at the time told him that he needed to simply go to a place where people were doing things and he found himself at 'The Arsenio Hall Show', which was an American late-night talk show. After attending 'The Arsenio Show' as a spectator, Will met Benny Medina whose life and journey 'The Fresh Prince' show is actually based around. Mr Medina invited Will to Quincy's home, where Will was given ten minutes by Quincy to prepare to audition for a role on 'The Fresh Prince' as Quincy Jones was one of the executive producers of the show. He was reluctant to even take up the audition due to the lack of time he had to prepare for it and tried to insist that he wanted a week to practise, but the people who were helping produce the show were so busy at the time, that doing the audition at any later point would involve a lot of rescheduling. So, Quincy told him that rescheduling may or may not be an option, or he could take ten minutes right there and then and change his life for ever. Using his instincts, Will took the hurried audition, 'let it rip' and was crowned as 'The Fresh Prince of Bel-Air', which was actually named using his stage name as a musician – 'The Fresh Prince'.

Now, there's quite a few things to take from this story. Mr Smith showed to all of us, through his confidence, courage and spontaneity, that things, dreams and goals do not always have to be routines or in a manner that people perceive them to be. At times, you may not even know who may help you get to where you want to be in life, or where you thought you could never even reach. That is why it is important to, depending on the situation, be open to every opportunity that you come across. You never know whether it may be your opportunity or chance to be the next 'Fresh Prince of Bel-Air' or 'The Fresh Princess of London'. Mr Smith demonstrated, vividly, how at times being spontaneous can work in our favour and lead to great things, as it did for him. Due to this series, Will Smith was already a household name, globally, by the age of 22. Will inspires me in so many different ways, including his capacity to try new things and build his skillset in many different areas.

As I just mentioned, Will produced music before he became an actor and still continued to produce music after his acting career took flight; and he made the most of both worlds. He was still quite young, but doing so much with his life and time already, and doing it in a manner and style that was not commonly seen before. Will never swore in his music, as most rappers and musicians usually did and continue to do. In addition, his ability to juggle the two careers of musician and actor is what I see as the new way of life. Will Smith, along with many others, has shown us and still demonstrates that us human beings do not have just one line of work, one talent or one gift. Mr Smith showed and continues to show us that being a professional footballer does not mean you cannot also be a model, photographer, or even a doctor. Will Smith did more within the first 30 years of his life than most human beings even dream of doing or becoming in their lifetime. He is a father of three children, a successful actor, film producer, musician, author and is globally recognised as a great person. He has taken the opportunities and ways of performing in life to the next level, in my eyes, and what attracts me to him most is the genuineness and the straight road he took to becoming the person he is today. Mr Smith has raised three good children, been there for them as a father despite his busy work schedule, and he has brought immense laughter, joy and peace to the earth through his talent for acting.

Will continuously tries to help others and bring out the best in them, even when they are busy trying to give him praise for good work that he has done. Above all, I think the thing which has allowed Mr Smith to go as far as he has in life is his humility. This man has so much humility and humbleness that it is difficult to dislike him. It is also hard not to be attracted to humble people and people who you can relate and talk to deeply. There was one particular event where I feel that Will showed immense humility. When he starred on the 1990 series 'The Fresh Prince of Bel-Air', Will was the star of the show. The show, at times, was mostly focused on him and his character, who had his real name, Will Smith.

For those of you who watched the sitcom, you would have most probably noticed that the character that played 'Aunt Viv' was replaced. Janet Hubert, the original 'Aunt Viv', used to play the mother to other characters in the sitcom and played the aunty to Will Smith's character, Will. However much of a family the cast of 'The Fresh Prince' appeared to be on camera, and even off camera, Janet Hubert decided to leave the show in 1993. She left because she was unhappy with a deal she was offered by the production company of the show, and there were feuds between herself and Will Smith, as well as with the actor who played the character 'Carlton', Alfonso Ribeiro. The dispute between Will Smith and Janet Hubert occurred at the time when Miss Hubert was pregnant and was interested in receiving a pay rise. She knew that Will was the main star of the show, so approached him and asked whether he could help by asking the employers of the show whether he and his other cast members could receive a pay rise similar to the type of pay rise that actors on the sitcom 'Friends' were granted – USD 1 million an episode for their remaining two seasons. Mr Smith's response to Miss Hubert was, 'My deal is my deal and y'all's deal is y'all's deal.' This may have not been the greatest or nicest of responses by Will and, if he did feel that way about salaries at the time, he could have articulated this in a much nicer way to Janet. After this, the hostility began to grow stronger and more frequent between the two. Miss Hubert said some unkind things to Mr Smith and envied him for his successes so early in his career as an actor. Mr Smith didn't help the situation when he said certain things to the press, such as calling Janet difficult to work with. At the time, stating that black women, which Janet was, were difficult to work with only ignited the racist and stereotypical fires that were already smouldering at the time. It soon became apparent that it was not possible to have both Will and Janet on the show together and they knew that finding a replacement for Will Smith, as the main character, would have been extremely difficult – especially because his name was actually his character's name. Miss Hubert decided to leave the show after they finished filming their second season. The argument continued between the two, especially whenever it was mentioned in the press, and only ended in 2020.

Due to the fact that Will had wanted to do a 30-year reunion with the cast of 'The Fresh Prince of Bel-Air', he felt it would not be complete if he did not settle things with Janet and, once and for all, end the 27-year feud. They had tried to do this at various times, but different things occurred that allowed the tension to remain between the two. Will had organised to meet up with Janet and talk about it, and what could be resolved, and they managed to do so in the end. The video of their conversation and the resolving of their feud was shown on 'The Fresh Prince of Bel-Air' 30-year reunion special that was aired on 18th November 2020. Both Will and Janet managed to put their fight to rest and were able to truly and fully hear one another and understand where each other were coming from during the time that the tension between them was the highest. They apologised to each other for things they had done and said, which they felt probably shouldn't have been said, and their relationship was revived. This was a moment that Will had purposely made happen and a relationship that he wanted to heal. The fact that he was able to do this after a 27-year feud that had caused the diminishing of a person's career and had many bad implications along with it, showed a lot about his true personality and how much he managed to grow as a person over the 27 years. It was a moment that I was once again inspired by Mr Smith and learned from him.

Ending feuds, tension and toxic energies between yourself and another person is a way of relieving yourself from bad energies, guilt, or any negativity that you have within yourself. It is a healing process that I believe both Will and Janet experienced and is a healthy process that anyone can benefit from. At times, the person with whom you have tension may not be ready to move on and may never ever be able to overcome some disputes, but the important thing is that you at least tried. Fortunately, Janet and Will had the courage and decency to put the water under the bridge in regard to their own issue and were able to both happily move on. If Mr Smith did not have the level of humility that he demonstrated by his ability to end his feud with Miss Hubert, it would be very difficult for people to picture themselves in his shoes in life and imagine themselves becoming as successful as he has grown to become. His humility enables other people around the world to regard him as a human being, as opposed to the Hollywood superstar who is interested in riches and his own world, rather than wanting to contribute and help the rest of the human family, which is how he always likes to refer to humanity. We do have a lot of great celebrities who have done great things, produced great music and done things that only a few human beings have been able to do before. However, the manner that Mr Will Smith has trodden his path for himself and his career, as well as for his own family, is something for which, I believe, the world needs to give him recognition and appreciation.

Reader Exercises:

- How often do you take up spontaneous opportunities and chances that come your way in life?
- Is there an activity in your life that you wish you could be doing alongside your job or studies but are finding it hard to put time aside for it? How do you plan to make the best of both worlds and manage your time to do the two things at once?

7. Mr Atkinson

'I used to wish I was older, until the day that I had got older' is a statement once said by Dave in one of his songs. I think this one really speaks for itself. Often, as children, many of us wish that we could become older in some aspect. We have a tendency to believe that older people are a lot cooler than our little 'insignificant' selves. When we see the 'cool kids' who get into trouble at school, but are still able to make the entire classroom burst into tears of laughter, as small children we genuinely see these people as role models. It is astonishing that the majority of children are more attracted to a child who misbehaves and causes trouble for others, than one who may be quiet and reserved and may be a bit of a bookworm. But you know, it is what it is – we live in the 21st century and that's just the way the cookie [sort of] crumbles, I guess. Now, I will not mention which child I was, but if you know me you already have an idea.

As Dave stated, I too wished to be older long before my time. I saw many people who were older than me as inspirational and something I hoped to be in the future. This was especially true for Afro-Caribbean people and those who were connected to me, either through family friendship or who were just around as I grew up. There was this one young man though, Mr Collin Atkinson, and he was a person I looked up to from around the age of ten to twelve years old. He was somebody I saw and just thought, Man, this boy is the guy! He had many things I did not have. For example, his ethnicity is Caribbean and Jamaican so his hair grew at a staggeringly rapid rate, as opposed to mine which took a much longer time. He was able to get all the girls too. Collin was somebody I searched for on my Facebook feed at the age of ten, and was a person I felt the need to discover things about due to the fact that, in a way, I simply was inspired by this guy. I never really got the opportunity to speak to him, but funnily enough his house was just a 15-minute walk from mine. I used to see his father and his little brothers, and I still see them today, but we were not close friends despite the fact that they were just another family living in the area I grew up in.

Over time, as I grew up in my local area and got on with life, I had the opportunity to finally meet the ten-year-old inspiration of mine, Collin himself. I cannot recall the day we may have finally talked, but I know for sure it may have been a big day for my young self. From the time we met, we have had contact with each other. This may have been through the football we have played on Sundays over the past seven years at O'Neil's, or when we both attended a family friend's function. Still today, many years later, I have this admiration for Collin, especially now that I have had the opportunity to meet him and know him slightly better. I have to say, this admiration for Collin may have stemmed from the fact that he was simply the fastest person I had seen run with a football across a field. His dreaded hair would brush past the wind as he made a sprint and he was a player that nobody would enjoy tackling due to his cut physique.

In 2019, I was surprised to find Collin at my friend's home. We shared a few words, but not too many. Before I knew it, it was time for me to return home. As time passed, I went to the same home and saw his face there once again. I was even more shocked this time, due to the fact that he was there and around so often at a place I definitely considered to be my second home. So, I asked my friend the question, "How come Collin is always here?" and I was shocked to receive the reply, "He lives here". I was immediately intrigued. Secretly, in my unconscious mind, what I really wanted to do is ask Collin face to face, "How come you are living here?". However, I did not do that. Living in the 21st century, we all know that not being fond of a person can get you into great trouble if you are asking questions that are perceived as overstepping the mark. Later, Collin and I finally got the opportunity my ten-year-old self was waiting for and that was to finally just talk. I enjoyed it immensely, the things he said and the knowledge he offered. It was a moment in my life that I realised, as Dave had mentioned, I had gotten older.

Collin, a couple friends and I were actually going to be heading to Portugal in the summer of 2020 for a festival, but due to the coronavirus pandemic, the trip was rescheduled to a later date. The only reason the trip was suggested in the first place was because Collin wanted to make his way to Portugal, and he asked that same friend of mine to go with him. My friend was interested in the idea and decided to go. Just then, in a sharp moment of spontaneity, Collin asked me to go with them. Initially, me being me, as unspontaneous as I may have been referred to in the past, I shut him down and told him, "Nah". Bear in mind that my ten-year-old self was searching through this same person's Facebook feed to see what he gets up to. Furthermore, the story did not end there. I decided to give Collin a few minutes more of my time and, with a promotional video of the festival and some persuasive language, I decided to think about it instead of completely shutting down his proposal. Sooner rather than later, I decided to take up his offer and booked my ticket for the trip.

It amazes me as I retreat back to the thoughts of my younger self and the shoes I currently walk in. If my ten-year-old self could look into the future and witness the conversations I had with Collin he would truly be amazed. I believe that the moral of the story shows that, whether we find Arnold Schwarzenegger as our inspiration or our neighbour from across the street, at times we need to have the confidence to break the ice and talk to that person who has influenced our life. Find out more about them, learn from them during conversations, and ultimately build friendship with them. Whether you think you are too young or not important enough is irrelevant. So, I invite other people, especially young children, to have the confidence to speak out to those who inspire them.

8. The Nazarene

Ever since I was a young boy, religion has always been a big part of my life. Both my parents were brought up in religious families that believed in Christianity and were practising Catholics. Through their upbringing and their own view of religion, they were also strong believers in Christianity. This was passed on to my elder sister who I live with and me from a young age. We were required to attend church with our parents from the time that we were born. We were baptised when we were babies, received our holy communion and were confirmed, as most Catholic children are. We were born into the Catholic church. From around age six, since I could remember actually attending church, I was against the idea of it. I never used to like going to church on Sunday mornings because it meant waking up at around 9am and having to get ready. This may not be an early time to wake up for most people, but for the six- to ten-year-old me it was early. So, at times when my parents would come into my room to wake me up, I was either still fast asleep, or pretending to be asleep so they may think that I still needed to sleep for longer and would, hopefully, let me remain at home and not attend church. I'm not quite sure how I thought this strategy was going to work, as I don't think my parents would have ever let me remain home alone between the ages of six and ten.

At times, when my friend Sean came for sleepovers at my house, both he and I knew that on a Sunday morning my mother or father was going to come into my room and tell us that we were going to have to get ready for church. Again, we would try the strategy of pretending to sleep, but it never worked. It was bad enough that I felt that I had to attend church with my family, but when I had to drag Sean along with me because he had slept over the previous night, I felt guilty because Sean did not want to attend church either. Even if it was my birthday or I had a sleepover with a few friends, my friends were also brought along to church with my family and me on Sunday morning. I think the main reason why I did not want to attend church was not because I wasn't a believer in God, but more or less due to the fact that it wasn't something that was trendy at the time. None of my friends at school would say to me that one of the highlights of their weekend was when they went to church with their families. At times, primary school classmates of mine would even laugh at the minority who stated that they attended church on the weekend and they viewed it as corny. In a way, church was viewed as uncool and at that age, I didn't want to be a part of anything that made me uncool. In addition, I also found church extremely boring! Despite these feelings I had about church, being so young meant I didn't really have a choice whether I attended or not, so I still attended church each Sunday of each year from the time I was born up until I reached 18 years old.

Before I had hit double digits in age I wasn't completely closed to the idea of church and didn't sit and sulk in the corner during the children's liturgy or anything like that. I was open enough to allow myself to learn what I was being taught during the children's liturgy each week. This was actually taught by the mother of one of my classmate's. It was comforting to be taught by a familiar face. As I made my way towards double digits in age and through to my teens, my perspective and views on church slowly began to change. I still had to take Sean with me to church if he slept over, but little did I know that throughout this change I was being influenced by an important person in Christianity: The Nazarene.

The Nazarene was a preacher and religious leader and plays a large role as a biblical figure in Christianity. He is extremely important in most Christian doctrines, Catholicism especially. The Nazarene has an important role in Christianity due to the way that he dealt with situations and challenges throughout his lifetime. He was kind to almost everybody, shared willingly with others, rarely got into any conflicts or fights with people, always forgave those who had done wrong unto him, and encouraged this behaviour among his peers. At the time he was alive, The Nazarene's way of life was not common among many people, so he stood out because of the way that he decided to live his life. One thing that The Nazarene managed to do consistently was pray. He was dedicated to his prayer and life as a holy man and even set an example of what it meant to be dedicated to your faith and beliefs through his relationship with prayer. It was between the ages of 11 and 18 years old that the stories and tales of The Nazarene had a significant influence in my life. As a result of what I was learning about The Nazarene and his way of life, being a believer in God, I decided to try and implement some of the ways he lived into my own life.

Before football games, I would start doing prayers on the pitch just before the whistle for kick-off was blown. I had seen other professional footballers confidently do it just before the game had begun, or just before they were being substituted in, so this may have also had an influence on my decision to pray before my games began. Initially, I would turn away from my teammates and do it closed by myself, while standing in my position waiting for the referee to blow the whistle. Over time, however, with practice, learning more about The Nazarene and growing in age, I began to build the confidence to not keep my before-match rituals hidden and I happily started to do it openly by the time I was in year 10, aged 15. I didn't worry or care as much that people looked or knew what I was doing. This was especially true after my experiences in Africa, which you will learn about slightly later on.

This wasn't the only way that The Nazarene was beginning to truly inspire me and influence my life. Early on in my secondary school days, I wasn't the most unpleasant of pupils, but neither was I the most pleasant. My friends and I would occasionally have a bit of banter with a few of our classmates, or one classmate in particular, and would make jokes about that classmate, or subtly irritate them as a group of boys usually do in most secondary schools. At the time, I did not realise that our actions would sometimes be extremely irritating towards our classmates, until they finally told us to stop or looked as if they were seriously upset. It was only later into my secondary school life that I realised I didn't want to do anything that irritated or upset another classmate of mine, due to what I was learning at church and from The Nazarene in particular. The Nazarene used to preach to people of his time that it was extremely important to love others as you loved yourself and, therefore, it wouldn't be right for me to treat anybody in any way that I wouldn't want to be treated myself. The influence of The Nazarene was something that I saw happen gradually, but was something that my teachers and classmates saw as quite a flip in my behaviour as, for the first two years of secondary school, I was viewed as a troublemaker and, after this, I began to show that there was another side to me that was very different from the behaviours I had displayed early on in secondary school. I knew this change in tune was due to the influences of The Nazarene, but since my faith wasn't something that I talked about everywhere I went, my classmates and teachers must have been clueless as to what it was that was converting my behaviours, actions and overall presence.

The influences of the Nazarene led to many significant events and moments throughout my life. During winter, I once decided to attend church on a Sunday morning when I was in year 11. It had snowed very heavily in my town throughout the week and, towards the end of the week leading up to that weekend, schools had shut because of the amount of snow on the roads, making it unsafe for students to travel to schools. Each student truly enjoyed the snow days of that week, probably did no work at all, and sat in their cosy homes and watched movies all day. When Sunday came around, churches were still open for usual Sunday masses. However, most people decided to not attend as they would have had to walk to church. My parents had decided that they were not going to attend church, as we lived a 20- to 30-minute walk away from our local church and were not able to drive there. My parents were also afraid of slipping in the snow. As a young and fit 15-year-old boy, I knew that I could walk to church with some good walking boots and that if I fell over it wouldn't have been the end of the world, so I decided that there was no real reason why I couldn't attend church that morning. So, I dressed myself in the correct gear and walked in the white, thick snow, finding barely any cars on the road, and managed to make it to church in good time in about 20 minutes. Once I got into the church, the first thing I noticed was that there were barely any people present and the ones who were there were local people who lived within a short walking distance. The second thing I noticed was that the church was quite dim, due to the snow covering where the natural light usually entered the church through its stained-glass windows. The mass was administered and it was the only mass I had ever attended with no more than ten people present. This action and desire of mine to walk through the snow on a Sunday morning, on a day that absence from church would not have been something to be frowned upon, was the influence that The Nazarene had on me. I did not notice it greatly at the time, yet my parents did. It is crazy to think that the person who pretended to be asleep on Sunday mornings to avoid church a few years earlier was the same person who happily trekked through the snow in order to avoid missing church.

Another occasion that actions and the way of life of The Nazarene inspired me to act in a certain way happened when I was walking home from school with my friends while I was in year 11. There were five of us in total walking together and, within a mile or two of our school, we came across an elderly man who seemed to be struggling to get up a short, steep part of path on his seated electric scooter. This elderly man was coming towards us as we were walking in the opposite direction to him. The man seemed to be in a desperate struggle, trying to move his scooter up the bit of path towards a level path where we had just been walking. He was almost at a standstill, breathless, when we had come across him. All five of us had noticed the situation and had decided to walk past him and carry on our way. Within seconds of walking past him and realising the situation, something within me made me walk back up to him and ask whether he needed any help. He politely nodded his head and looked slightly shocked that I had offered to help him and, being as young and energised as I was, I managed to pretty much run up the short, steep bit of path he was struggling with. I moved the scooter to a flat area for him to continue his journey. He kindly thanked me and went on with his journey.

I had seen that my friends had kept walking and had waited for me after crossing at some traffic lights. When I reached them, one of my friends asked me, "Why did you help him?" I replied saying, "Did you not see how much he was struggling?" The same friend then asked me, "That's not the point Neo, did you not see the white supremist flags that he had attached to his scooter?" The real answer is yes, I had seen the confederate flags, which represent white supremacy, attached to the elderly white man's scooter, but I did not have full knowledge of what the flags actually represented. I had some idea and knew that they had some bad connotations, but I was not definitely clear about the fact that it was a white supremist flag. My four friends all came from black-African descent, as do I, and seemed unwilling to give any help towards that elderly man who potentially saw people of our background as inferior to people who had the same skin colour as him. I was able to understand where my friends were coming from and, after learning about the flag, I later pondered by myself, after telling my parents of the experience I had earlier that day, whether I would still have acted in the manner that I did with full knowledge of what the flag meant. Hypothetically speaking, I believe I would have decided to act in the same manner due to the influence of The Nazarene.

The Nazarene encouraged individuals to love their enemies and treat every single individual with love and respect, no matter how many times they may have made you upset, angry, or carried out acts that people viewed as unforgivable. It is this teaching from The Nazarene that I believe helped me to ignore the flag, which I had little knowledge of, while helping that elderly man. It is this teaching that I still believe would have persuaded me to go and help that man, even if I completely understood the meaning of his flags. In that situation, the elderly man may have had white supremist flags attached to his scooter and he may have even thought that I was interior to him while I helped him move his scooter, but all I saw was a person in great struggle, requiring assistance and I knew that if I allowed myself to head home that day and walk past the man without even offering any assistance, I was going to feel like the bad guy.

It is this type of influence that The Nazarene has had in my life, from the time when I was a young boy, up until a more vivid influence in my later years, that led me to have a different perspective of people, the world, and my own endeavours on a day-to-day basis. It is this influence from The Nazarene which leads me to get down on my knees each morning and night to enter a period of prayer. The influence of The Nazarene makes it impossible for me to lazily miss church without feeling completely guilty after doing so. I feel that the influence of The Nazarene and my faith have played extremely significant roles in my success and achievements throughout my life thus far. I think they also have roles whenever I am recognised positively and whenever any good has managed to cross my path throughout my life. I can't see myself being half the person I am today without the influence and help of The Nazarene and Christianity. The Nazarene is a person who has made known his name throughout history, long after he left earth. He is most probably the most talked about human being in human history. His birthday and death day are known to almost every single person that has walked upon this earth. Despite not having social media, the internet or even phones during his time, he still manages to make an appearance in all of these areas regularly. In the bible he is also referred to by another name that he is commonly known as among many people around the world and throughout human history. That name is Jesus Christ.

9. My Mother

My mother's name is Mrs Agnes Chiku Kalungu-Banda and she upholds a lot of values and qualities as a person. She is kind, selfless, respectful and disciplined. However, she does have one strength that she applies frequently to the rest of my family members. That is her capacity to clean and remain tidy and presentable. My mother is one clean human being. As the firstborn among her many siblings, she had the pleasure of experiencing, first-hand, the whole process of cleaning up after her elders. This involved cleaning the house every day and especially every evening after her parents and she had finished dining. Fortunately, my mother kept this trait of being clean and has passed it on to my siblings and myself. In my household, Saturday is always cleaning day, so each time the weekend comes to pass we all have our assigned roles within the house that we need to tackle. Mine is to hoover the entire house. My mother has instilled into both my elder sister, Bobo (who lives with me), and I that we cannot leave our rooms untidy or with our beds not made. I don't know about Bobo, but it took me just under the first 18 years of my life to master this skill. It is such a difficult skill, in my opinion, due to the busyness of everyday life. You just want to rush out of the door in the mornings at times, not be late, and get to where you are meant to be. Over the course of my life, my mother and my father too have trained me as a human being to keep myself clean, and this ranges from wearing clean clothes, being clean and presentable while out in public, always having clean hair and, overall, being as tidy as I can while I walk out among society. Although it has taken me such a long while to master this skill, I am so grateful that I have been taught it.

Cleanliness and tidiness are privileges that some people take for granted. Not everyone has the availability and opportunity to purchase cleaning items and so have to struggle when it comes to eradicating dirt in their homes. So those of us who have been blessed with access to good and healthy cleanliness should be grateful for the position we are in and even more grateful if we have a parent or, even better, two parents who emphasise the importance of cleanliness. It is a skill that remains with a person throughout the course of their life and influences other aspects of their lives too, other than just being able to make a bed and maintain a tidy room.

10. My Father

My father, who goes by the name of Mr Martin Mugbanga Kalungu-Banda, told me that when we first arrived in England, travelling from South Africa, he used to watch me kick a football in our garden at home. He had later told me that my kick was quite strong for a three-year-old. One of my closest friend's late father had actually encouraged my parents to take me to a club at that age. From what I have been told, I discovered that I was given the opportunity to take my talents elsewhere at a local football practice. Where this story got most interesting for me is when my father told me one time when, during those moments of seeing me have the ability to kick the ball the way I did, he thought that the purpose of my family's move to England was for me to pursue professional English football. The interest of the story for me is not the fact that my dad once believed I could become a professional footballer at the age of three – it was the openness and belief in me and my abilities that my dad decided to share with me in that moment, that it was possible his son was potentially destined for success in professional football. I was truly inspired by my dad after I learned that he did not choose to think in a narrow-minded way, but that he thought laterally in that moment when he saw me there, playing in the back garden at the age of three.

I have decided to tell this story as I think that it fully represents the type of belief that my father has had in me since the day I was born. My father believed that it was possible for me to play professional football just through the way I kicked the ball at such a young age and has believed in me on many other occasions throughout my life. My father's belief in me is not something that I take for granted at all. It is not just his belief that I am able to achieve things, it is also the fact that he does not put limitations on me either. I remember, vividly, once while I was playing for my local club, Banbury Irish, that I had a discussion with both my parents about my school grades and the time that I was devoting to football during my early years at secondary school. My father shared his belief with me that he thought I would not make it as a professional footballer because I wasn't even the best player in Banbury Irish. This broke my heart at the time. Having someone you know and love tell you that they did not believe you had what it takes to achieve your dreams, is something that truly hurt to the core. However, these were my father's thoughts. He was entitled to believe what he believed and, in the end, he was correct.

At the time, I intended to prove him wrong through working relentlessly on my footballing ability and trying to progress as an overall player. This didn't play in my mind too much as I went along my football journey, as you will learn about later. My father's doubts and thoughts went into the category where I placed the doubts that other people had while I was trying to pursue professional football. Unconsciously, I knew that peers of mine thought that it wasn't possible for me to make it, along with anybody else who also played football locally. My own teammates were among this group of people, but I tried to never allow this to affect my mind, thoughts and intentions. My father has a lot of belief in me, but only for things that he thinks are within my reach. One of those things was writing this book.

Initially, when my friend Gilbert introduced the idea of writing a book, I had to give it a few days to play in my mind and see whether this task was actually achievable. I definitely had the time for it because, as he mentioned at the time, my A-level exams had been cancelled due to the coronavirus pandemic, and I now had a full 24 hours each day to spend as I wished. After practising a bit of writing on the subject I actually wanted to write about, I realised that the speed at which I wrote and thought were of a good standard and the way I managed to narrate stories was not too bad. Therefore, I shared some pieces of my writing with both of my parents and they were impressed. I hadn't told them of my intentions to write a book at the time, as I was still experimenting on what the book would be about and the idea of it was too wide and open; I had to narrow it down slightly to specific topics. After I managed to find a topic that I was interested in, I sat down with both my parents and told them what I intended to do. As my father has authored three books, I thought it might have been best for me to let him know my intentions very early on and have his guidance throughout the process. Both of my parents were on board with the idea and were interested to see and read what I was going to write about. This was the first sign of belief I saw from my father, as well as my mother, about me writing a book.

When I revealed my intentions, they never told me that they thought the task was too difficult for me to achieve, or that I didn't have what it takes, or even that I should wait until I start university or read a few more books before deciding to write my own. Both my parents knew that I was not a big fan of reading and rarely did it. Despite this, bearing in mind I was almost 18 years old at the time, they believed in the idea proposed by Gilbert and were ready to help me.

In the early stages of writing, I decided that I wanted this book to focus on celebrating people who have inspired me in life and what the rest of the world could learn from them. So, I followed protocol and led my writing with this idea. It was after I completed writing about the people who have inspired me in life, that my father came up with the idea that I should also share times, moments and events in my life where I have been an inspiration to others. Immediately, I thought to myself, what have I done that is inspirational? My father then went on to mention some of the times when I have been an inspiration to others and this opened multiple doors in my mind. During that moment he had switched on a light bulb in my head and the book was now going its own way and creating its own path.

This, again, was a moment that I reflected on and thought that if it was not for my dad's suggestion of this new idea and section of the book, most of what you are about to read would not have been written. At that moment, when he told me that I was an inspiration to others and gave me examples of why, he actually believed in me and my stories more than I did or have ever managed to. It was the belief my father had in me and my experiences that inspired me and led me to tell the stories that are about to be told.

So, it is from this experience that I encourage parents, grandparents, great grandparents and friends to have and share the type of belief that my father had in me for writing this book. This belief can be in friends, family members, or anyone you are close to. You never know what great things could come to surface with the belief you uphold.

11. Mr Proudfoot

I think that a big reason for writing this book is my year 9 science teacher, Mr Proudfoot. He taught me science while I was preparing to choose my GCSE subjects. In year 9 I was not a super student nor was I a student who was considered to be above the average. I was viewed as an average student. Most people do not mind being an average student and viewed as average by their teachers and peers but, fortunately, I did mind. The problem with me was that I minded about being average and not being the best in my class, but I simply did not act on my own account. There was a period during year 9 science classes when a classmate of mine, Giovanni, who now is a friend, was beating everyone and topping the class in every single end of unit test. We would be tested on a chapter we had just completed and, each time we received our results, Mr Proudfoot would always tell us who came top of the class and this was almost always Giovanni Ambrosio. At the time, I did not feel envy or negative feelings towards Giovanni, however, the feeling of being beneath him in some way had got to me. I was not able to understand how he was consistently scoring top of the class in each and every test.

Each time I received my own results, scoring a solid average score, I just felt a numb response. Deep down, I knew that I wanted to be sitting in the same position as Mr Ambrosio, topping the class in every single test, or at least scoring highly for my own personal reward. Eventually, my day came.

It was in April 2016 that I finally decided to pick up my science revision guide and prepare as well and as fully as I could, so that I could write the end of unit test coming up and achieve the highest grade possible. It was a physics end of unit test based on speed, velocity and time. The day we received our results back happened to be my birthday, 21st April. When Mr Proudfoot named the person who topped the class, I heard the first syllables of my name and a great bubbly feeling came to the core of my body. A feeling of untouchable happiness. My immediate response was not to react and instead show the class and my friends that I was calm and content. I did smile due to the happiness Mr Proudfoot had given me in his announcement, but I tried my hardest to contain my happiness and buzz. I remember saying out loud to myself, "So revision does work." Mr Proudfoot heard me say these words and smiled at me greatly saying, "Yeah! It does." It was from that day, when I had finally topped the class, was recognised as the best and seen as more than an average student, that I continued attempting to obtain more of the same feelings.

Towards the end of the academic year and my transition from year 9 to year 10, my one aim was to do as well as I could in all of my subjects, predominantly in science. I preferred science above my other subjects because I viewed it as one of my strongest subjects. It was from that one experience and positive reinforcement of studying, then achieving success, that I was enticed to continue working hard to become the best in my science class in years 10 and 11. Over the two-year period, there were predominantly two people who managed to come top of the class in end of unit tests and they were Mr Ambrosio and myself. In the end, I managed to top the class the most out of my entire class. It was a feeling that I just could not get enough of.

Doing well and scoring highly was not enough to fill my satisfaction at the time. I had to hear from my science teachers that I did the best in the entire class. It did not even matter to me at times if we all failed, as long as I was above everyone else, I was happy. So, tracking back all the way to my year 9 self. That average student is grateful to Mr Proudfoot for using language in such a way that inspired me to learn more about the concept of competition and working hard, and the importance of trying to be seen as above average. That small trigger of naming the person who came top of the class was the defining factor which inspired me to pick up that revision guide.

For me, the moral of the story is not that either Mr Ambrosio or myself were above the rest, or that Mr Ambrosio dominated the rest of us during his glory days in year 9. The ideology is that an individual can usually apply themselves to tasks either completely or incompletely. I was not applying myself enough to achieve the highest grades possible in year 9, nor was I working hard enough to be recognised as the best in my year 9 science class. Giovanni was the one doing that. So, when my turning point happened it was due to my complete dedication to achieve and truly do my best. Previously, I was recognised as just another average student in my year 9 science class because I was not doing anything to be recognised as otherwise. Given chances, on multiple occasions, and finally taking them led to my achievements in those two years. If the same average-achieving Neo can do it, tell me why anybody else can't.

Reader Exercises:

- What stories can you trace back to in your own life that laid the foundations for your success and drive in life?
- Are there times in your life when you feel as if you are not applying yourself fully to your studies or your job and, if so, why do you think this is?
- Are you seen as average among your classmates, work colleagues or in your respective industry and, if this is the case, what can you do to move yourself up in the rankings?

With Mr Proudfoot at prom

12. Michael Jordan

'The Last Dance' is a Netflix series that I began to watch soon after it was released on 19th April 2020, during the national lockdown of the UK and most countries across the world. I saw it one time while flicking through Netflix and I soon saw it again on multiple social media platforms, and on 'Good Morning Britain' due to the media attention it received soon after it came out. After watching English broadcaster Piers Morgan do an interview with Dennis Rodman, who stars in the show, about what the Netflix series was about and their views on it, I soon hit play and began to watch the series myself. Now, when I can, I try to refrain from starting or following series due to the addictive effect they have on me. If I really get into a show, I have the capacity to sit and watch back-to-back episodes for twelve hours. So, when starting watching 'The Last Dance' I said to myself that I would only watch a maximum of two episodes a day, as each episode is fifty minutes long and I only intended to give myself two hours of television a day during the lockdown period. Despite this principle that I decided to place on myself, after watching the first two episodes in one day, I couldn't help but click onto the third. It also didn't help that Netflix gives you ten seconds to back out before the next episode automatically begins to play. Before I knew it, I had finished the ten-episode series within three-to-four days, but I had no shame in spending all those hours to watch the show due to the abundant number of valuable lessons that it taught me.

'The Last Dance' series tells the story of how the Chicago Bulls Dynasty basketball team played their last season together, in one last attempt to win their sixth NBA Championship. If they did so, this was going to be the Dynasty's second threepeat, which means to win three NBA Championships in a row, in the seven seasons that they spent playing together. Different shots of the series were filmed during the 1997–1998 NBA season, which was named 'The Last Dance' by the head coach at the time, Phil Jackson. Throughout the series, it goes back to look at the start of different players' careers and various events that occurred. As you get more and more into the series, you come to see how the spotlight shined upon one man, Mr Michael Jordan. For those who do not know him, Michael Jeffrey Jordan is a basketball legend and member of the Naismith Memorial Basketball Hall of Fame. He is considered the greatest basketball player to ever play the game and one of the top ten greatest athletes who has ever lived. He played the lead role in helping the Chicago Bulls to winning five championships in the '91–'92, '92–'93, '93–'94, '95–'96 and '96–'97 seasons. Having only seen a few highlights of Mr Jordan and reading people's comments describing him, I knew very little about him before watching 'The Last Dance.' 'The Last Dance' shows some of Michael's mouth-watering plays and how he made a full team of legends look average compared to himself. Importantly, it also shows how Mr Jordan rose to the level that he did in terms of basketball, as an athlete and, especially, as a winner.

The series reveals where it all started for Mr Jordan, which was in a small port city in North Carolina called Wilmington. Michael's parents insisted that all of their children participated in organised sports in order for them to stay out of trouble and learn more about life. This is where Michael was first introduced to the game of basketball. His first sport was actually baseball. Soon, he began playing basketball and quickly fell in love with the sport. Due to the racism in North Carolina and the entire United States, and in Wilmington especially, Michael stated he wanted no involvement in it and wanted to excel outside his hometown. For him, athletics was his strong point. So, early on in his basketball years, he tried out for his high school team and did not make it in the trials. Michael mentioned how this cut him and how he no longer wanted to play any more sports. However, his mother comforted him and told him that if he really wanted to make the team he would need to work hard over the summer. Mr Jordan did so and, with the help of puberty, grew quite a few inches taller too. He was immediately picked the following year and was seen as one of the best players competing for his high school as a junior student. He was soon invited to the University of North Carolina (UNC) for a basketball camp and, within just five days, they thought that he was the best player of his age in the whole of America. After graduating from high school, Michael was enrolled at UNC and was soon playing for the varsity team as a first year in the hope of being the best player to have ever played there.

James Worthy, a teammate of Michael's at UNC, said how, after two-and-a-half hours of hard practice, Michael walked up to him and asked him whether he wanted to play him in a one-on-one to see where his game was at. James stated that he was better than Michael at the time, but it only lasted for two weeks. This was due to the hard work Mr Jordan put in, on and off the court. From then on, Michael only continued to improve. He learned more, soaked up information, and added all of this to the raw talent and athleticism he already had. In this same year, Michael and the UNC basketball team made it to the NCAA Championship final which was played against Georgetown. Michael was described as a great player by then. He had played a good game so far, but in the last 32 seconds of the match his team was down by one point at 61-62. The UNC coach at the time, Dean Smith, made a play which would've resulted in Michael having a clear shot at the basket. Smith told Michael that if he was able to get the shot off, he should take it. Michael stated that this gave him the green light. The play was administered and it occurred as coach Smith intended. Michael was free on the left side of the court and the ball was passed over to him. He caught the ball and took the shot that Georgetown were not expecting. The shot went in to make the score 64-62 and UNC was crowned as the 1982 NCAA Champions. Prior to the shot that Michael scored in the last second, he was known and referred to as 'Mike' or 'Mike Jordan'. It was after that game-winning shot that his name changed from 'Mike' to 'Michael Jordan'. Michael states that this gave him the confidence he needed to excel at the game of basketball. After this, he simply continued to improve as a basketball player, exponentially, and continued helping his university achieve different successes, as well as winning at an individual level such as varsity Player of the Year.

After his first year of university, Michael planned to return to school to finish his bachelor's degree in Geography, but coach Smith recommended that he should go and play professional basketball. At the time, he was likely to be among the top three or four players to be chosen to play for teams in the NBA. On 4th May 1984, Michael decided, within an hour-and-a-half, that he was going to leave UNC in his first year and take up the opportunity of playing professional basketball. Before that hour-and-a-half, he was 50-50 on what to do but, after speaking to coach Smith and with his parents that same morning, they all decided it would be best for him. On 19th June 1984, it was the 1984 NBA draft – the annual event that teams in the NBA get to choose players who are eligible to play. The players are usually college players who have either finished their college degrees or, like Michael, have decided to put college on hold or leave college completely to become an NBA player. Michael Jordan was the third pick and was chosen by the Chicago Bulls. This is how he made it to becoming a professional basketball player.

Soon after the draft, Michael was chosen to represent the USA men's basketball team at the 1984 Olympics held in Los Angeles. Here, the USA team managed to achieve a gold medal and this was another occasion at which Michael Jordan truly made a name for himself and began to bring more attention to his game. As the preseason began for Michael's first season with the Bulls, the '84–'85 season, he did not know that most of his team were players who had gotten themselves involved in drugs. Despite this, as soon as it became apparent to Michael, he decided to be independent when it came to being a part of the Chicago Bulls team. At the time, the Bulls were a very poor franchise and had a very poor basketball team. The team was used to losing, the stadium in Chicago was barely filled each game, and they hadn't won a championship for 16 years, only having one NBA Championship under their belt. A lot of people believed that Michael was Chicago's way out of its own death and had come to lift the franchise, almost like a new, fresh seed being planted in infertile soil. However, people and players had their odds against him, including his own teammates. Some of Michael's teammates would tell the press that he was not tall enough to completely carry a team in the NBA. His own manager at the time stated they wished he was 7ft 1" compared to his height of 6ft 6". Soon, it came to the first day of practice for the preseason and Michael knew that he had to earn his respect, despite all of the talk around him. He just went in and gave the court all he had. Michael's teammate at the time, Rod Higgins, stated that during that first day of practice, within a short period, you could see that Michael was the best player among the team. Higgins further stated, "This cat is different."

Michael's mentality at the time was that he was aiming for whoever the leader was on the team and going after them for their position, but he knew he could only do it with his game because he had no 'voice' at the time. Shortly into the season, Michael earned respect during their third match. The Bulls were losing to the Milwaukee Bucks and they were heading into the last quarter of the match. Michael stated that his teammates would usually get down, and just give up looking forward and being hopeful to the next game, but Michael saw it in a different light and would say, "The game is not over with." One of Michael's teammates sensed this and continued to pass the ball to him. Soon, Michael managed to score the majority of the points to put the Bulls in front and they went on to win the match. After this match, Michael's teammates realised that, despite his youth, he would not allow them to lose and they knew he was the best player they had. As Michael played more and more games and began to improve and perform each match, numbers in the stadium grew to see him play. Within a matter of matches, the Chicago Bulls' stadium was sold out. That same season, Michael Jordan was recognised as the Rookie of the Year for the '84–'85 season. However, due to the way he played, some wouldn't necessarily call him a rookie.

In the following seasons, Michael continued to grow as a basketball player, an athlete and a person. He remained as the Bulls' best player despite the multiple changes the team underwent and, in the process, recruited Michael's best teammate that he's ever played with, Mr Scotty Maurice Pippen Sr. Pippen assisted Michael tremendously throughout his career and was there both defensively and offensively whenever Michael was not able to be. Pippen was the Robin to Michael's Batman. While Michael still proceeded to be Chicago's biggest leader and impact player on and off the court, there were several factors that led him to gaining this position. One of them was his desire to win. Ever since Michael was young, competition had been a big part of his life. Michael's father stated that Michael's siblings and he have always been very competitive between themselves when it came to sport and, especially, losing. This is where Michael feels the desire in him to win was initiated and, as he grew more and more as a player, he experienced winning and received many other awards too. These were contributing factors that added to his desire to win. By the time Michael was drafted to the Chicago Bulls, he had a 'win at all costs' type of personality. Even if it meant winning by himself. When Michael first joined the Bulls, he already had a high level of confidence and told the people of Chicago that, by the time that he left they would have become NBA champions. It was in the '88–'89 season that Michael Jordan was seen as the best player in the NBA, under new coach, Doug Collins. He won various awards, such as most valued player of the league (MVP), MVP of the all-star match, defensive player of the year and the slam dunk competition winner across the three years for which Mr Collins coached him. Due to his successes and consistent ability to score points and help in leading the Bulls to victory, Michael developed a mindset during the '89–'90 season where, after a teammate complained that he wasn't passing the ball to his teammates enough and that there was no 'I' in 'team', Michael replied, "There isn't an 'I' in 'team' but there is one in 'win'."

During that season, a new head coach was enrolled to take over from Doug Collins – Phil Jackson. Mr Jackson took a different approach to Mr Collins, who was more or less focused on "getting the ball to Michael", in that he wanted the ball to be shared around the team a lot more but still understood and knew the value that Michael held. Michael states that, initially, he felt as if his new coach was taking the ball "out of his hands" whereas Mr Collins had put the ball into his hands. He was also anxious about the fact that he would no longer be taking each last second shot that could help his team to win. However, after more guidance from Mr Jackson, there was a moment when Michael was able to look more deeply into what it was that he was trying to achieve as a coach, and Michael was able to change his philosophy. He realised that his scoring a lot of points in a match and chasing individual accolades was not going to help Chicago bring a championship home. He realised that there was no individual in a team and that he did not need to have the ball in his hand all the time. This is what helped contribute to the Bulls winning their first championship in the '91-'92 season. Before this, Michael and the Bulls had undergone a close run towards being champions of their conference and so had the opportunity to be NBA champions in the previous season. However, they suffered a loss to the Detroit Pistons, their rivals at the time. It was a huge loss for the Bulls and, especially, Michael, as it was another championship opportunity squandered. At the time, Michael was truly seen as one of the greatest players of all time. However, he was not on the level of other legendary players such as Magic Johnson and Larry Bird because they had won championships and he was yet to achieve that.

Meanwhile, before the Bulls' first championship winning season, instead of going on vacation after the match against the Pistons, they all returned to practise to prep themselves for the following season and finally beat the Pistons. In the process, Michael began to gear his winning energy and desire towards his teammates, but it wasn't in the nicest way that people may want to be encouraged to win. Michael began to push his teammates to really dedicate themselves to off-season training and working hard to ensure that, during the same season, they were not going to be runners up but champions. Teammates of his describe how he was on their case, entertained no mistakes, screamed at them if they were to make mistakes and belittled them at times – all with the aim of ensuring they won and were successful that season. That same season, the Bulls met the Pistons in the final of their conferences and completely whitewashed them, beating them 4-0 in the game series. The Bulls proceeded to play the Los Angeles Lakers in the NBA final, where Magic Johnson and Michael Jordan were going to meet for the first time. In a process that involved Michael trusting in his teammates to make important shots in the fifth match against the Lakers, the Chicago Bulls team rose to prominence by winning their first championship 4-1 in the series. After they had finally became champions, Michael went into the Bulls' locker room and began to cry heavily. All of his emotions that he had bottled up to keep the focus on winning had poured out after that game. His teammates were extremely shocked to see him in such a state as they had only known the 'win at all costs' Michael Jordan, they had never seen this side to him. Throughout several years of watching him play and playing with him, they had thought that he almost wasn't human and had no feelings, until the moment they saw him in tears after winning his first championship. Michael mentioned that, when you finally cross the finish line and know that you have won, you can let out all the emotions that you kept inside. He was finally put into the category of Magic Johnson and Larry Bird.

Starting with the following season, Michael's teammate Benjamin Roy, better known as B. J. Armstrong Jr, felt as if Michael never played basketball anymore, instead he just figured out how to win the game. Mr Armstrong added that he knew how to steer the game and get momentum going, along with influencing his teammates. He felt as if Michael was playing a different game to everyone else. Michael still played with his teammates, but was simply there to win the game. The Bulls had managed to make it to the NBA finals once again and had the chance to win back-to-back championships. Jordan always looked for different ways to keep his competitive nature and winning mentality fresh. At the time, he was being compared to a player he was playing against in the final, Clyde Drexler. Jordan took offence to this comparison, as he felt that Clyde was a good player and a threat, but still felt that he was a much better player than Mr Drexler and used this as a motivation to perform well and show who was the better player. As the series commenced, Michael used this as motivation for each game and, as a team, the Bulls managed win back-to-back championships that season.

Now that Michael had two back-to-back championships to his name, the thing that would separate him as a player from Magic Johnson and Larry Bird, who had won several championships each but had never won them three times in a row, was to do a threepeat the following season and win a third championship. Therefore, during the '93–'94 season, Michael had his eyes on the prize of becoming the only player in his era to win three in a row. The Bulls managed to get to their third consecutive NBA final once again and faced the Phoenix Suns. Normally, there is no game seven and usually one team would have managed to reach four wins and win a series. However, in this particular instance, the series was 3-1 to the Bulls, and they had the chance of winning the championship at home to make it 4-1 during game five. However, they did not win, and the series was scored at 3-2. They had to fly to Phoenix to play game six, which was where they had another opportunity to win the series and become champions. As the Bulls got onto the plane, Michael had a cigar and wanted to speak to his teammates. At the time, his teammates were dreading going back to Phoenix to play game six in fear that they could lose and would have to play the last game of the series, game seven, in Phoenix. Michael was, once again, thinking in another light. He said to his teammates, "I don't know about you guys, but I am only packing one suit. We're going back to win one game. I'm not going there to play two games." In the remaining seconds of game six, a game-winning basket was scored by one of Michael's teammates, putting the Bulls to a one-point lead that they were crowned champions. That same basket was the only shot scored in that last quarter by a Bulls player other than Michael. Phoenix's best player, Charles Barkley, stated that, "Michael had the ability where he was not going to let them lose."

It was the confidence Mr Jordan showed that truly inspired me. This mentality of constantly winning, winning at all costs and keeping an extremely high level of competition led me to admire him so greatly. The fact that Michael only packed one suit as he travelled to Phoenix shows the level of confidence he had in himself and his teammates to win game six. I believe that type of confidence can be extremely beneficial to anyone, in any field of work they are in.

Soon after the threepeat season, Michael unfortunately lost his father and announced his retirement from the sport of basketball. He took a year out and went to play professional baseball. During the end of the '94–'95 season, Michael began to work out with his old teammates and soon decided to come out of retirement to play once again. It was suggested that he was even more goal-oriented and focused on winning a championship once again after having time away from the sport. However, the Bulls didn't manage to even make the final of their conference that same season. This was quite disheartening for Michael, as he wasn't able to make a great return and help the Bulls win a championship. Despite this, Michael used it as his motivation for the following season. In the following two seasons, the Bulls were able to win back-to-back championships once again and were now into another season heading for their second threepeat.

There was one event where actions taken by Michael simply

blew my mind. It was during the '96–'97 season when Chicago had met Utah Jazz in the NBA finals. The series was tied at 2-2 as they headed into game five being played in Utah. The night before, Michael had gotten hungry late in the evening, around 10pm, so ordered a pizza. Five people showed up to his hotel room to deliver the pizza, which was rare. Michael's trainer had a bad feeling about the pizza as he paid the delivery guys, but Michael ate all of it himself. In the middle of the night Michael woke to throw up and he was soon to discover that he had food poisoning from the pizza. He was comforted by his trainer who saw him curled up in a ball and shaking. Later on, the day of game five, he was still very sick and his mother insisted that he did not play. However, he could not fight the urge to play in such an important match. That day, Michael had to remain in bed all day and did not eat a single thing because, each time he did, it would just come back up. So, he played game five on an empty stomach. Utah began with a lead over Chicago and, each time out, Michael was described as looking as though the life was being thrown out of his body as his head and shoulders dropped. He was completely fatigued. It was after the time out of the second quarter that Michael was described as having gone somewhere within himself and found 'a switch'. He got up, played and performed as he usually would, and began to help the Bulls take the lead. The Bulls ended up winning the match and going on to win the series in the end, but it was after that match, which Michael Jordan played while being sick, that he truly showed what it takes to win and, despite being sick, he was still the best player in the world.

His desire to win was not the only thing that inspired me about Mr Jordan. His incredible work ethic was also something I admired greatly about him. During the era that he played, there was no highly efficient technology or social media to promote you or put you on all of the platforms. Despite this, he still managed to become one of the most powerful and iconic athletes the world has ever seen. A cultural figure and influence among many people across the world, simply due to his great capacity to perform on a basketball court. Michael Jordan managed to lead a poor 1984 Chicago Bulls team in rising to greatness over the years and win several championships. He changed the franchise forever. As he sweetly puts it, it only took one match, the NCAA Championship final, for him to light the entire fire. He is completely right. At times, it only does take one match to light an entire fire, such as the reign of the Chicago Bulls dynasty from 1991–1998 and who knows, whether it's in business, sports, or film, with similar qualities to Michael, you may one day rise to that success and discover your own match to light.

Reader Exercises:

- When faced with failure, how often do you go back and give things another try in the hope of succeeding?
- When competing in sport, for a job or a new role, how much confidence do you have within yourself to come out victorious? How can you improve your level of confidence?

13. LeBron James

LeBron Raymone James Sr is an American professional basketball player for the Los Angeles Lakers of the National Basketball Association (NBA). He has won four NBA championships and has managed to break multiple records and do things that no other human being has ever done in the sport of basketball. He is among the four players in history to have won an NBA championship with three different teams. He is also known for securing what could potentially be called one of his most special NBA championships, after he returned back to the team that drafted him when he first became an NBA player at age 18. Namely, when he returned to the Cleveland Cavaliers, he helped them to end their 52-year drought of not winning an NBA championship. Potentially, this could be argued to have been the pinnacle moment throughout LeBron's career as a basketballer. To return to the first team that he ever played for as an NBA player, 11 years later, and help them end their 52-year drought, as he said it himself in an interview, may have made him the greatest player ever to play the game of basketball.

I have never really been interested in basketball as a sport, but I have always been interested in LeBron and would watch some of his seasonal highlights on YouTube. I soon gained a bigger interest in basketball throughout the first lockdown in the UK in 2020. My friend Sean decided to purchase a basketball and started playing at a basketball court in a place called Hanwell, which is local to where my friends and I live. Soon after this, other members of my friendship group, known as the mandem, decided to join Sean in playing basketball and began to start arranging to meet up and play throughout the UK's period in lockdown. I saw this on their Snapchat stories and was cautious about playing at first due to coronavirus, but as the restrictions in Britain began to slowly relax, I joined them in playing basketball. Other members of the mandem also got involved and we made it a thing that we would play basketball from late afternoon up until it got dark around 8pm to 9pm. Usually, there was only a maximum of six of us, to adhere to COVID-19 restrictions, but basketball was our go-to throughout lockdown. Some of us even decided to purchase our own basketballs as we wanted to practise by ourselves from time to time, to be improved when we came to play against each other when we met up.

Since we were now playing basketball, as opposed to our usual sport of football, the tables turned with regard to who were the best players. It was no longer my friends called Jekhio and Gwin sitting at the top. It was now Sean and Champ who were the most valued players (MVPs) when it came to basketball. This new interest in basketball, stemmed from playing it socially with my friends, led me to learn more about the sport as I intended to try out for the University of Leicester basketball team once the semester began. However, due to coronavirus, I was not able to try out for the varsity basketball team as the university was not able to hold trials. Despite this, I was still playing basketball at a local park at university with some of my new friends from Leicester. Around the time that I had begun university and was playing basketball every other morning, the NBA playoffs for the 2020 season were still going on and the final was being played in October. The two teams that made it to the NBA finals in the 2019–2020 season were the Miami Heat and the Los Angeles Lakers. LeBron James played for the Lakers at the time and played the leading role in their campaign to win an NBA championship that season. As I was so interested in basketball by this point, I decided that I would put time aside to watch the NBA finals, for the first time ever, as well as learn a thing or two from the two best teams in America at the time. During this period, I witnessed LeBron

James display behaviours that inspired me greatly.

I never used to watch basketball, or even any big NBA finals, due to the time difference between the UK and America. Basketball games were and still are played around 7pm or 9pm American time. Due to the fact that the UK is five hours ahead of the States in GMT to UTC time zones, you usually have to stay up late into the following day to watch any basketball matches that are being played live in America. As I was a first-year university student and it was still within the first month that I had begun university, and most lectures and teaching were online due to the pandemic, I thought there was no better time to stay up late and watch the NBA finals. So, within the period that games were being played between the Heat and the Lakers in the NBA finals, I managed to watch the remaining two games of the finals. The Lakers were leading 3-1 in the finals and it was clear that the Heat were more than likely going to lose this NBA series. LeBron and his troops had done enough damage during the series to put the spirits of the Heat heavily down and also make them think that their NBA finals were soon coming to an end. In the NBA finals, the two teams usually play up to six games in a best-out-of-six match series. The Lakers were sitting in a very comfortable position and only needed to win one more match to be crowned NBA champions for the 2020 season. At this point throughout the series, LeBron was one win away from grasping his fourth NBA championship. In game five, the Heat had other plans and ended up winning the match, forcing a game six which left the series at 3-2 to the Lakers. It was now the first to reach four between the two teams. Usually, if an NBA series gets tied at 3-3 between the two final teams, it ultimately forces a game seven to be played where a winner will be crowned after the match.

Having watched a few interviews with the Heat star Jimmy Butler and leading Lakers player LeBron James throughout the NBA finals, I had learned quite a lot about the two. Mr Butler was mostly interested in winning, and winning his first NBA championship ever. In an interview after the Heat won game five, he calmly told the press that nobody should have counted the Heat out by thinking it was all over for them. Mr Butler also stated that he didn't care about the fact that he was probably giving some of his best performances he had ever given on a basketball court as a player, and that it didn't matter about his crazily good match statistics, all he had in mind was winning each match. On the other hand, I saw a slightly different tone from Mr James. In his interviews, before and after game five, he also seemed very calm and relaxed, and especially focused. He told the press that he was simply on a mission to bring a championship back home to LA with him and his teammates, and that he was in a deep mode of complete focus on the task and the goal in hand. Even being 3-1 up in the series at one point, Mr James relentlessly stated that the job was not done yet and there was still plenty of work to do. He knew this especially because he had been in a position where the Cleveland Cavaliers were 3-1 down against the Golden State Warriors in 2016 and managed to bring it back and force a game seven, ultimately winning game seven and ending Cleveland's drought of 52 years without winning an NBA championship. LeBron and the rest of his teammates came back from a two-match deficit and were crowned NBA champions that season. So, LeBron knew that the journey was far from over despite the Lakers leading 3-1 in the series after game four.

After winning game four, the post-match interview revealed a certain level of focus in LeBron that I hadn't seen an athlete display for some time. He stated, during the interview, that he was not going to sleep or rest until the job was done and that he didn't care about sleep or rest. LeBron said this in such a relaxed fashion, as though it was perfectly normal and something that was commonly said among many people. When he said he would not sleep, he didn't mean this literally, he was still sleeping and recovering for his matches, but he was probably just sleeping a lot less than he usually would due to the intensity of the period. LeBron, along with the rest of his Lakers teammates, were playing matches every two days and each day they weren't playing matches they were in the film room analysing their previous matches. The NBA finals are a very intense and fast-moving period for both players and coaches. An individual cannot afford to lose focus, as this could cost the whole team their entire NBA finals run. Mr James clearly wasn't looking as though he was going to lose any focus, nor was he interested in anything at the time other than bringing home his fourth championship and a championship for the state.

During the time that LeBron was playing in the 2020 NBA playoffs, a video of his oldest child, LeBron 'Bronny' James, surfaced on the internet. At the time, Bronny was 15 and the video was of Bronny smoking marijuana. He had recorded himself smoking the drug after his father's team won their first conference finals match, which was going to allow them to proceed to the NBA finals after winning the series, and he accidentally leaked it to his millions of Instagram followers. LeBron must have seen the video because of the media hype, but did not react in any way towards Bronny or the media, other than posting a video on his own Instagram of him playing a sad and moving tune on the harmonica. Bronny seemed to have been enjoying his time and freedom, while his Dad was away and playing in the NBA playoffs. Despite all of this, LeBron kept his focus throughout the NBA playoffs and all the way through until he reached game six of the finals. As he said in an Instagram caption and an interview at the time, he kept 'on the edge' at all times and allowed his mind to be focused and razor sharp. This focus is what led to the Lakers becoming the 2020 NBA champions and is what allowed LeBron to grasp his fourth NBA title and be crowned as MVP throughout the NBA finals. He kept his focus throughout the entire finals, from the round stages and qualifying stages, all the way up until the closing seconds of the final, and he played the leading role in helping his team to win a championship. It was within the remaining seconds of game six when I saw LeBron and his partner in crime, Anthony Davis, celebrating together like kids on the bench, receiving rest after playing countless minutes throughout the series and the remaining game. The Lakers had managed to play so well in game six that they didn't need their two star players on the court for the remaining minutes of the match. After the final whistle had blown, I watched, late at night in my university accommodation, Mr James and his teammates fill the stadium with energy, happiness and joy as they were crowned champions of America. All of the focus and 'on the edge' type of energy LeBron kept throughout several weeks of making it to that point had finally been let go and he was relieved now that he had reached the finish line and completed the job. Watching this and seeing LeBron so happy and relieved, smoking cigars during the post-match interviews after game six, I saw and felt inspired by a man who had delivered a promise to himself, as well as the state of Los Angeles.

In the end, with his high level of focus and determination, LeBron was able to deliver his first NBA championship to the LA Lakers and retrieve his fourth championship as an individual. Now that he had accomplished that, he was definitely in the conversation of the greatest player to have ever played basketball, along with other greats such as Michael Jordan, Kareem Abdul-Jabbar and Wilt Chamberlain. It has been a constant and ongoing debate regarding who the better basketballer has been in the entire history of basketball, between Michael Jordan, who has six NBA championships to his name with the same team, and LeBron James, who has four championships to his name with three different teams. The fact that LeBron James won an NBA championship with three different franchises showed to people that, wherever LeBron James went, an NBA championship was going to follow. LeBron was able to have this type of effect as a basketball player due to his extremely high and efficient work ethic, but also because of his outstanding ability to focus when required and his raw determination to win and deliver. The type of focus and determination LeBron showed during the 2020 NBA finals was completely unprecedented and rarely ever seen in previous NBA players and athletes. This type of focus and desire to simply win and come out on top is what allowed him to be so dominant and such a force each time he walked onto the court. It is what allowed him to grasp his fourth NBA Championship title.

Having this type of focus and determination is likely to help you be successful in whatever it is your heart desires. Focusing on a task as carefully as Mr James did during his quest for his fourth title, will enable you to conquer it and get your set job done. Not allowing yourself to rest until the job is completely and truly finished, to its best form, is only going to yield good results for an individual. It sure did for LeBron during the NBA finals. It is not the idea of working yourself to death or until your bones break, but it is the idea behind knowing and understanding that all of your focus, attention and energy may be required at a certain period of time to deliver on something. LeBron knew this and he stated in an interview that, after the finals had passed, he would be able to sleep for eight hours, wake up, eat, and go back to bed once again. He knew that rest was just around the corner after the finals was complete, but also knew that he couldn't allow his mind, focus and determination, aimed towards winning that title, begin to rest and fatigue during the time when those attributes were most needed.

The same philosophy can be applied to many other events in life. Say you are studying and preparing for your exams, but you are beginning to tire slightly and lose focus. If you understand that a two-month summer holiday is just around the corner, this can enable and inspire you to continue to study and complete the work needed to put you in the best position to execute and produce results when you write your exams. Despite the difficulty and long duration of the task, you still need to keep a razor-sharp focus and stay determined until the end of your final exam. The same theory can be applied to people who go to university and need to hand in assignments, or those who have a job and need to complete tasks by a certain deadline. Understanding and knowing that your energies and hard focus are required for a certain period of time, maybe even an extended period of time, but that it is not forever, is likely to enable you and may even inspire you to continue to keep a focused mindset until the job is done. Maybe too, after you have completed and delivered your set task, project or work, you can sit back, relax and light a cigar.

Reader Exercises:

- When trying to achieve a goal you have set yourself, do you allow your entire self to be completely focused on attaining that goal?
- Are you prepared to give up rest temporarily in order to attain your goals?
- Are you able to identify periods in your life that require your complete focus and all of your energy?

14. Barack Obama

Barack Hussein Obama II is an American politician and attorney who served as the 44th President of the United States from 2009 to 2017. Obama's presence as a person and a presidential candidate came around by the time I was six years old. At the end of President Obama's eight years as President of the United States, I was 14 years old. Many children, especially millennials, seem to be getting more and more interested in subjects such as politics, news, and what occurs outside of their own nations around the world. I was not one of those children until my later teens. By the time I had just hit my teens, I knew that President Obama was the President of the United States and, from my parents', peers' and other black celebrities' reactions to this and opinions on this, I knew that it must have been quite a big thing for black people and people of colour. I knew the importance of President Obama becoming the first black President of the United States and his wife Michelle Obama the first black First Lady, but I was not very involved in this process or truly understanding of how much every second of that event meant to black people. I was just beginning my first years of secondary school and was just over half-way through it by the time President Obama left office on 20th January 2017. As I grew older, I soon came to realise and understand more about how significant it was for African Americans and black people as a whole, having begun to learn about what President Obama and First Lady Michelle Obama did as the leaders of America. As I watched more episodes of American TV programmes such as 'Black-ish', I soon truly realised how much it meant to people of my race.

Over time, as I began sixth form and headed into my final year of A-levels, I began to gain more of an interest in politics, news, and things that were going on in my own country, as well as in the rest of the world. Throughout the 2020 presidential elections between Joe Biden and President Trump, I tried following and learning more about the two candidates as it came closer to 4th November, the day when votes were being counted for each candidate. As time moved on, the world soon came to know that President Trump's four-year period as President of America was finally up and that President-Elect Joe Biden, who served as Vice President to President Obama for eight years, was soon going to be the 46th President of the United States. During Joe Biden's presidential rallies, which followed COVID-19 guidelines that were in place at the time, (compared to President Trump's campaign which allowed mass gatherings of people), I saw Barack Obama with Joe Biden, supporting him by giving speeches and talking on behalf of the Biden campaign. This was one of the few times that I was able to sit down and fully digest what President Obama had to say and believed in. It gave me a glimpse of what the people of America and the rest of the world, who were attentive, got to experience and hear from President Obama over his eight years as President. I got to hear what President Obama believed in, how he believed in America as a nation, and what this special and history-making President was all about.

This wasn't quite the first time that I had properly seen and heard President Obama speak and address the nation. During the time that President Trump was president, President Obama had recorded and uploaded videos of himself speaking on certain issues in the hopes of getting Americans to vote for Joe Biden to be the next President of the United States. This also gave me an opportunity to learn more about President Obama. My father was and still remains a big fan of Obama and is the person who shared these videos of President Obama addressing the nation with my family and me. When I came back from university in December 2020 for the Christmas break, I had seen that my dad had updated his book collection and purchased a few more books. One of these books was 'A Promised Land' by Barack Obama. Once I had seen this, despite its daunting, thick nature of over 600 pages, I was intrigued to get my teeth into it and learn more about President Obama. I knew at the time that I wouldn't be reading his newly released book for at least another year, because I had some other books lined up that I needed to get through first. Previously, I had never gotten through one whole book in one year, let alone a 600-page book!

During my late teens, I developed a big interest in President Obama, both as the 44th President of the United States and as Barack Obama the person. I was intrigued to learn the steps he took to become the first black President of the United States. My interest grew further during the time President-Elect Joe Biden was voted to be the next President of the United States, and his previous boss, President Obama, was mentioned here and there in CNN News. I discovered more about Obama whenever news presenters on CNN discussed him. I came to learn from news presenter Fareed Zakaria that he was well read, and I thought to myself: 'Well read', what type of term is that to describe someone? It then dawned on me that President Obama had read a lot throughout his lifetime and in the lead up to becoming the President. I already knew that President Obama was among one of the best students of his time at Harvard Law School. He was elected the first black President of the Harvard Law Review at the age of 28. This role is considered the most prestigious student position at Harvard Law School. Harvard University is also one of the most prestigious learning institutions in the world. I was already aware of this because I had decided to use President Obama as one of the people who had inspired my campaign in an effort to become head boy at my school in September 2019 at the start of year 13. As mentioned earlier, I did not know that much about President Obama as a person or as a president, but I decided to use him as my inspiration simply due to what he had managed to achieve as a person.

President Obama broke the chain of 43 consecutive white

Presidents of the United States of America – white male Presidents, specifically. He was the promise and hope that African Americans and black people were hoping to see sometime throughout their lifetimes. He was the first black President of the United States! Achieving this as an individual, whether I knew him well or not, was enough to give me the inspiration and belief that, as a black boy myself, I could go on to become the next head boy at my school.

I did not become the head boy in the end and only managed to become a joint head of house for my school pupil leadership team. I did see the benefits that this led to during my last year of sixth form though. However, it was the initial courage, belief and confidence that President Obama displayed when running for President in 2008 and being elected that inspired me to act on a similar thing on a much smaller scale at my own school.

Through being elected the first black President of the United States, President Obama gave so much hope for the younger generations of black people and children. It demonstrated that it was also possible for them to do similar things with their own lives. He was among many of the most influential characters in black history, such as Doctor Martin Luther King Jr and Malcolm X, who had shown younger children and people of colour that there was hope, that we had a voice in areas such as being world leaders, and that it was possible for black people to achieve anything that any other person of any other race had managed to achieve. It was around the time that I applied to become head boy and later, during the US 2020 presidential elections, when I reflected on what the true specialness was of President Obama becoming the first black President of the United States of America. During the inauguration of President-Elect Joe Biden that took place on 20th January 2021, I saw President Obama and the First Lady Michelle Obama at the ceremony. As I was on the sofa in my living room, sitting next to my dad, I saw the Obamas and other former US Presidents, such as President Bush and President Clinton, in a completely different way to how I had seen other people, including famous people. I saw them as something slightly higher than human beings when they were together as one, collectively in the same environment, catching up after the inauguration was complete. I even turned to my father and told him that usually, I try not see celebrities and famous people as anything more than human beings, as I and many others simply are, and I try to not put them on a pedestal above humans. However, for some reason in that moment of seeing the previous presidents together as one, I felt that there were categories. I told my father that it seemed as if there are humans and, above that, Presidents of the United States.

Now, this was very specific to US Presidents. To clarify, I didn't feel as if there was a big difference between world leaders and humans per se, but I did feel as if there was a difference between US Presidents and humans. I viewed world leaders such as Prime Minister Boris Johnson and the President of France, Emmanuel Macron, as ordinary people in positions of power. However, when I saw these three previous US Presidents and First Ladies together in a group, they appeared to be in a completely different league to the rest of humanity. I believe that I saw them in this way because, after the presidential reign of Donald Trump and his questionable moments throughout his presidency, I realised that being President of the most powerful country in the entire world is a very tough job. I realised that, when you allow a businessman or somebody who doesn't really actually know what they are doing into the White House to run America, it can lead to a fast-spreading fire in the nation. When I saw President Clinton, President Bush and President Obama all standing together at the inauguration, I saw previous presidents who had managed to at least show decent leadership among the American people during their time in power and, for me, this is what put them into a different league above other humans and above other world leaders.

It was when I saw President Obama and the former First Lady, in particular, that I felt a different type of hope compared to seeing President Clinton and President Bush. When I saw the Obamas, I felt a deep sense of hope for the nation of

America, as well as the rest of the world. This was especially true after the year that America had just experienced in 2020 (as well as other countries across the rest of the world). When I saw them, it felt as if I was looking at two angels who were among the minority of influential people in America who were going to help in leading the nation through and out of its struggle with the coronavirus pandemic, along with the leadership of now-President Joe Biden and Vice President Harris. The reason I felt this way about the Obamas and President Obama in particular, is because of how they behaved as individuals throughout their time in office and after this period passed too. They were humble individuals and world leaders from 2009 to 2017. They wanted to do what was best for America and the world. In doing this, it showed the people of America and the rest of the world what type of people Barack Obama and Michelle Obama truly were and still are. Of course, they made mistakes during their time in power and at other points in their lives, there is no human being who hasn't. Despite this, they always had the intention of giving their best to the country and giving their best to the people of the nation. It is because of his humble nature and overall presence that President Obama is able to connect well with others, including music stars such as Drake; NBA players such as Stephen Curry; and many other people around the world who are not involved with government or politics, and those who have created a status and name for themselves. People who aren't involved in politics but who still have a large status as individuals in their own fields, genuinely like President Obama and look up to him. This is not just because he was President of America, but because he actually treats people with respect, care and love.

After the inauguration of Joe Biden, I watched a short clip of a YouTube video that popped up on my screen one day. The YouTube video was a snippet of Barack Obama sharing a few things about his life, his upbringing, and any advice he could give to young people for them to do well in America. He was accompanied by some young men and NBA player Stephen Curry. President Obama shared a few words about his thoughts on masculinity. He shared his views on what it means to be a man and stated that it means you are reliable, respectful, hardworking and compassionate. He also suggested that males who require hundreds of women around them, dancing and giving them affection and attention must have issues with their sexuality and a need to prove that they were manly. President Obama then went on to say that he only had one woman who he was very happy with – Michelle. In this moment, it hit me and made me think about the fact that some men require so many women around them, and so many women at once in order to either feel good, feel wanted, or show that they are manly. When President Obama said those words in that short YouTube clip, I was once again inspired by him through his virtue, humility and the way that he treated others, women especially.

To conclude, President Obama is an extremely influential individual whose words mean a lot to any ears that listen to them. I think it is fair to say that, during his period as President of the United States, he did a good job for the nation and showed great leadership, and still continues to do so after his presidency. President Obama made history in 2008 and changed the narrative for America and the rest of the world regarding where black people stand when it comes to questions such as who should be elected and voted to become world leaders in different countries. He played a huge role in what is now seen as normal for Vice President Kamala Harris to become the first female, and female of colour, to serve the President of the United States in the year 2020. President Obama has lived his life, so far, in a certain way that makes me view him as being above the rest of humanity. The responsibilities that he has had to fulfil and the decency with which he did this requires my applause and my sheer admiration. I still have a lot of things to learn about President Obama, but his actions and words have already taught me so much about him. As an individual, if you are able to adopt and display half of the humility and care for people that President Obama has displayed throughout his life, I am sure it will lead to crowds of people always wanting to be in your presence. Being able to use your voice and influence a way in that leads to good and real change in the world will only lead to you being recognised as a good leader. Lastly, having the confidence, courage and ambition to go and achieve something as big as becoming the President or Prime Minister of a country, let alone the first black leader of a nation, will generate an even greater legacy in your name.

Reader Exercises:

- Do you have the courage to do or achieve something that will change the narrative in your respected field, community or the world?
- Are you viewed as a person who tends to display a lot of humility?
- Do you do things in life which lead you to be viewed as role model?

15. The Mandem

A mandem (a term which I used in an earlier chapter) is a slang word that originated from Caribbean English and is used popularly among most millennials around the world. It is defined as a gang or a group of male friends. Many people have mandems across the world and, especially in the UK, it has grown to become a culturally shared word and idea through YouTube series such as 'Mandem on the Wall', along with its use in music produced in the UK. A mandem doesn't always necessarily have bad connotations regarding 'gangs' and the aims of particular mandems across the world isn't to associate themselves with bad connotations, either. Most people in the generations before the year 2000 may see a mandem all together in a shopping centre and immediately associate it with violence, gangs, and many other negative things. It is true that some mandems do try to portray a bad image and behave in a manners that they think is cool by causing disruption, selling drugs or being violent, but not all mandems have this intention. I sure know that my mandem did not have this intention while we were growing up together.

I grew up with a group of friends with similar ethnic backgrounds to me and a few who even came from the same country as me. Many of us attended the same primary school and the majority of us were studying at the same secondary school at one point. My group of friends are not all of my age. Some of them are in the year above me and others are two years above me. No one in my friendship group is born earlier than 1999. We all managed to become friends and grow a friendship group together, because some of our parents knew each other when they came to the UK from different parts of Africa. We grew together and saw each other grow from the time we were around one or two years old, until the present day. Initially, there were only a couple of us who knew one another and had been together from this age. Friends of mine called Champhe, Sean, Gwin, Jekhio and Farai, were all boys I knew from when they were very young and grew up with until my secondary school years. By the time I had started secondary school, I made a very smooth and peaceful transition because I knew the likes of Gwin, Jekhio and Farai, who were in year 9 while I was starting in year 7. I would hang around with them at school occasionally and managed to build friendships with some of their friends. At the time, other children in my year group saw the type of relationships I had with some of the people in older year groups and this is what led to the growth in my popularity and coolness.

I was fortunate enough to be invited to Jekhio's 15th birthday party in September 2013, where I entered an environment that I had never ever experienced before. The party took place in the evening at Jekhio's home and my dad had dropped me off. When he saw the party that was going on in the back garden and heard the loud bass of the music, he said to me, "Wow, now this is a party!" I was just hoping that he didn't feel the need to take me home after he saw how big and lively that year 9 party was, and whether it was too mature for my little year 7 self. Fortunately, he didn't feel this way and allowed me to go and enjoy myself. I walked into the party full of year 9 students from my school, girls and boys. I was extremely out of my comfort zone being around all these older children and soon went to find the likes of Gwin, Jekhio and Farai. Once I found my friends, I felt more at ease in the company of 50 to 60 year 9 students. I kept close with one or more of these three throughout the evening and therefore managed to experience one of the best nights of my life, and one that has remained with me years after it occurred.

As my time throughout secondary school continued to move on, I made friends in my own year group and built strong relations there, but all my other friends from different year groups, who I grew with, were my true closest friends. Champhe and Sean also went to the school down the road from BGN – Warriner – so I saw them a lot less than the boys in year 9. Champ and Sean were only in the year above me, so I had a much stronger connection with them and our families were also very close. By the time I was in year 9 at secondary school, the likes of the boys two years above me were preparing to sit their GCSEs. When I transitioned into year 9, a friend of mine called Warren had transferred back to BGN after he had left for a year to experience Banbury School, a school that was next door to BGN. I was extremely happy to have Warren back at BGN after he had left in year 7, as a friend of mine called Tyrell and I, together with one other boy, were the only boys from our year group from a Black Asian and minority ethnic BAME background. Warren was also from a BAME background as he is Jamaican. Warren was quite surprised at how welcoming I was towards him during the start of our year 9 days, as he recalled vividly that I was horrible to him during our time in year 7. I remembered the way that I behaved towards Warren and apologised for my actions towards him. I told him that I was still young and foolish at that stage and still had a lot to learn about life and how to treat people. I also asked him how he allowed me to treat him the way I did since he was at least a whole foot taller than me back in year 7.

From the time we began school as year 9 students, throughout our remaining years at secondary school, Warren and I were the closest of friends. Warren also soon became friends with the likes of Gwin, Jekhio and Farai as time passed during our school days. I had seen one day, on Jekhio's phone, that he had some sort of iMessage group chat with a few friends in his year group. I asked him about it and he told me that it was, in fact, just a group chat with himself and a couple of his friends from his own year group. This sparked an idea in my mind. I thought that, because we were all close friends, a group chat including Gwin, Jekhio, Farai, Warren, Champ, Sean and myself would be a good idea and a good way for all of us to communicate. So, we created the iMessage group chat and began to use it and talk in it. However, the iMessage group chat was not used as frequently as I had expected and soon became of little use. We all then decided that it was best we transfer to Snapchat and create the group chat there, because that was the app that most people were using at the time to communicate with each other. This was especially true after Snapchat had undergone updates and incorporated group chats onto its platform. We soon created the group chat on Snapchat. Snapchat gave the option to add a name to a group chat and we all decided that we would call the group 'Mandem', with an ocean wave emoji which signifies a certain level of supreme coolness. We also created our Mandem group chat on Instagram.

Over time, as we all continued with school, sports, and everything that we were doing during our secondary school years, we made more friends with others similar to us. One of those friends was a boy called Javah. Javah went to a school called North Oxfordshire Academy, which was local to where Champ, Sean and I lived, and was in the same year group as Sean and Champ. We had seen Javah around from time to time, at sports events in particular, as we used to see him play for his school football team and run for his athletics team in the long-distance races. One day, Sean, Champ and I had managed to talk to Javah for the first time and built a friendship with him. Sooner rather than later, Javah was added to the Mandem group chat and was another member of our group. Javah mostly knew Sean, Champ and me, and didn't really know the others as he hadn't really met them. Initially, we were slightly cautious about adding Javah and contemplated whether we had added a random person that we didn't really know, just because he had a similar background to the rest of us, being fully Jamaican. However, we soon realised that Javah was not just any random person when we got to know him better and he became the comedian of the group, making us laugh heavily with his crazy thoughts, funny impressions and bubbly nature. Over time, as we grew, we began to use the group chat a lot more frequently, for meeting up, cracking jokes, and just sharing whatever it was that we felt the need to share. Soon, we began to use our group chat name when referring to ourselves as a group and the mandem name was soon born and adopted among my friends and me.

Our mandem is a group of boys with very high levels of ambition, and it is for this reason that many of the people in the group, along with the group as a whole, have had such a great influence on my life and have managed to inspire me on countless occasions. During our youth days, while many of us were still at secondary school, there was one summer in particular when the mandem did something collectively which helped each member to have one of the greatest summers of our lives. During the summer of 2016, we all decided to go to the football court one day in an area of Banbury called Bretch Hill. The football court that we played was in a park called Princess Diana (PD). Since the most of us, but not all, were aspiring professional footballers, we all decided that we wanted to go to PD and play football as a group. We did this one day during the summer months of July and August and had some of the best fun and played some of the most competitive football any of us had played in a while. We would play all sorts of football games and matches, almost with the intensity of a proper football training session, but it was fun and you were with your friends. All eight of us (now we had Javah) would go to Princess Diana park to play football from around 2pm until 8 or 9pm at times, due to the long days, and we each experienced one of the greatest and most fun summers of our lives. We were together all day, nattering about all sorts of things, in the scorching hot sun and having fun doing it while we played football for close to five hours every other day. It became something that we did religiously throughout the summer and we all continued to return to Princess Diana park because we all enjoyed our time while we were there.

We invited Tyrell, another friend from my year, to join us in playing football at the park throughout the summer and soon we also added Tyrell to the Mandem group chat. It was truly a special summer for each one of us. Where the mandem showed ambition during this time, is when we would all compete with one another while playing football, or whenever it was one of us versus another member to see who could get the ball into the goal past the goalkeeper and avoid going into goal for the next game. We were extremely competitive with one another and wanted to prove to ourselves, as well as our peers, that we were good players and/or better than the person we were matched up against. We would compare ourselves to each other, say who was better than who, say who was the best and the worst, and we would be completely upfront about it. The likes of Warren and myself were usually better than some of the boys in the year above us, but we found it very difficult to match up to Gwin and Jekhio who were extremely good footballers at the time.

One of the things that I felt most inspired about by Jekhio, as an individual, was his capacity and talent to play football. The type of skills he would display while we played at PD together were completely out of our league and difficult to match up to. Jekhio had always been this way ever since he was young; he was one of the most dominant players on the pitch during some of his early years of playing football for local clubs such as Banbury United and Banbury Irish, and he was known as one of those players who you did not want to be in front of while they shot a football. He was the overall complete package for a footballer: tall, strong, fast and skilful. He was completely dominant against his opponents and against the rest of the mandem. So, the mandem was able to grow more and more ambitious to become better footballers as we saw the likes of Jekhio, who was on a far better level than many of us, as an inspiration to grow towards. It is this ambition from everyone else that also inspired me to continue to practise my own football ability and put the work in to improve as a footballer. This was especially true as I had just managed to sign for the younger squad of a new semi-professional football club that played quite a high level of football, called Brackley Town. That summer taught us quite a lot about ourselves and about other members of our mandem.

Another time that I have been inspired by the mandem is when I had the opportunity to play for the BGN first team in year 11. Sean and Champhe actually decided to transfer to BGN to complete their A-levels, as they knew that the likes of Gwin, Jekhio and Farai were all in year 13, about to finish their A-levels. It was an extremely happy moment for me to have two of my closest friends finally at the same school as me. It was such a big thing because we had all spent one year in Oxford together between the ages of one and two years old, and when my family decided to move to Banbury along with Sean's family, which moved us away from Champhe's family, we were only able to see Champ every now and then due to the 40-minute car journey from Banbury to Oxford. So, when Champhe and his family moved to Banbury after he had completed year 7 at school, this was some compensation for not having seen him as often, but when he joined my school as well as living in the same town as the rest of us, we were all extremely happy.

I played football for the school sixth form team, along with Warren and a couple of our other friends from our year group who were also very good footballers. Sean, Champ, Gwin and Jekhio also played for the BGN first team, as it was a mixture of the best players from year 13, 12 and 11. Gwin was chosen to be captain of our school first team by our PE teacher, Mr Orton. Playing with the BGN first team, let alone alongside all of the boys who I grew up with, was a pinnacle moment during my years at BGN. I had wished to play with the likes of Jekhio and Gwin whenever I could, due to the fact that we were extremely close friends as well as them being very good footballers. Having the wish fulfilled was truly a happy moment for me. It even inspired me to go on and aim to be captain of the BGN first team when I had transitioned into year 13. While I was in my last year of sixth form, there were not many options available for year 13 regarding footballers who could represent the school. BGN's new PE teacher, Mr Michno, had put the responsibility on me to find and create a team for the BGN first team, so that we could begin to compete in matches. I selected the players who I thought were best at the time, from years 13, 12 and 11, and managed to find enough players to form the BGN first team. Most of the good footballers were in year 12 and there was only one other boy in my year group, in addition to myself, representing the school from year 13.

Once we began to play more games, we soon realised that we needed to appoint a captain. Mr Michno would have probably been fine with me taking the lead as captain, being the second oldest footballer in the school and having experienced representing the school football team on countless occasions across several year groups, both my own and that of the years above me. However, I decided that I wanted to give the team a voice in who was to be pronounced captain. So, I set up a vote and asked for the names of possible captains to be written on Post-it Notes and handed to me one lunchtime. Initially, I feared doing this, as I thought that most of the year 12 footballers would have chosen one of the best players in their year because they were friends with him and they didn't really know me personally. Once the votes were counted, it was very close between myself and the year 12 player who I thought might receive more votes than me but, in the end, I was voted captain. It was a moment that I felt a sense of huge gratification and achievement as I hadn't taken the captaincy by force, but was voted in, which felt a lot better on my side and showed me that my teammates believed in me as a footballer, as well as a leader.

My friend Farai, who I mentioned earlier, has played football throughout his life, but never really wanted to go down the route of becoming a professional footballer. He was always more interested in other things and one of these things were his academic studies. Among the mandem, when it came to school performance and who thrived most in that area, it was hands down Farai. Even when we compared GCSE grades, Farai scored above the rest of us in all subjects. Many of us, especially those of us who were in the years below Farai, looked up to him throughout secondary school as the ideal type of pupil we all aspired to be, especially due to the similarities Farai shared with us. One thing Farai did that truly inspired me, was when he put himself forward for head boy at BGN during his last year in sixth form. When Farai told me that he had applied for this role it was initially quite a big shock to me because it deviated slightly from the type of activities members of the mandem usually decided to put their time into. These activities were usually just school, football and girls. Applying for the sixth form pupil leadership team, let alone head boy, was a step in a different direction that we were all witnessing. The likes of Gwin and Jekhio had not applied to be on the student council, as they simply felt it was not for them. Unfortunately, Farai did not manage to get the role of head boy in the end, but he did manage to get the role of joint deputy head boy.

This action by Farai, in itself, regardless of the fact that he didn't become head boy, is what inspired me to apply for head boy when I transitioned into year 13. Applications were open by the time we were about to complete year 12 and I sent mine off. I decided not to tell anyone about this, not even my parents, because I wanted to keep my application quiet so I would not get distracted or side-tracked by the competition of my other classmates. I simply wanted to focus on myself and helping my own campaign, in aiming to become BGN's next head boy. Soon, I was not able to keep my campaign secret after it was announced in front of my tutor group that I was among the people who had made it through to an interview with our Principal at the time, Mr Long. Even when my classmates had asked me whether I had applied, I told them that I hadn't. Therefore, they were soon coming back to me again after they found out that I was among the people shortlisted for an interview. The interviews went ahead and we were waiting for September to roll along to find out whether we were chosen to be on the pupil leadership team. As you would have learnt previously, I didn't manage to receive the role of head boy but was given the role of joint head of house. I was immensely distraught about this, as I had wanted to become head boy for myself, my family and, in a way, to redeem what Farai had started when he applied. However, I guess it just wasn't meant to be. Nevertheless, it was Farai's action that inspired me to apply to be on the student leadership team in the first place and I was grateful both he and I decided to take the actions we did, regardless of the outcomes.

Overall, the mandem has grown significantly over time. New members and friends of ours have been added to our group chat and more group chats have been formed. Other friends of mine, as well as other mandem members –Michael, Zay, Munair, Gilbert and Effiom – have all been incorporated into the mandem. On Boxing Day of 2019, most of the names previously mentioned came to my home for an evening full of chilled vibes, catching up, rapping and laughter. During February half-term 2020, Champhe, Gilbert and I met up one day for lunch at a pub called the Falcon, just outside Banbury. Gilbert was an aspiring musician at the time and I knew that Champhe had a lot of knowledge about the music industry. I had been helping Gilbert, who is known by his stage name 'Tembo', with regards to ideas for his music and the way that he could balance his school life and his music career. So, I thought it would be a good idea for Champhe and Gilbert to meet up one day to exchange thoughts on what it is that Tembo could do for his career in music, and how he could push on to becoming an established musician. The two of them clicked immediately and a trio was formed between the three of us, known as the 'Innovators'. This was another reason for an additional group chat to be created. We use the Innovators group chat to share with each other how we were doing, but also to share what was happening regarding the things we were aspiring to become and do. Whatever we were working on at the time, be it a freestyle or song for Tembo, or ideas for this book for my benefit, we shared it with each other and sought advice and help on different things.

This has been extremely useful to the three of us and has truly helped each of us to progress towards becoming what we wish to be in life and achieve. We still use our group chats today, especially during the time I wrote this book. Seeing either of the two of them, as well as other members of the mandem, work towards their life goals and act in doing this, inspires me to continue doing similar kinds of things with my own life. It is for all of those reasons, stories, and events mentioned earlier, that I feel the need to tell the story of the mandem, because it has played quite a big role in the things I have managed to achieve in life thus far and the things which I wish to go ahead and grasp in the future. Having this set of people around me as I have grown has resulted in me becoming a more ambitious and hungrier individual. Each of them, in their own way and as a group, have sparked moments of inspiration in my life which have literally led me to write this book. If it wasn't for Gilbert just wildly challenging me and telling me to attempt writing a book, I may have never decided to write any of the information you have read or any of that which you will later go on to read. It is because I have been around such level-headed individuals and ones who wish to do more with their lives, that their own characters have reflected towards me and helped in building my own.

Therefore, I encourage you to seek to be around the type of people who you believe will help you progress in life and go on to achieve your wildest dreams and goals. I encourage you to surround yourself with individuals and create circles of your own with people who only have your best interest in mind, all the time, and who want to see you reach your potential, grow and become the best version of you. Surrounding yourself with people such as this is going to help you move in one direction in life – upwards and onwards.

Quote from Champhe Pelekamoyo:

> Throughout the 2016 summer holidays, we would go play football at Hanwell Courts. Usually it would be me, Neo, Sean, Tyrell, and Gwin. We would often play quite intense games, with the aim that we leave everything on the court. Play with our hearts on our sleeves. Throughout the summer we had been trying to improve our footballing abilities;

we had dreams of making it as professional football players. There was this one session that I remember in particular. It was a hot summer's day; it was the usual group of players and other people that we had met at Hanwell Court that day. I had gone in goal as a result of losing the crossbar challenge, which involves hitting the crossbar of the goal from a specific spot. The person who's shot is furthest away from the crossbar ended up in goal, and that person happened to be me. I remember so clearly that, every single time Neo collected the ball, whether it was from the goal kick from me, or whether he had tackled somebody, I remember so clearly Neo dribbling through everyone as if he was Lionel Messi. Neo would often dribble through people up and down the court and not score because, in his own words 'it's too easy' and from my goal keeper view, it honestly looked effortless. This was the first time I had seen Neo in this state of flow, where everything just clicked. It made me realise that the hours Neo spent working on his dribbling and his footballing knowledge was paying off. He carried himself in a particular way. He wanted everyone around him to be better so he could test himself and be better. This is one of the days Neo inspired me.

Reader Exercises:

- What type of personalities do you have within your own close friendship group?
- What type of things come up in conversation between you and your friends? Are they topics which are positive, insightful and helpful in life?
- Are you surrounded by people who seek the best in themselves as well as in you and help you achieve your goals in life?

Sean, Me, Tinashe (Champ's older brother) and Champ
sat on a sofa playing at Sean's house

Me, Jekhio, Munair, Javah, Gwin, Champ, Taimun, Sean and Micheal
(squatted) after Champ's surprise birthday meal in May 2019

End of Section Reader Exercises:
Considering the chapters you have just read, I invite you to ask yourself the following questions and meditate on the answers that come up. I also invite you to take action on these, in order to realise your highest potential.

- What are some of the key things that have inspired you from this section?
- What have you learned from this section and the people mentioned in it?
- Who are some of the key people in your life that inspire you and what inspires you about them?

SECTION TWO

SHARING INSPIRATION I HAVE FOUND WITHIN MYSELF

16. Perception is Key

Perception is the use of all of your senses: your sight, touch, smell, taste and hearing. Fundamentally, perception is the way that an individual interprets or understands something. Everyone's perception is individual and specific to them. You may be watching TV with your family and each of your family members may be hearing and seeing something different to you, from the same TV, while you are all watching the same programme. This is a thought that I had regularly while watching television with my parents. I used to think to myself: I wonder whether they see what I am seeing right now. Most of the time, people do tend to perceive the same things as those around them if something is blatantly clear and obvious, but this is not always the case. Understanding and interpretation are processes that are slightly above the level of simply seeing, hearing and touching things. Understanding and interpretation go deeper into one's mind and overall being. They are a completely different ball game. These two factors are the difference between someone feeling happy or sad on a rainy day and contribute to whether people are successful in whatever they do and, overall, whether they are successful in life. If used correctly and mastered to some extent, your understanding and interpretation can lead to you becoming an influential force and a great contribution to humanity.

When I was at my first primary school, St Joseph's, my father recalls a specific evening after school when I asked him to help me with the homework my teacher had given me. My task was to come up with as many different transport methods that an individual could use to go to school. Initially, my father was upset with me and thought that I was being lazy. He told me that the task was extremely easy and there were many ways that people can go to school. I replied to my father, stating that I just wanted to hear his thoughts and ideas about the different ways to travel to school. To prevent me from taking advantage of his thoughts and being told the answers, my dad stated that we would both come up with our own ideas of different transport methods and share them after we had written our individual lists. After my father checked I was done with writing my list, we shared our lists together. My father had come up with typical transport methods such as cars, buses, walking and trains. I, on the other hand, had a slightly different list of transport methods to my father. I had listed going to school by scooter, roller blades, Heely shoes, a skateboard, or using a bike. We had completely different ideas about how one could go to school simply because we saw things differently at that time and had different perceptions and understanding of forms of transport to one another. My father was immediately shocked after he saw my list of methods of getting to school, because my adolescent ideas had not come to his mind at all. He realised, in that moment, that his world and mine were completely different and that there was a lot that he and others from his generation could learn from myself, and from others of my generation. My father tends to use this story at times during his work as an example of how important it is to listen to the youth of today and what they have to say and contribute to the well-being of the world.

A more recent event, which occurred in 2021, was a discussion that I had with my mother and father after our church service on the last Sunday of January (the 31st). The message from our church service had me thinking about a big topic that I think a lot of people tend to think about, but rarely ever voice their opinions and thoughts about. The church service that I attended with my parents that day sparked the thought in my head about what happens to all of us after we die? As Catholics, my parents and I believe that, after one dies, they either go to join God in heaven or, depending on how they lived their life here on earth, they go to a place that most people would not like to go to. Typical Catholics and Christians tend to believe that if you are a good person you go to heaven and if you are a bad person on earth and have done extremely bad things and feel no remorse for these things, you go to hell. Personally, I am not too keen on the idea of it being as simple as individuals either going to heaven or hell. I think too much goes on in one's life for it to be as simple as either going to join God in heaven and have a great time, or going to hell to suffer immensely. I don't think it is as simple as just saying "You are a bad person and you have done bad things, so you are going to hell". People of a similar faith to me – and myself – believe that God is a loving and forgiving God; I do not believe that God doesn't forgive. A lot of people have done very bad things, whether that's to others, themselves, or the world itself. However, there is always reasoning behind people's decision making, and it is too simple to place someone in a category for something bad they have done, no matter the magnitude. God doesn't see human beings that way and we shouldn't either. God is loving, forgiving and caring. An individual can do 100 wrongs, but it only takes one apology for all of these things for God to put water under the bridge for that person. Well, this is what most Christians believe.

To me, therefore, the concept of heaven and hell isn't as black and white as most Christians tend to suggest and the bottom line is, Christians and any other human being that breathes air on this earth simply don't have the answers to such big issues. This idea of not knowing is commonly found in many things to do with religion; humanity doesn't know whether there is a God or not, because they have never seen a God, whether that same God may be a 'He' or a 'She'. Nobody born after the year 300 AD has ever seen Jesus Christ, or any of the people who wrote the bible. All of these issues are simply down to our own perception and understanding of whether we believe these things – or anything for that matter – or whether we don't. Furthermore, my parents and I broke into discussion and I asked them: "How do you guys feel about the idea of going to join God in heaven and knowing that you will be there forever and ever?". I asked my parents this question to learn more about the perception of two people that I consider extremely wise and thoughtful on a topic that constantly plays on my mind. As our discussion escalated, the three of us sat there in our living room, on our sofa, talking about many different concepts and potential ideas for life after earth. We considered what Buddhists believe in regard to dying and then coming back to life in a different form, or becoming a God. Buddhists believe that individuals can be reincarnated in six different forms, which range from a heavenly God to a human, an animal or a ghost. Buddhists believe that the form of living creature, or God, you reincarnate into depends on how you decided to live your life here on earth . Those individuals who lived good, respectable and kind lives are believed to be reincarnated in the top three best realms out of the six: Deva (heavenly God), Asura (demigod) or Manusya (human), whereas a person who may have not been kind or respectful to others could be reincarnated in either of the three realms of Tiryak (animals), Preta (ghosts) and Naraka (sent to hell). My parents and I thought that if an individual returned to earth, they would have no recollection of their previous life and it would simply be the way we all live now, thinking and believing that we've only had our current life. My father even stated that this could potentially be a reason why some individuals are labelled as old souls; maybe this wasn't their first time living life but they just have no recollection of their previous life.

These were only ideas and thoughts that the three of us were having and were sharing with each other. I was still definitely being pulled more towards the idea of human beings living one life, dying, and either being reunited with God or not. In addition, my thought process had changed over time. I had previously thought that it was as simple as either going to heaven or hell, due to the fact that this is what is preached in my church by local priests. However, over time, and with deep discussions about religion and faith, I thought to myself that a loving God, who I believe in, see and love as a parent figure, would not want their children to suffer for eternity and be away from them. So, after having some of these thoughts, I am leaning more towards the idea of individuals suffering slightly for their wrongdoings and behaviour on earth, which includes practically all of us, but after the suffering is served, one can go and join God. I do not believe that an individual will be completely banished from God's presence for not living a good life on earth. In my opinion, God still shares the same amount of love for each of his children, no matter how great or bad they are as people.

Moving on with our discussion, my parents continued to give me insights into their thoughts about the idea of life after earth and what the idea of 'forever' may feel or seem like, and we raised a good point between the three of us. We thought that many people, including myself, don't like to think about the idea of death, life after death, or forever. The idea of something lasting forever is foreign to human beings because we have lived our entire lives with time limits and durations on each of our activities. From the time we are born, we don't embrace the idea of forever in our lives. We age each time 364 days go past the day when we were born so never remain the same age for over 365 days. We attend school for the most part of our childhood and adolescent lives, but each school day always ends at a particular time. After our days at school and further education, we go into work for a good number of decades of our lives, but this never lasts forever either because we soon grow older and retire as working people. Human beings have constantly lived their lives around the clock, ever since it was invented. Even before time was invented and used as frequently as it is today, humans would still only do things for a certain amount of time and would use the rising and setting of the sun and the moon to figure out what time of day it was and how long they could do certain activities for. Nothing a human has ever done before has lasted eternally – not one single thing.

Therefore, this idea of looking at 'forever' in the face and even thinking about it is extremely tough for humans; I know it is for me at times. Even as a believer in God and a man of faith, the idea of going to heaven and being with God forever and ever, no end, no time limit, no school bell to tell me that my day has finished, is slightly daunting. The idea of heaven is not daunting, however, the idea of heaven is great and is a place I only dream of being invited to go and stay. It is the idea of this never ending which worries me slightly. This concept of something never ending, for me, is something that my limited human mind finds extremely tough to come to terms with and, in some form at least, tough trying to understand. It is something that I have never been exposed to before – nor has anyone else – and it is simply something that I am still trying to learn and understand.

During my discussion with my parents, however, my father said something to my mother and I which truly inspired me. He said: "You know, the reason why God has probably just allowed the earth to be as it is for the past billions of years, is because He may simply just truly enjoy and be at peace with what He has created. Therefore, for Him, one billion years could be an extremely short period in time due to the fact that He is simply just enjoying himself." This philosophy struck a nerve deep within my mind. My father continued, saying that it was the same as people going to parties, on holiday, or spending true quality time with their friends, and soon realising that a five-hour party feels as if it has passed in a matter of minutes, or a two-week holiday overseas feels as if it passed in two days. This is the same concept as being God at peace with His creation, His earth and universe, for billions and billions of years. The idea of one billion years is simply indigestible for human beings to comprehend. Most people can't even imagine what one billion years looks like, and to think that the earth and different species have been here, or are still here, for that amount of time is simply mind boggling. It makes our 70–90-year lifespan almost seem insignificant, or almost like just a day in that timeline of the history of the earth. Of course, as we live each day of our lives on earth, waiting a week or two weeks for an event to come around, it feels like forever. Or waiting to open one's Christmas presents feels as if time has slowed down completely. So, we don't feel or see that time moves like this, but when you are actually not breathing, or a living organism, or present on earth, it kind of does move this fast because you're simply not there to see it pass by.

So, after my father raised this point and enabled my mother and I to see the idea of forever in this way, I had come to some level of peace and calm with the concept. As long as I managed to live in a way that was pleasing to God, to allow me to be with Him for however many billions of years are to pass long after I am gone, as long as time continues to fly by me as it does whenever I used to play football with my friends at Princess Diana park, or whenever I am back in Zambia with my family and friends, forever can last for however long it wants.

Overall, perception is a key aspect in life. It has so many implications far beyond our five senses. It taps into how we behave as individuals. It affects our mood and emotional and mental state, and it is something that each individual should take care to be aware of and detect whether they are happy with the way they perceive and understand things. It constantly dawns on me that some people walk this earth and never have even thought about the idea of why they are on earth, what their purpose is, who brought them here, and what the history of the earth is. They simply go about living their lives, getting on with day-to-day things, never really thinking about things and concepts beyond life on earth, or higher thinking beyond the surface of the present day and current time that they are living. These same people are most probably likely to reflect about different moments and events that occurred throughout their life, but that is as far as they reflect and think about certain concepts. However, these same people may be extremely happy in life and content with what they have and how they are, and they may not feel the need to think beyond to concepts such as why or how the earth was created, or what we are actually doing here, and that is completely fine. Those same people see the world and life in the manner that they do and they are happy with this, that is the most important thing – happiness. As long as you are happy with yourself, your life and your situation, more often than not, all will be well. You are very unlikely to be happy and jolly at all times and through each hour of a day, but if you are overall happy with your life and how you perceive yourself and the world as whole, then this is a good thing.

It is all down to perception. However, it could be argued that the way that I perceive the world relates to the way I've been brought up. Despite this thought, I would much prefer to perceive the world and my place in the world in the way that I do, as opposed to the example mentioned above. Those people with simplistic perceptions and understanding still have the capacity and opportunity to perceive life in a much deeper way. They would just have to either choose to be exposed to this thought process and begin to see things in a slightly different way, or purposefully choose to find materials and information that helps them to perceive life in a deeper form. On a day-to-day basis, as an individual, you have the choice each second of your life to perceive matters in a way you feel is suitable and correct for you. This can go from perceiving your long friendship with a close friend, who you have grown up with, as worthless because they are beginning to do bad things with their life and are going down a bad route, or you can choose to see your relationship with your friend more distanced, simply keeping in touch with that same person from time to time to stay connected. Your perception can lead you to believe that a person who likes to dress similarly to you is trying to be you, or that they just truly admire the way that you dress and like to wear similar clothes to you because they like your fashion sense. Perception is a choice, it is down to you to choose what works best for you.

17. My Locked-Down Expedition Adventure

Having found the inspiration to finally write this book about the inspirational people who have had an effect on my life, following a particular event that took place, my parents suggested that I ought to share inspiration I have found from within myself, as well as that from the people who have been mentioned in this book. I decided, early on during lockdown, that it was a time to completely challenge myself. I was off the hook with regard to school due to graduating early from my A-levels, and therefore I had a full 24 hours a day, day in, day out. I was a free boy! Initially I was drawn towards the idea of not only socially distancing myself from people physically, but also digitally. The idea of camping out in my garden for a few days came when I witnessed, from my window, my next-door neighbours doing exactly that one night. The lockdown measures in the UK were still strict, restricted to leaving the house for only one hour of exercise per day as we approached the end of April 2020. Despite this, I thought to myself that it was possible to experience a wildlife lifestyle by living in the garden and organising my food rations as if I was in the wild trying to survive with just the resources I carried with me. I intended to go trekking for one hour per day and explore the different sites, footpaths, villages and countryside areas in my local town. Overall, I had the idea of a locked-down expedition that I was wanting to carry out. Meanwhile, I decided that one hour of walking a day simply would not be enough and being in the garden all day with a tent was not necessarily an explorative expedition and adventure. So, I decided to let the idea remain in the air for some time and focused on other things instead.

It was to my surprise that on Sunday 9th May 2020 the British government announced that the people of Britain were now allowed to exercise and be outdoors for an unlimited amount of time starting on Wednesday 12th May. I realised quickly what this meant for my plan to go on my own personal locked-down expedition and I began organising it. I decided that the first weekend after the government was easing some of the lockdown measures was the weekend I was going to start my adventure. I first had to get in touch with my school as I knew they had detailed maps for expeditions and walking, because they always took part in the Duke of Edinburgh's Award scheme. Once I had collected the maps left inside the school gates by my PE teacher, my next job was to seek a tent from my neighbours. They were kind enough to allow me to use it and said they would leave it outside their door first thing in the morning of day one of my expedition. Throughout all of this preparation, the one thing I had forgotten to organise was my food rations! This only came to my attention late on the Thursday night and I asked my dad whether we could go early in the morning so I could pick up my bread and cheese for my cheese sandwich lunches for the next three days.

Day One: I woke up at 7am on the Friday morning and began to try and prepare myself and organise what I was going to carry with me as I stepped out into the wild. I had planned to set out for 10:30am and remain outdoors for a minimum of six hours. It came to around 10am and I was almost ready for action. The clothes I was using for the next three days remained in the garage while I was out walking. My two cheese sandwiches were enclosed in lunch boxes, and all that was left was slipping on the old walking boots. These boots have served me throughout two expeditions I undertook in Wales with my school while completing my Gold Duke of Edinburgh's Award from 2018 to 2019 (I write more about my Duke of Edinburgh adventures later in this book). Despite the fact that the soles of my boots slide under my feet and upwards along my Achilles heels, I was not prepared to walk in any other shoes.

So, my route on day one was fairly simple. It was just around my local area and was initially only meant to be ten kilometres. However, due to my inadequate map reading skills, I ended up going down the wrong footpaths at times and misjudged the length of certain roads and distances, which led me to having to use my phone to locate myself and my surroundings more often than I had intended. As it was the first day, my thoughts weren't able to simply wander due to my concentration and focus on map reading, and ensuring I was definitely following the route I had set. However, what I most certainly enjoyed about day one was the weather, as Banbury's high temperatures really made the walk a lot more enjoyable. I enjoyed the sights I was able to view around the local area of Drayton and the occasional animals I saw each time I crossed a farm. Just the opportunity to be out in nature, away from social media and interaction, with time to just reflect, was truly fulfilling.

Later, I arrived back home, greeted my family, and asked them to open the back gate to let me in. I really tried to challenge myself and remain strict in my guidelines of what I could do and had access to. I ensured that, unless I was having breakfast or dinner, I would remain outside of the house, either in the tent or just in the garden. The rations of food I decided to take with me, which were just snacks and bars, were the only food I was consuming outside of mealtimes. My parents decided to join me for a meal of rice, vegetables and chicken for the first night. They insisted that I slept with a duvet, at least, in my neighbour's wide spaced and large four-man tent. My mother even insisted that I put a mattress in the tent for the night, while my father and I laughed, thinking I was only able to use a mattress if it was able to be compressed in the rucksack that I carried with me. There are no mattresses in the wild! They would be far too much weight to bear, and you are making a much larger investment by filling mattress or duvet space with food or clothing. I was not able to carry the tent, my clothes or my sleeping bag in my backpack as I did not have a large enough bag – how on earth could I carry a duvet or mattress too? My parents and I came to an agreement that the duvet would at least sit in the corner of the tent while I lay on my roll mat, inside my sleeping bag, with it pulled up to my neck.

It was a shock to see my parents' surprise of how rough camping can be if you are on an expedition, especially due to the fact that my classmates and I had recently survived far worse nights and conditions in October 2019 in Snowdonia. During my first night it got to around midnight and I was doing well. My hat and insulated clothes were tucked away deep inside my sleeping bag and I don't know whether it was the sound of the main road, around 200 metres from me, or my sister's loud singing in the conservatory that woke me up. However, I found myself looking at the white duvet which was in the corner of the tent and, within seconds, I felt the cold temperatures of the night and pulled it right over my head and over the entire sleeping bag. I sighed in great relief. With a tent of such size and airspace, I don't think my teachers who ran the expeditions at my secondary school would have shamed me in my duvet indulgence.

Day Two: I was woken at around 7:30am by a surprise good morning from my parents. I guess they came nice and early to ensure their son hadn't frozen to death overnight. I had aimed to set off at 9:30am. The route I had chosen to walk on day two was fairly simple and involved going slightly away from home, looping back around and trekking some footpaths on the opposite side of the town. It was also quite short, no more than eight-to-nine kilometres. So, as I began my journey, I managed to follow my route accurately with the small help of my phone, but it was highly unlikely that I would have failed to achieve this as I was walking along pathways and roads that I use every so often. It was when I came across my second footpath in an area called Hanwell that I began to head off route. By day two I still did not realise, while I was searching for my footpath, that it was roughly 200 metres from me as opposed to 20 metres. This caused me to go down another path which didn't lead me too astray from the footpath I should've originally been walking along, but it did lead to more confusion as I came to the realisation that I had taken a wrong turn.

By day two, making the same mistakes I had already made

on day one got to my head slightly. It just didn't feel good to have gone off the path I set for myself and then have to find it again after covering the walking distance. At times, I even decided to retrace the distances I had walked and find the correct footpath that I was supposed to have headed down, to get that feeling of satisfaction of having 'gone the right way'. The most interesting part of day two happened early on, when I decided to exchange it with day three. As I was approaching a loop in Hanwell that would bring me back to base, I was also standing near the path that was on the schedule for day three. In this moment, I paused. I had originally planned to visit a lake that was 100 metres away from me, but I could not find any nearby paths that would take me to it. During this pause in my journey, I remembered how many kilometres I had set myself to walk on the final day and it was over 20. Meanwhile, I also recalled that, whenever I had been on an expedition with my school, the last day is usually where we cover the least ground and day two (or three, on a four-day walk) are usually the heavy days. Using this knowledge, I decided to walk 20-kilometres on day two instead of day three. I had set out early enough to return to camp by 6pm or 7pm. In that moment, I also had this feeling of simply wanting to challenge myself and explore this adventurous route I had plotted for myself. I planned it thinking that, by day three, my map reading skills would have improved to their best level and so that is when I could walk slightly further outside of my local area and into other villages on the outskirts of Banbury.

As I began to make my way to my first village, Shotteswell, I stumbled upon another issue with map reading and finding the correct route. I had really wanted to ensure that I was walking along the right footpath to Shotteswell, as it was quite a simple route which required me to just follow all the way until I reached the village. However, once again, my phone came to the rescue after 30 minutes of trying to find out where the correct footpath was. I made it into Shotteswell and I was very excited by the journey so far, after walking through a field of sheep and lambs as well as being able to see some cows. As I walked through the farm that kept cows, I saw a dark-looking animal in a gated pit in the near distance. It glared its glowing hazel eyes through one of the gaps in the gate and locked eyes with me as I made the noises of closing the gate to the field I had just passed through. In that moment, my body and mind felt a slight sense of fear and a large amount of intimidation from this creature that I was failing to identify. As I continued towards the gate that led me out of the farm, I came to discover that it was either a matt black hornless bull or a matt black cow. At the time I did not know, but after arriving home and searching the difference between the two, I am sure that it was a bull.

Moving onwards, I stopped for a ten-minute lunch break in a park that was just in front of the farm. It was only as I was leaving the park that I discovered a sign which prohibited people from using any furniture in the area due to COVID-19 restrictions. One of my checkpoints on the journey was crossing a bridge that went over the motorway. My ability to navigate myself to such a point felt like quite a large achievement due to the fact that I had never ever done this before, or walked across a bridge that went over the motorway. After this, I found myself in another village, Bourton, which is where I was going to find my way to meet the Oxford Canal Walkway, leading me all the way back into Banbury town. Once I had found the canal, after taking various footpaths, it was a one-way route home. While walking along the canal a lot of thoughts passed through my mind, now that I did not have to use the map or my phone for help. The thought of an alligator leaping out of the water to snatch a part of my leg came to mind, and this may have been due to my discovery of the Netflix series '72 Dangerous Animals Asia' during lockdown. I wondered, if I decided to jump into the canal, what sort of creatures and wild beasts I would find in there, and how deep, in metres, was the water?

By then I was also facing a dilemma. My phone was on 3% battery charge and if it ran out of power I would have had to walk home once I reached Banbury, as opposed to calling my dad to come and pick me up as originally planned. At the time,

I was still about six kilometres from Banbury, so I was either going to have to pick up my pace to ensure I reached Banbury with a phone that was still working so I could make the call and end my 20-kilometre journey, or allow my phone to die and walk an extra five kilometres to reach home. As you may have guessed, despite the rising levels of lactic acid in my legs, I chose to walk as quickly as I could so there would be some level of charge in my phone when I reached Banbury. At that point, the only thing running through my mind was wondering when I would have to make the call to my family to say my phone was almost out of charge, and that I would be returning home at an estimated time. However, I was blessed to see the sign that read 'Welcome to Banbury' and again experienced that sense of achievement. Immediately, I took the nearest path leading to normal-levelled ground and I now was familiar with my surroundings. Fortunately, my phone was still on 3% charge and I was pumped full of excitement after completing a challenging walk.

I decided to try and take a shorter route I had never walked before to reach my final check point of some local shops in Hanwell. I was displeased to find that I ended up actually walking further away from my home and very much further away from the local shops I intended to arrive at. I guess, in that moment, taking the familiar and longer route would have worked out best. Nevertheless, I managed to call my dad in the end to be picked up by Aldi shopping market. I found myself sat on the bench outside the store, trying to stretch a little to remove the lactic acid in my legs. I shared my experiences with father as we drove. He listened with great attention. We arrived back to camp and my only thoughts were to set up the tent, get inside my sleeping bag and rest, and I did exactly that.

Day Three: Day three was the shortest day both in kilometres and in time spent outdoors. When I woke up on the last day I was in high spirits as I knew the finish line wasn't so far away anymore. I geared up on the Sunday morning, underwent my usual routine and was ready to go. Day three had plots of many of the same footpaths and routes I had completed on days one and two. I decided to do this because I wanted to ensure that I had finally walked along the original routes I had plotted for myself. In a sense, day three was more or less a day that I was truly looking to improve my map reading skills, by going back to see where different errors and misjudgements were made while I trekked during the previous two days. I began my journey following the exact same route as the one I walked on day two. Due to the fact that I was familiar with this route, the use of my phone and the map was very minimal. Soon into the walk I met a footpath junction that I had previously encountered on day two. On day two I misjudged the small distances that the map portrayed and ended up following the wrong footpath, which led me to having to use my phone to relocate myself and get back onto the correct route.

On day three I remembered this error vividly and stopped before trying to follow the correct path. With the tiny help of my phone and good judgement, I chose the correct path that I had originally planned to walk along. Once I reached a path that was taking me downhill for just over a kilometre, I felt at great peace, knowing I had managed to organise myself and follow the correct route. It was such a good feeling. I also felt at peace because, in the midst of walking down through acres of farmland, I was learning and calculating the distances a map portrays and how much that same distance is in real-life for the next time I encounter a similar situation. As the long footpath came to an end and began to curve left, I had reached the point where I decided to change route on day two and this is where the route followed a different path.

This path led me through a forest that looped back to my original starting point of the footpath junction in Hanwell. As I followed the path that was leading me through the forest, my eyes and ears were not ready for what nature was about to reveal. The long and high-branched trees shaded most of the forest. Sunlight was only able to shine through the small cracks between the many branches and leaves. Birds were singing and tweeting to add a musical chime to this moment of pure bliss and peace. Each footstep I took only got slower and slower, as

I was amazed by my incredible surroundings. As I began to walk uphill and out of the forest, I knew that soon after the expedition I would have to make a return and that it would be cruel of me to not invite my friends or family to enjoy the same experience as I did. Furthermore, as the journey continued, I was about to head into the familiar territory of day one. As I approached these footpaths, I began to dwell on the thought that so many people who live in my town, mostly the youth, throw shade at it for being a terrible place and having nothing exciting about it. However, just like myself, I don't think these people have had the opportunity or taken the time to explore all that the town has to offer. It was such a great shock to me that Banbury town had all of these sites, scenery and tiny spots of beauty to be seen.

As I met a footpath that I had walked along on day one, I approached an area where my map reading skills had truly failed me, leading to complete confusion. The issue that I faced on day one was not that I literally did not know where I was, it was the fact that I knew exactly where I was in real life, but I simply couldn't locate myself on the map and seek out the route that I was supposed to be following. On day one, that brought a great sense of hopelessness. So, I brought out my phone and tried to remain as concentrated as possible. I began following a footpath that my parents and I usually use, that loops you round to a main road leading back to our home. As I stood at the beginning of a path that I was extremely familiar with, I was hoping to find a footpath on my right in a small village near to my home called Drayton. This was going to take me on my final detour before I reached home. The footpath that I was meant to turn into was around 50 metres in front of me, but I was not able to see it from where I was standing. I knew that I was extremely close to my home and that, if I failed to follow the exact route that I had plotted for myself, there would be a great sense of disappointment. So, as I stood there in complete wonder as to where the footpath was, I was delighted to see, out of the corner of my right eye, two elderly people walk out of a small passage. I looked down at the map, did a rough calculation of distances, and knew I had finally found it. It was surprising to discover that I have walked and cycled around that same area and its paths before, but not ever seen the footpath that came to my rescue while trying to complete the expedition.

Soon, I was walking downhill into a farm and I crossed a small field of horses. I continued along the footpath and found myself at another familiar place where I had been many times before, in the area that I was most familiar with was where things headed south. I met another footpath junction that I had seen before and was looking for a footpath that would have looped back round to connect with a straight path led to the Southam road that would take me back home. However, when I met the junction, I could not see the footpath that connected to my final path. I ended up searching for this footpath and it was nowhere to be seen. I turned to my phone for help, but it was no use – I simply couldn't find it. I then found a path that was going to loop me back around and began to follow it. As I trekked upwards along this path, I looked ahead and saw my connection point that led to the road home. I also looked at my phone and discovered that I was walking on the wrong side of an enormous area of vegetation. Immediately I was upset, as I knew I had gone off route – again. I went to explore along the other side of the vegetation to see where the footpath I had been searching for actually was, but when I reached the other side of it, the side I should have been walking along, there was no footpath.

Ultimately, I discovered that the path I was longing to searching for simply wasn't present in real life, but was on the map. This added a great sense of relief and joy to my spirits. It added relief because I was not to blame for going off route, but it also added joy because I had developed an eagerness to learn. When I saw my connection point and realised I had gone off route, I could have simply said, "Ah well" and continued on home to finish day three. However, I didn't do that. Instead, I wanted to learn and see where I had gone wrong, which misjudgement I had made and which footpath I had missed and, thankfully, it wasn't my fault. If I had never walked around the vegetation to discover that the path I drew directions for and intended to walk along no longer existed, I may have felt that my map reading skills were still poor and that I had only mildly improved them. That was truly a highlight of the expedition for me. Despite having to cover more ground, I was satisfied by my actions and decision. As I contently walked towards my connection point to Southam Road, I knew exactly where I was and put both the map and my phone in my backpack. I knew I had done it. I knew that it was finally complete and I could go home and sit down, feeling that I had accomplished something over these three days. When I reached home, I was greeted by my father with a great smile and an "Aww!" and that was just enough to say, "You've done it".

This experience truly did have an impact on my life, my determination, resilience and ability to rise to a challenge, having walked just over 40 kilometres in 3 days. Among the many sources of inspiration I have around me and have found, this event happened due to the inspiration within me. So, I challenge anyone who has taken the time to read my story to seek the opportunity to challenge yourself daily, whether that be small or large, or whether it is during a lockdown in a pandemic, or during normal times. The idea is to never stop testing yourself.

Reader Exercises:

- How often do you decide to step out of your comfort zone and test yourself?
- Is there something in your life that you have thought about doing or achieving, but have just been worried that the task is far too challenging? How can you overcome this and take that leap of faith?
- Are you a person that tries to challenge themselves in some shape or form each day, whether that be a big or a small challenge?

Outside of my neighbour's tent during my lockdown expedition adventure

18. Stop Caring

Most people usually tend to care what other people think about them, say about them, or say to them. Many people allow someone else's opinions or comments about them to bring the mood of their day down. After people feel as if their day has been brought down by someone who voices opinions about them, they may go on to say that they have had a bad day due to the hurtful comments they have received. This is where they are wrong, however. Yes, the person who voiced their unkind opinions may be slightly harsh and cold-hearted in doing so, but they are completely free and entitled to voice their opinions about whatever they wish.

The person who said they had a bad day due to the comments of another person allowed another person's opinions get to them and bring their day down. Each individual has a choice in whether they listen to or entertain opinions from other people, and they also have a choice to decide whether or not they are going to put their energy into caring about these opinions. Most of the time, people tend to put their energies into things and situations that do not benefit them whatsoever. They tend to put time and effort into worrying about what their friends think about them, or what their new work colleagues may be saying about them behind their back. The responsibility of the responsibility of either having a good day with good energies and thoughts, or a bad day with bad energies and thoughts, is completely up to you. You have the choice – each individual does.

I have faced this choice often in my life, as I believe many other people have too. Over time, throughout my childhood and right up until the first year of my adulthood, I have tried practising not allowing the opinions of other people to affect me or get to my head too much and disrupt my days, thoughts or goals. It has taken time over the years to master – in some areas of my life it took close to 18 years – but I soon got the hang of it through persistent practice.

Ever since I was young, my hair, and hair in general, has always been a big thing for me. I have always cared about the way my hair was cut, styled and the way it grew. For most of my childhood, up until I reached year 7 in secondary school, my hair was always extremely short, to the degree that most of my classmates would look at the hair on my head and say to me, "You haven't got any hair." They were wrong in these claims. I did have hair, it was just that it was so short that they couldn't see it clearly unless they were standing close to me. Coming from Africa, it is usually the case that boys have their hair cut nice and short. In most African countries, short hair on boys is viewed as smart, as opposed to long hair. Girls from most African countries are encouraged and allowed to grow their hair, simply because they are girls. The idea of boys having very short hair and girls having long hair is more of a traditional thing that has been carried on throughout several generations. So, while I was young, I rarely had a choice in whether I grew my hair out or not and usually had it very short. I used to like having short hair though; I thought I looked nice and I was more or less used to it. None of my other friends I have mentioned earlier, such as Gwin, Sean, Champhe or Farai, had long hair either while we were children, so it wasn't as if I was the only one with short hair.

So, it is commonly seen that black males usually have short hair, whether they are young or old, it is more of a culture aspect. By the time I had begun year 7 and was a few school terms into it, I started growing my hair out as I was tired of short hair and had seen many other black boys from my school who had grown their hair out slightly. My hair didn't grow at a very fast rate, so it took a few months before you could see the difference between my short hair and my slightly elongated hair. My hair grew, however, and I began to like life where I had some hair on my head. I always grew it on top as opposed to on the sides, which I got cut frequently. One time, while I grew my hair out on top, I decided to do something that a few other black boys had done to their hair and that was to relax it. When a black-African or African-American person relaxes their hair they put a certain type of chemical and hair product in it, which allows their tightly coiled, curled and textured hair to relax and practically converts their hair into a straight or wavy type of hair texture. So, I decided to relax my hair after seeing that many other boys and girls from similar backgrounds to me had also done it. I ended up having slightly less tightly coiled hair and more of a loose type of curly hair that you usually find in mixed-race boys. I liked the way my hair looked when it was relaxed. The effects of relaxing your hair do not last for that long though, usually only one to three months, then your hair slowly goes back to its original texture. Relaxing your hair also makes it look a lot longer, as it becomes more stretched and less coiled.

The only disadvantage of relaxing one's hair is that the chemicals can lead to disruption in the way a person's hair grows, leading to abnormal growth in some areas, which could result in some areas of the hair growing more slowly than other areas. This is exactly what happened to me. When I relaxed my hair I made it go completely straight and my hair was slightly damaged by this chemical process. Afterwards, the growth of it was slightly abnormal. I had a lot of hair in some places and not so much in others. This resulted in me having to once again cut my hair very short to stimulate the growth and allow it to grow naturally and properly again, in the correct proportions. Now, the reason that I decided to relax my hair on several occasions in the first place was because my classmates at school, both girls and boys, liked it quite a lot and said how it looked 'way better' when it was relaxed. However, in spite of these nice comments from my friends at school, I knew that the effects of the relaxer on my hair would not last for that long and if I wanted to maintain the look of having relaxed hair, I would have to relax it every so often, which ultimately led to dysfunctional hair growth. So, by the time I was in year 10 at school, I decided to stop relaxing my hair due to the damage caused by the process.

At times, my friends would say to me that I should make it straight again and that it looked a lot better that way, but I knew it would only lead to damaged hair and I simply told them that, and said I wasn't going to do it for this reason. So, I had long hair throughout the last two years of my secondary school days and I usually just combed it out into an afro on top, as that was the neatest style I could have. Occasionally, I would try out other styles and, again, my classmates would like it and would pay me compliments. Styling it differently, as opposed to just combing it out, definitely took much more of my time in the morning. I never really used to like spending too much time on things such as my hair, because I felt that I could attribute the time I spent on my hair to more productive things. So, while I used to style my hair in the morning, this may have taken 10 to 15 minutes, which is probably not much time for most people, especially females, but I still felt as if this was quite a bit of time every morning to dedicate solely to the way my hair looked at school each day.

I knew why I was devoting time to do this. It was because I kind of liked my hair looking this way, as well as the fact that I enjoyed the compliments I would receive from my peers. In some way, when they complimented me about my styled and twisted hair I felt it was validation that I looked nice. This is where I allowed the opinions of my peers to control the way that I felt and behaved. Allowing them to have control on whether my hair looked nice or not, or whether I looked nice or not, resulted in more mornings of trying to style my hair. If I did not care about what they thought or their opinions about my hair and my appearance, I would have just combed it on the mornings I didn't want to dedicate time to styling my hair instead. This would have been much more convenient for me. However, I knew that friends of mine at school liked my hair styled and therefore I continued to do it, even when I felt I didn't want to give time to it.

As I reflected later in life and realised this was the relationship I had with my appearance, my peers and myself, I realised there was one problem with that relationship – the inclusion of my peers. I realised that I shouldn't have allowed the opinions of my friends to affect the way that I wished to style my hair each morning for school and that, instead, I should have styled it whenever I felt that I wanted to dedicate time to it and simply combed my hair on the days that I didn't want to. I realised that I alone should have been all the validation I needed to determine whether I looked nice or not, or whether my hair was styled to a degree that I liked personally. After discovering and learning this, I put it into practice during my time in sixth form.

When I began sixth form, I had medium-length hair on the top of my head and had it cut very short on the back and sides of my head – a typical schoolboy haircut. I started my time in year 12 with a hairstyle that I previously had throughout year 10 and 11 but, at one point during my early days of sixth form, I felt that my long hair on top was just not the type of look I was going for and I began to dislike the shape of it very much. So, by November of the school year, I decided to cut it all off on top and, once again, go for a short hair type of look. This time I decided to go short on top on my own account and had decided this for myself. I was tired of my hairstyle and wanted a change. I even decided to attempt to get my short hair on top to form waves, which is a certain type of cool hairstyle for boys who come from BAME backgrounds and is commonly found among people, boys specifically, with short hair. This was one of the reasons I also decided to cut my hair short; I wanted to attempt going for this new type of hairstyle that I had never attempted before. Once I walked into school on picture day, the day after I cut my hair short, quite a few of my classmates had said to me that my hair looked good and that I looked nice and smart. One boy from the year below me, who I only knew of, stopped me in the school corridor as we walked past each other and told me that he liked the way I looked with short hair. This was a very nice moment and an enjoyable one, receiving compliments from my peers, but I already knew myself, from the time that Mr Bell cut my hair short, that I was looking pretty fresh. I was happy, comfortable and confident with the way my hair looked and was not ready to allow anyone else's opinions or thoughts affect that.

I kept my short hair for the entire time I was in year 12, during which I attempted to form waves in my hair. This was a very difficult process, because it involved a lot of brushing to form the waves by folding the small strands of hair over each other, and it was extremely time consuming. You also need to sleep with something that covers your head each night, to avoid the waves being ruined and the style going back to normal short hair. Forming waves on your head is very high maintenance. For this reason I decided that waves were no longer something I wanted to maintain either. It required over 15 minutes a day of brushing, every day. So, I kept short hair for the latter part of my time in year 12 and I was content with it, as I still felt as if I looked nice and the hairstyle suited me. The only problem that I experienced with short hair was that I much preferred it when I had just gotten a haircut, because I looked extra smart after this, but once it had been over a week since my last haircut, my hair began to grow on top and on the sides and this is the part of having short hair that I least liked. To look smart and good the majority of the time, while keeping your hair short, it is necessary to get haircuts frequently.

Despite whether I thought I looked good or not with short hair, some people from my school still had opinions and thoughts that short hair made me look as if I had no hair and looked like a skinhead, or my head looked like a ball due to my round head shape. Even when I went on my school trip to Lourdes, when I was in year 12, a classmate of mine said that I didn't even have any hair when she saw me brushing my waves on the bus after a few people had commented that my waves looked nice. I didn't allow these comments to affect my feelings and thoughts about my appearance, and my hair especially, because I simply didn't care what they thought. As I transitioned into year 13, I still had short hair on top of my head but, as time moved on throughout the year, I began to let it grow – slowly. I had made the decision again that I was done with short hair and wanted to move back to medium-length hair once again. So, as the year went on, I was happy with having some height of hair on top of my head because, when my hair on the side of my head began to grow, I still was happy with the way I looked and still managed to maintain a pretty fresh appearance.

As the year 2020 came around and we headed towards the time during which the coronavirus was spreading around the entire world and the UK specifically, my hair was a short-to-medium height on top of my head. Once the lockdown was announced in the UK in late March, my hair was still at medium height and I didn't think much about it, or care about it, due to the fact there was a global pandemic going on. I had seen on social media that people were cutting their hair completely bald for the sake of doing it, as quite a large proportion of the world was now in lockdown and it was not possible to visit a barber or a hairdresser. I considered cutting my hair too, but this time going completely bald and having a head of skin as smooth as a baby's bottom. This idea was enticing to me and it felt as if I was going to go through a spiritual experience of cutting my hair down to skin and letting it grow freely again in a new cycle, until my friend Gilbert suggested otherwise. I was on Facetime to Gilbert one day during the early weeks of lockdown and he had also seen on social media that people were cutting their hair and was confused by this. Due to the fact that Gilbert also had short hair at the time, probably just shorter than mine, he thought that a better thing to do than cut one's hair completely bald would be to allow it to grow out completely and fully during the time in lockdown. After Gilbert suggested this idea, I immediately scrapped the thought of cutting all of my hair off and thought, instead, what better time to grow my hair out than during lockdown.

I didn't necessarily have that much hair on the top of my head at the end of March, but I thought this was the best time to allow my hair to grow and just see how it grew over time. I was excited, because this time around, when I decided to let my hair grow out, I planned to let it grow on top as well as on the sides and I was going to allow it to go freely. Before, when I wanted to grow my hair out at school, I usually had to comb it every morning for school in order to look smart. I later learned that this was a contributing factor to the slow growth of my hair, because combing my type of hair texture resulted in small curls of my hair coming out and, for this reason, I also preferred to simply have short hair. After all, whenever I wanted to grow my hair out, it took such a long time that I was never interested in doing it. Now that I was in lockdown and didn't have to worry about looking smart for school, there was no need to comb my hair and so it could grow freely and in the manner it wanted. So, I went ahead with allowing my hair to grow all the way, starting in March up until and past the later lockdowns, lifting of COVID-19 restrictions and many other things that occurred throughout the lockdowns. I did not cut it until it was time for me to prepare for starting university in October. I decided not to cut my haabyir between the lockdown in March until the middle of August. I only cut my hair in August because my aunty had put it in plaits for me and a haircut was going to just outline the shape of my haircut and make it look smarter. I also cut it in late September, to look smart for when I first arrived at university and to make a good impression on my new peers. Other than that, I did very little to the hair I grew out from March 2020, all the way past the start of 2021, until the present day.

As a result of this, my hair grew a lot during this period and ended up being the longest hair I have ever had on my head. It is long! Typically, you wouldn't see the length of hair that I had at the time, and still have, on a boy's head in Africa, simply because this was not the way it was done over there and was not traditional, and still isn't. Having long hair as a black boy is more of a western-cultured thing. My parents and grandma are shocked whenever they see the length of my hair after I have taken it out of plaits. They say it is truly long. The experience of growing my hair has been one of the most liberating things I have ever done. It has barely cost me anything, apart from buying hair products such as essential hair oil, conditioner and shampoo. It has been such a wonderful journey to watch and I view myself completely differently with this new look. It almost also feels spiritual in a way, and I feel so connected with my hair when I wash it, oil it, and put something over it when I sleep to protect it at night; I almost feel at one with it.

I even fear, sometimes, that my mother may come into my room at night while I am at home, and cut off some of my strands of hair simply because she wants me to go back to having short hair and look like her baby boy once again. My mother isn't the only one who wishes I would go back to short hair. Even my friend Gilbert told me that he much prefers me with short hair and that short hair is more suited to me. I don't disagree with him, or my mother, in the fact that I look nice and smart with short hair and suit it, but I also feel the same with long hair. So, whenever either of them, or my aunty, tells me that I should go back to short hair, I listen to their opinions but that is as far their opinions go with me. I enjoy my long hair and do not care whatsoever what anyone else thinks or feels about it. I am completely happy with the length of hair on my head and my goals and aims for it, and am not prepared to start cutting it or changing it in any way because of the opinions of those around me. As long as I look smart and presentable with it, it doesn't register in my emotions whether people like my long hair or not. They are just opinions that I push to the back of my mind and life, and simply listen whenever they are voiced to me.

It is my different experiences with my hair and its different stages in growth and state that I feel the need to share with you, and show how allowing other people's opinions to dictate the way that you think, behave or live is not the correct way to go about your life. You should be able to live the way you choose, doing the things you wish to do and believing in the things that you wish to believe in. You're entitled to this, it is your life! You have the free will to either decide to care or not care about what others think about you, or think about the way that you do certain things in your life, from the way you decide to dress, to the way you spend your days and the way you wish to act at times. People, especially secondary school children, tend to mock other children for trying too hard, either in class or during a PE lesson, but this shouldn't prevent the 'try hards', as they are called, from continuing to put maximum effort into the things they do. The opinions of those mocking pupils may be listened to and recognised, but that is as far as it should go. They shouldn't start entering into one's mind and affecting the way that one behaves. That is how you allow the opinions of others to affect your life. People's negative opinions are usually built on jealousy and envy of others and are reflected and voiced to those individuals towards whom the envy is felt.

There is also something called the principle of 'crab mentality', also known as the 'crab theory'. When crabs are trapped in a bucket and one of them tries to escape, its efforts will be undermined by the others, with the other crabs pulling it back down into the bucket again, ensuring the group's collective demise. In human behaviour, this compares with when members of a group or those of a particular mindset will attempt to reduce the self-confidence of others who achieves success, or do something outside of their collective way of thinking or behaving. 'Crab thinking' is best described by the term: 'If I cannot have it, neither can you.' The emotional drivers for this are often envy, resentment, spite, or strong competitive feelings – sometimes even conspiracy.

These opinions are not constructive and listening to them is a waste of time. Not all opinions are like this, however. Some are very constructive and can teach us to learn more about a specific thing, or even ourselves, at times. That's why it is always important to at least listen to the opinions of others, but those which don't seem to be of much use or add much to your life do not need to be registered in your mind or receive any of your energy. Developing a confident and carefree attitude to these types of opinions and views will truly help you in the long run and help you to conserve energy and use it in more productive areas of life, as opposed to spending it on people and opinions that are of not of much use. Therefore, I encourage you to develop a more confident and carefree attitude to the opinions of others and stop allowing useless thoughts from other people dictate your life. Instead, allow yourself and your thoughts, and the good thoughts of others around you, to be in control of what you do.

19. GCSEs

> I used to have so many friends, me and them went different ways. Some man wanna drink and party, me and them got different aims. And when you cut man out, people say you changed. Nothing changed here, same player different game.

This is a very well-known quote that was rapped by a popular British rapper, Dave. Now, some people may find it difficult to understand the language used here, so I will convert it into proper English. Mr Omoregie states here that he used to have many friends. However, they all decided to take different paths in life. Some of his friends wanted to enjoy themselves and party a lot of the time. Dave, on the other hand, had different aims. For example, he was aiming at pursuing a career as a musician. Dave goes on to say that when you distance yourself from these people who have chosen to live life very differently from yourself, , they begin to accuse you of changing as a person. He finishes by mentioning, "Nothing has changed here, same player different game", which can be interpreted as Dave, as a person, has not changed, but the stage of his life that he is currently living, 'the game', has.

I had an experience similar to the one Mr Omoregie mentioned. When I was preparing to sit my GCSES, aged 15–16, two of my closest friends, Warren and Tomasz, did not quite understand why I was giving so much of my time to prepare for my exams. When I initially started preparing for my GCSEs in September 2016, I knew that I wanted to excel and be known as the best in my subjects, especially science. However, this also meant that I was giving a lot of my personal time towards preparing to sit these exams. During timetabled lessons, very few people from some of my classes decided to use their time effectively. Meanwhile, I saw lesson time in school for most subjects, not all of them, as an opportunity to build myself up and absorb as much information as possible. In classes such as science, which was my strongest subject at the time, it was sometimes only myself and another person from my class who would respond and engage with the teacher who, evidently, was doing everything he could to teach us the theory of biology, physics and chemistry.

Moreover, to contribute to my goal of 'being the best', towards the end of my penultimate year at BGN, I decided to spend more of my free time preparing for my final exams that were in less than a year's time. Now, where the role of Warren and Tomasz comes into play is when they decided to question me as to why it was that I was giving so much time towards these GCSEs. I told them, repeatedly, week after week, the same answer, "I simply need to revise." The interesting thing in this story is that Warren understood why I took the precautions I decided to take, but Tomasz, on the other hand, still was not completely on board with what it was that I was choosing to do. I made the decision, at age 15, to sacrifice everything I had in order to be the best version of myself. I did not tell everyone about this decision. I do not even recall telling my own parents. It was just a decision that was between my conscious and unconscious self. So, as the story moves forward, I continued trying to achieve what I had set for myself, with or without the support of my friends. As a result, distance grew between my friend Tomasz and me. The thing is, I did not want or choose for this to happen to our relationship. My view is that it was destined for both of us to pursue what life was leading each one of us into.

Because Warren understood what I was seeking to achieve, we did not grow as far apart as was the case with Tomasz. Warren and I still kept some form of contact during this stage in my life. However, even with Warren, the distance between us grew as the time for final exams drew nearer. Unfortunately, Tomasz and I stopped keeping in touch with each other and this resulted partly because of my lack of commitment to keep in touch with him too.

For me, the moral of this story is that, as Dave said, some of us have different aims in life in comparison to our friends. I was interested in being the best version of myself at school and excelling as a student, whereas for Tomasz, this may not have been his biggest concern at that stage in his life. Therefore, when when a distance began to grow between us due to his attitude towards my personal goals and overall attitude towards school at the time, he accused me of changing, of not being fun, not being "the old Neo" and running away from "my old ways", which links back to Dave's concept of "people say you changed". However, two years down the line, I realised that I was not in the wrong and that I had not changed in how I treated Tomasz as a friend and Tomasz did end up telling me that he knows that he was in the wrong for saying that I had changed. I was "the same player" but, in the September of 2016, I was simply, "playing a different game."

Quote from Javah Bowen:

> It's hard to comprise the times I've been inspired by Neo because it's happened many times. I will say this, however. In Neo's GCSE year, the dedication he showed was more than admirable. He would study for hours and hours a day. It made me look at myself and think about how I could apply that sort of drive to my own life by putting in hours and repetition after repetition. Neo would also skip out on social activities to invest in his future. Anyone can use this advice to better themselves and I appreciate and thank Neo for that because I don't think he understands how inspiring he can be. His attitude to life is something else, he knows when to have fun and when to be serious. He's got a good balance in that aspect.

Reader Exercises:

- Do your friends, at times, question changes you make in your behaviour in order to better yourself and, if so, have you asked them why they do this?
- Are your friends supportive, understanding and encouraging towards your set goals?
- Are your aims in life completely different to those of your friends and, if so, what type of differences are they – do these differences affect the way you relate with your friends?

20. BGN: The Transition

One part of my secondary school years that I have not yet mentioned is the beginning. I did not have the typical easy-going and trouble-free start to secondary school that they recommend for your first year. I definitely made my name known early on at BGN. It was within my first 30 days of year 7, during a French lesson, that I said something inappropriate to a classmate of mine about another classmate. Little did I know that the words I had shared were discussed between this person and their group of friends, who came to the decision that it was best to report me to our Deputy Head of the school at the time, Mrs Rolph. It wasn't too soon later into our next period in the day that an office messenger came into our class and asked whether I could go and see Mrs Rolph and bring my bag along with me too. I had never been called to see the Deputy Head, let alone any teacher, before this. So, as I was escorted by the messenger I was walking in confusion and curiosity as to why I was being called to see her.

I arrived at her office, which was next door to our Principal's office and she began to question me about the incident that had taken place during French. I immediately put my guard up and tried to defend myself for my actions and words but, being older and wiser, she understood every word that I said about both of my classmates. At that moment, I had never felt so much fear before. My heart thumped against my ribs after I realised the seriousness of the situation that I had thrown myself into. After a telling off for the words I shared and trying to weave my way out of it, Mrs Rolph concluded our discussion by telling me that I was going to have to sit in internal isolation for the rest of the day. For those of you who do not know what an internal isolation is, it is where you are inside the school but you are put in a room by yourself, or near the staff room by yourself. You are provided with a table so that you can complete your school work for the day and an office messenger is required to visit each one of your classes to collect your work for each period. You do not get to go out for any of the breaks during school, you only get an escort to the canteen to collect your food. I vividly remember the moment Mrs Rolph mentioned that I was going to be sitting in isolation and that the school was going to inform my parents of my actions – tears began to roll down my face immediately. So, as I sat there, experiencing my first ever internal isolation and my first trouble at secondary school, tears continued to roll down my face as teachers walked past behind me to get to their offices. One of the worst parts of that isolation was that I was placed right outside my Principal's office, Mr Long. It was almost impossible to avoid him seeing me. When it finally came to the moment when Mr Long was walking to his office, he saw me and locked eyes with me. He didn't say or ask me anything, he just looked at me sternly and continued on to his office. That was the first time that we had, in some way, fully met.

Just before the bell for our last period rang, Mrs Rolph came to me and told me that I was also going to be internally isolated the following day too, so that I could be fully isolated for an entire day over the two school days. Now, when I heard her say these words, again, the tears began to run down my face as I pleaded and begged that I had already served a punishment for today. She simply responded that I would need to come to the same location immediately after I entered school the following morning. I was not allowed to go anywhere else, and just return to the same spot as soon as I entered the school gates.

By the time I reached home my parents had already received the call from my school informing them of the events of the day and my parents were shocked, disappointed, and embarrassed at having received such a call. This was especially true as it had occurred within my first month of secondary school. For the rest of that same evening all I could think about was the fact that, when I walked into school the next day, I wasn't going to be able to speak with and be with my fellow classmates, share jokes and laugh with them or do any of the normal and fun things that are accessible to you on a daily basis. I was going to be alone, and glared at by teachers as they walked up and down past me throughout the course of the day. I was going to be isolated. That was truly a horrible feeling, simply knowing that tomorrow you weren't going to experience a normal day like everyone else, and you knew what awaited you as you walked through those school gates. It came to the following day and I did as Mrs Rolph asked. I arrived at the same spot as the previous day and I waited for her. When she arrived, she had told me that I was going to be isolated in a different area, at the table just outside the staff room.

As I sat there, trying to complete each task for the different periods I had throughout the day, it was a much tougher isolation to serve as it lasted the entire day. The fact that I was just outside the staff room meant that many more teachers were walking past and glaring, hourly. That same day Mrs Makwezva, a religious education teacher who I have known my entire life and is the mother to my good friend Farai, came to me and asked what I was doing there. I told her that I had said something inappropriate to a person in my class and she simply replied that she shouldn't see me here again. It came to the end of the day and I was once again a free man. That experience truly showed me that the words I said and shared with people could have a big impact and that I needed to be extremely careful about what I said to people and who I said it to.

After the incident, my parents, the school and I all hoped that it would be the last one. Unfortunately, it wasn't. I served two more isolations during my time in year 7 and another two when I made the transition into year 8. Throughout year 7, it came to the point where if I was able to go a whole term without a phone call going home, that was an achievement for me and a relief for my parents. It wasn't the greatest of experiences though, each time an office messenger came into any of my classes my heart would immediately begin to start racing, even if I knew I had not been involved in any events recently. The thing was, I would never get into trouble for doing things such as bullying, swearing at teachers or fighting. I got into trouble for things such as being in the wrong place at the wrong time, or saying the wrong thing to the wrong person. When I moved into year 8, we had a new Head of Year called Ms Fisher. She would have already had an eye on me due to my track record in year 7. She even said to me, "I am going to be watching you like hawk" after I was called into her office for another incident. Throughout year 7 and year 8 I was not working alone in creating a bad name for myself. I had my two friends, Sidney and Sonny. This trio formed when I moved to Sid and Sonny's primary school in year 4. Ever since then, we were a troublesome three. Most of the time I would get the isolations by myself, but for smaller things such as detentions, bad behaviour, or after-school detentions was where the influence of this trio would come into effect.

We would misbehave during class, complete our schoolwork occasionally, pick on other children, and ensure that we did it as discreetly as possible. When I say pick on other children, I do not mean every day and every minute of each day, but during class we would make jokes about fellow classmates, irritate them and so on. Typical things you find in most secondary schools. We just saw it as banter. In addition, we were not salient with our disruptive ways, we always ensured that we did it while the teacher had their face turned the other way, or when we knew it was not possible to get caught. It is hard to imagine that, despite all of my bad behaviour during this time in school, I was still eager to be in the top sets for maths and English. It came to the point where teachers would have to ensure that we sat separately during class in order to prevent disruption and distraction. When heading to school assemblies, teachers would split us up if we decided to line up together. We were simply three very naughty boys who were in the same tutor group and so in the same class for each subject. The teachers in the staff room would talk about us and how troublesome we were as a three. We were tough work, but one day that all changed.

Ms Fisher must have had the thought, along with the suggestion from other teachers, of splitting the three of us up by moving either of us to a different tutor group. However, she had never instigated this. A boy in our tutor group, called Benjamin Lewis, who also wasn't a completely trouble-free student and actually got me isolated with him on one occasion, had gone to tell our Head of Year that the three of us, predominantly Sonny and me, were being troublesome towards him throughout year 8. This was the final trigger to cause the split of Sid, Sonny and me. An entire process was carried out where we were spoken to individually by Ms Fisher and told where we would be going. Sid and I were moved to two different tutor groups and Sonny remained in our original one. After she contacted our parents to inform them of this action, the move soon took place. The trio was broken. Initially, I was very against this move in that I knew I was going to have to make new friends and bond with the new people I was going to be learning with, talking with and laughing with in this new tutor group. I was familiar with people in my new tutor group, but I also knew that I didn't have a single close friend such as Sonny or Sid and so I would almost be alone. Despite these feelings and although I didn't realise it at the time, this move was potentially the best thing that could have happened to me during my time in secondary school.

My new tutor group gave me a new environment, a fresh start, and another opportunity. I wasn't around people I was very fond of or close to, therefore there was minimal room for me to misbehave, be distractive or disruptive. Normally, I was able to do those things with either Sonny or Sid but, now that I was alone, if I wanted to do that I would have to do it alone and I just saw no use in that. There were other troublemakers in the tutor group, but I was not close enough friends with them to feel the need to join them in their actions. I served my first internal isolation in my new setting, but that was also my last one too. As I sat there, for the fifth time, thinking and reflecting on this cycle I was in – normal school time, incident every two to three months, office messenger walks in and calls for your name… isolation – I thought deeply about it and said to myself, "There is simply no need for this." As I thought about some of my older friends in the school who I looked up to, Mrs Makwezva's son included, I didn't recall them sitting where I was and getting into trouble the way I did. I just thought on that last time I was sat there that I didn't need to be doing this anymore. I didn't need to be involved in such things and repeatedly getting myself into these situations.

So, with persistent effort and caution in my actions, words and thoughts over time, I began to get into less trouble; this is where the real change began. Once I moved into year nine, I had a goal of not getting a single isolation for the entire year and I achieved this. Each time the office messenger walked into the room there was still a slight fear due to my past experiences of them walking into my classrooms but, over time, this fear slowly decreased as I increased the amount of time since I had served my last isolation. Also, since I wasn't focusing on being troublesome anymore, I was able to put more of my energy and time into my school work. Throughout the period that Sid, Sonny and I were split, we gradually all went off along our separate pathways. We saw much less of each other throughout the school terms, apart from break time and lunch time. Even then, I began to build bonds with the people in my new tutor group and began to spend less and less time with Sid and Sonny. We also had different interests outside of school which contributed to the gradual breakage of our bond as a trio and as friends. In addition, Sonny departed from BGN in the spring term of year 9, which only weakened our friendship further.

Soon, it came to the point in the academic year where Mr Proudfoot played a big role in my school career and from then on, the story only went upwards for me. It took me an entire academic year to lay low and begin to convince the teachers, my parents and myself that I was more than just a troublesome kid. It was from the point of the science story and during my two GCSE years that I really learned how to focus and apply myself correctly, enjoying the success that my disciplined attitude delivered. My teachers also finally began to see me in a brighter light.

At the time I had begun to actually start writing my GCSEs, just before the beginning of the first week of exams, my school traditionally holds a leavers' mass for the year 11 students who are leaving school that summer. At the end of the mass, they also give out an award called the Sean Concannon Cup to a student who has truly lived up to their potential throughout the academic year. Merits include those of a student who has involved themselves in a lot of the activities the school has to offer and who simply gives it their best, day in, day out. This award is in memory of Sean Concannon, a former student at BGN. That year, I was fortunate enough to be a runner up, alongside a girl in my year group, for the cup. In our Head of Year's speech, we were both described as "mature and reliable Prefects, wise beyond their years and popular among both staff and pupils."

After exams had passed, we entered into a new academic year and I was now a sixth former at BGN. I was invited to my school's annual prize giving award ceremony for my achievements and efforts during year 11. I had never ever been invited to a prize giving awards ceremony throughout my time at BGN and saw it as an event for only the truly exceptional students from my school. Different children from each year group would be invited, with the opportunity to win prizes for outstanding effort and achievement in all different subjects and acts in and out of the classroom. As I sat there, as a prize winner, watching all the other winners head onto stage to collect their deserved awards, I wondered upon the prize I was going to win. I was initially called to win a prize for Outstanding Effort in Religious Studies and, as I sat down, I thought that was the end of my night. To my surprise, a description that somewhat fitted me caught my attention. It was for an award in memory of another fellow pupil from BGN, called Paula Walsh, for Outstanding Personal Achievement. The description followed, "The winner of this award is a shining example of what can be achieved when you make the most of the opportunities every day brings. Some of his teachers would say that he had a slightly 'bumpy ride' lower down in the school..." By then, I had some knowledge that it was me being described on that paper and a few of my classmates began to stare and smile at me. Receiving the Paula Walsh Cup was truly a special moment for me. With the addition of the description, it felt as if I had reached a milestone from when I began my transition at the beginning of year 9. I felt, in that moment, that I had finally convinced my teachers that I wasn't all bad.

Meanwhile, throughout my first year in sixth form, I had been asked by teachers to mentor two male students – one in year 9 and the other in year 10. These two boys were getting into similar situations and troubles as I had, at times even worse, and the teachers at my school thought I would be the best mentor for them due to the similar start that I had during secondary school, but also due to the big transition I had decided to make in my later years. At the time, when I realised my teachers saw my past as an example of how someone can change and go the other way, I knew that I was truly being seen in a completely different light by the teachers and pupils at my school. This gave me the confidence to talk to other children in the lower years who may have been going down a similar path to my previous self, and tell them that it didn't lead to anywhere they were going to enjoy.

After the academic year finished and I moved into my last year of sixth form, I was fortunate enough to get a place on the pupil leadership team and, as a result, I was automatically invited to the prize giving award ceremony to receive a certificate for being a part of the pupil leadership team. In addition, I was also required to be of service to the guests, parents and pupils attending the ceremony. I only received a letter home mentioning that I was attending the ceremony on behalf of the student council, and I had not received the letter that stated I was a prize winner so did not attend any of those necessary meetings. I had felt slightly disappointed to know that I would be attending without winning a prize, however, I also knew that I didn't perform my best during my first year in the sixth form, which you will learn about later. As the evening commenced, I sat there along with the other members of the council, applauding and cheering the prize winners. It then came to the awarding of the oldest and largest cup in the entire school. This cup is called The Father Brabazon Cup for the Scholar Who had Contributed the Most to the Well-being of the School. The description followed, "The cup continues to represent all that BGN stands for in recognising that the development of the whole person and academic achievement go hand in hand. He has been the role model that others were to him when he was that boy in the corridor or dining hall, and he has been a diligent mentor." I was fortunate enough to be the person who was awarded this prize but, initially, it was a shock to me. I thought I was not going to be awarded with a prize at all that evening, as I had not received the prize giving letter at home. I was also in shock because I had found it extremely hard in my first year of sixth form, in regard to achieving high grades in my A-levels. However, that award showed clearly to me that it wasn't just about studies and how well I performed, it was also in recognition of how I was as a person and a fellow classmate to my friends and other pupils. It was an award to show that the same kid who received several isolations very early on in his days, had another and better side to him. I feel the award authenticated that.

Due to the coronavirus pandemic, a lot of things and events have had to be cancelled, postponed, or adapted in some way. My year 13 prom was one of them. My classmates, teachers and I were all supposed to celebrate the complete ending of our secondary school years at the Whately Hall Hotel in my local town on Thursday 26th June 2020. However, due to the prohibition of mass gatherings and the closure of many places, we were unable to celebrate in the way we had hoped. Instead, my school decided that we would still go through with a prom/leavers' celebration, but a virtual one instead. Normally, to end our time at BGN, the leaving year group is given a leavers' mass as well as a prom, so my school merged the two together. At the leavers' mass, you celebrate and pray together during a normal mass and, at the end, there are awards again as there normally are in the year 11 version. At the prom, you simply dance, hear speeches, and there are more informal awards as well as the crowning of the Prom King and Queen. So, our leavers' celebrations and prom (combined) still went ahead on June 26th, but it was just virtual. The dress code was not as strict either, as we were all going to be attending from our homes. Despite this, I still felt the necessity to dress up as it was still a big celebration and event.

The evening began with greetings from the heads of years and the different teachers who attended and our Principal gave a short speech. The stage was then given to our chaplain priest to say a few words about us and, after that, it was over to the head of the lower sixth form to begin the formal awards ceremony. There were five different cups available to win. Three were voted for by members of the sixth form and the other two were voted for by teachers. I won't lie to you, I was very much hoping to have been voted to win a cup and a particular one for that matter. So, the first cup up was the Shining Light award. This award was voted for by our cohort of year 12 students, as opposed to my year group. It was for an individual who had 'shone their light' on both sides of the sixth form common room. It was mentioned that, in gathering the votes, it was clear to see the regard and admiration that this person's peers had for them. Some of the quotes contributed were: "Always a motivational and friendly person"; "They are a huge inspiration to do well and achieve our life's goals"; "Clearly goes out of his way to help and advise those around himself, whether they know them well or not"; and "They are a confident, hard-working and an overall good person who served the BGN community well." When I began to hear descriptions of this person as a motivational and inspirational person, I began to get a large hint that the person being described was myself. Then it was this line, said by one of my classmates, that sent it home for me... "They are the most dapper student in sixth form!"

After hearing those words, with my camera off, I began to do a little dance as I continued to listen from my living room sofa. If there's one thing that my classmates and teachers liked to comment about me, it was the way that I dressed. Soon the speech came to an end and, as it led on to mention my name, it revealed an increasingly true description of me. I was extremely grateful to the year 12 students who had voted me worthy of winning such an award and it was the perfect start to a celebratory evening. As the evening came to an end, our Head of Year reminded us that we were going to have to return any resources that we had used or been awarded over the academic year, and that big cup which I had been awarded last September was on the list too. Yet, with the winning of the newly awarded cup, I was only going to give one award back to receive another, once again, and that was a truly happy moment for me. Knowing that, in my past three years and my last years at BGN, I had been awarded a cup consecutively in recognition of different acts, felt like such a big achievement.

There are definitely one or two things to take from my experiences throughout secondary school. All of these awards and praises I gratefully received would not have happened if I had been too stubborn and not conformed to what was best for me during that time when I was in year 8. I give uppermost gratitude to Ms Fisher for making me move tutor groups, for I don't know what would have happened if I had continued along the same path. It is because of this special move she made for me, that I encourage other people or pupils who may find themselves in a situation similar to mine, to make the correct decision. If a move away from an environment that you're not able thrive is available, take the chance. Where a fresh start and new opportunity is only one word away, say yes! I encourage you, if you are ever in a situation similar to mine, be bold and courageous enough to trust that the move will work out in your favour and is truly in your best interests.

With my Aunty Rebecca in
January 2014

My first day of year 11 at BGN

At Prize Giving after receiving the Father Brabazon Cup for my contribution to the well being of the school while I was in year 12

With my Dad at Prize Giving after receiving a prize for my effort in religious studies and receiving the Paula Walsh Cup for Outstanding Personal Achievement in September 2018

21. My Relationship with Fashion

Ever since I was young, clothes and fashion have always been a big interest of mine. Having cool shoes, a cool jacket or t-shirt truly meant something to me and it still does. It is just something that I seemed to have installed in my behaviour and mind very, very early on. It was jackets and coats which I used to value so highly too. On countless occasions I would see my friends wearing a jacket which I really liked, and would just wish that I had a version of the same jacket myself, or wish that the exact jacket they were wearing was mine. Even when they let me try it on, or even wear it at times, it just made me happy to be wearing such clothing. Clothing and dress has always been something that I have been conscious about. From the time that I began to dress myself, I was only interested in looking cool, stylish and trendy. Even on non-school uniform days, I would plan what I was going to wear days ahead and give a good think on what outfit I could pull off best from the selection of clothes in my wardrobe.

I remember, vividly, my first non-uniform day in secondary school. It was in the first two months of school, on 8th November 2013, and it was called to raise money in memory of the patron of our school and Catholic martyr, George Napper (also known as Napier), as it was the day before he died on 9th November 1610. BGN celebrates this day each year as BGN Day. I already started planning what I would wear as soon as I found out we were going have a non-uniform day. However, all the planning was a shambles on the day, as I realised my sister had borrowed the jeans I had intended to wear with the rest of my outfit. So, I had to quickly put something together in the time I had remaining and, therefore, in my opinion, my outfit was not as co-ordinated and flashy as I had intended it to be. I wore a navy-blue fleece with baggy grey jeans, with black, red and white Nike Air Jordans. At the time, I felt the Jordan shoes didn't go with the outfit whatsoever. I despised the fact that I was wearing baggy jeans, at the time skinny jeans were trending, and I wore the fleece because I thought it was one of the coolest pieces of clothing I had. As the day escalated, I remember feeling not as comfy as I would like to be, while I also felt that my outfit wasn't all that good and I simply didn't feel that I looked 'cool enough'. I also remember a classmate of mine coming up to me on that day and telling me that she did not picture me wearing the clothes I was wearing. She thought that I was going to be wearing green shorts and a t-shirt, which was definitely something I would not wear. At that time in school, I was considered among the popular kids due to the people I spent my time with and the connections I had in school, so that may have been a reason why my classmate pictured the type of outfit I was going to be wearing.

Clothing and fashion was such a big thing to me that it changed how the rest of my Christmases occurred after one specific Christmas. When I got to the age of about eleven, I no longer wanted toys, games and consoles for Christmas and actually took more of an interest into what I wore. One Christmas I wrote a list of the type of clothing I wanted, which was most likely some Nike jumpers and some cool shoes and so on. However, when it came to Christmas Day, I received many clothes but they were clothes that I felt didn't truly express me or meet my idea of 'cool'. So, that Christmas, I was slightly disappointed. It was the case whereby I was opening my presents and putting on the smile and joyfulness a person normally shows when receiving a present they hoped may have been slightly different. My parents could see that my true hopes had not been fulfilled and we came to the agreement, on that day, that instead of them going out to purchase presents which they thought I may want, they would give me a sum of money and allow me to purchase the things I really wanted. Ever since that Christmas, it has been this way for both myself and my sister.

As the school years went by, my attitude to clothing and fashion remained the same. When I entered my last year of school, year 11, I started to form ideas in my mind of what I was going to wear to my school prom very early on in the year. With months to spare, I was mostly focused on how my date, who I was yet to ask, and I were going to arrive at the scene. I had recalled a group of boys from one of my older sister's year group who had arrived in a helicopter to their prom, and that idea was definitely a contender. I also looked at prices of arriving in either a Lamborghini, Ferrari or Bugatti. As you can see, I was not holding back! I wanted us to be the most dashing and flashy couple there. The prices of all those things were far too expensive, however, and a lot of them were sold out already. So, we managed to get in touch with one of my mum's connections who was involved with cars and he was able to help us out with quite an offer – a ride to the prom in a matt black Bentley for a price we could not refuse.

By then, I had asked a girl from my school who goes by the name of Miss Maddy Measures to accompany me to the prom. She kindly accepted my invitation after I publicly gave it to her on a card which read 'Prom?' in bubble writing. This was on our school field, in front of her group of friends and half of the entire school. At the time, I knew that everybody had either simply texted the person they wanted to go with to the prom, or had organised it long in advance, but I wanted to take a different approach, a more American and old-fashioned way of asking Miss Measures to the prom. So, in preparation for one of the most memorable nights of our lives, I left my prom suit search extremely late because I wanted to solely focus on my GCSE exams, as well as the fact that I worried my weight could fluctuate throughout the year and I wanted my suit to fit perfectly. Maddy and I had already discussed that we would be wearing the exact same colours, so if she was wearing a green dress, I would have to find an entirely green suit.

Normally guys just wear a tie, bow tie, or handkerchief and tie of the same colour as their date's dress, but I wanted Maddy and I to go all out and be the couple people could not take their eyes off. Maddy had already bought her dress well in advance and she told me that the colour of it was burgundy. I insisted that she did not show me the dress, or show me what it looked like on her, so that on the day of the prom when I saw her for the first time, I could simply be wowed.

Nine days prior to the prom, which was scheduled to take place on 29th June 2018, I travelled to Reading to visit my aunty and uncle. My mother saw this trip as the perfect time to shop for my burgundy prom suit, as Reading was going to have far more options. We ended up searching in a local shopping area, Bicester village, for the suit. When I told my aunty and uncle that I was looking for full burgundy suit, they were quite shocked and were not sure that I would find one – especially this close to my prom. We searched around various shops and the most we could find was an expensive burgundy suit jacket, but no full suit. The option of buying the coloured suit online was proposed and, by the end of the day, while still being 'suitless', I went with the idea. By then, I was feeling extremely worried that my plan of matching Maddy's dress was going to crumble completely. As soon as we reached home, I did my searching immediately. After looking at Next and M&S, ASOS was the saviour I had been looking for. I searched on the website and found a full burgundy suit. It had sequins sewn throughout both the jacket and trousers and it quickly grabbed my attention. I ordered it within minutes and, fortunately, my aunty was able to get next day delivery. It arrived the following the day and fitted me perfectly. In the photos on ASOS the person was wearing black loafers with it, so I had ordered those as well. To my misfortune, the loafers were a size too small for me, however, I was still able to get my foot into them and it was too late for me to try and exchange or return them. I knew I only had to wear them for the prom and they matched too well with the suit for me to wear anything else. At last, I was at peace and was now fully ready for my school prom. My aunty, uncle and I knew that my suit was one which you would not find anyone else wearing, and would truly separate me from the crowd.

When it came to the day of prom, I was thrilled with excitement. My hair was cut to precision, my suit was on point and, with Maddy next to me, the picture was simply going to be complete. Maddy arrived at my home for the 'pre-prom ceremony' and she truly did wow me as I had expected. Together, her dress and my suit made a perfect match. Soon, we made our way to the prom. I made sure that we were among the last few to arrive so that: 1. Everyone could see us arrive; and 2. I wanted to arrive fashionably late. Despite this desire, I really do wish I had the opportunity to see everyone else arrive from the beginning and just get the full experience of the excitement and the moment of the evening. Once we arrived at the prom, driven by the person who provided the car for us, I saw a mass of my classmates, parents and people to my left. Our driver opened my door first and, without even realising and only knowing when I watched the videos back over, I hopped out of the Bentley and within seconds a loud "Woo!" came from the crowd to my left. There were multiple cheers from people and one person even said I looked like Michael Jackson. That was most probably due to the loafers, white socks and suit trousers which only went down to the bottom of my ankles. In the midst of the exciting and energy-filled environment, I managed to hear bellows from my two closet friends, Sean and Champ, stating, "That's my guy!" and "That's my boy!". I then cautiously walked towards the car door nearest to where Maddy was still sitting and opened it for her. She stepped out and the crowd again cheered and roared for her too. She stepped to the left side of me, we locked arms and made our way to the red carpet for our photo. That, in itself, was truly one of the best moments I had ever experienced in my life.

The process of pictures continued until we were seated inside the hall of The Great Barn, a place in Aynho which was local to many of us and was where our prom took place. Prior to this, once we were all inside the building, teachers who were present at the prom announced that the voting line had opened for the King and Queen of the prom. Now, I initially thought that in England they do not do Prom King and Queen and that it was an American thing, so it was a shock to me when I heard this. Once this was announced, I heard a couple of my friends saying that we should all vote for one specific person from our friendship group as a joke, so I thought that, with the mass of votes that were going towards our friend, from our friendship group alone, he would come out as the Prom King. I did not even manage to place a vote for either King or Queen, as I got too caught up in taking pictures. I knew who I was going to vote for though. It was a classmate of mine who wore a smashing baby pink suit with tinted glasses and a girl who I had a crush on throughout most of my secondary school years, who was wearing an eye-catching baby blue dress. Later, it came to the award ceremony where people were granted awards such as 'Most likely to become Prime Minister', 'Biggest Gossip' and other entertaining accolades. Soon, it came to the last awards of the evening, the Prom King and Queen award. At this point, the atmosphere levels were high. People were making their predictions as to who would be crowned King and Queen.

I was standing right at the back of the large crowd of my peers, away from the centre stage and frontline view of all that was going on. Firstly, the Prom Queen was announced. The winner was my close friend Molly Nugent who had truly stunned everyone that evening with her dress in royal blue. Next up was the winner of the Prom King award. I had four people in mind who were contenders for this award. Firstly, it was my friend who had received some automatic votes from my friendship group, second was myself simply due to my suit which was not commonly seen, third was my other friend who wore the baby pink suit, and fourth was a friend of mine who was wearing a baby blue suit. My science teacher, Mr Savania, began to request a drum roll from the audience; he then paused midway through the drum roll asking for a louder drum roll, which greatly increased the suspense of the moment. Two of my classmates, who were standing next to me, started videoing me as they believed I was going to be the winner. There was one last drum roll before my teacher announced, "The Prom King award 2018 for year 11 goes to… Neooo!"

Screams came from my two friends who I was standing with as I made my way through the mass crowd of people, towards the royal thrones to sit alongside my Queen and be crowned. I was extremely happy and filled with joy to be crowned as King, because I knew that what I had chosen to wear to the prom had managed to wow people to the extent that I gained enough votes to be their Prom King. Many people mentioned to me, afterwards, that it must have taken some bravery to wear such a suit due to its loud nature, but I did not see it that way at the time and still do not. I do not see wearing something that stands out, or that is just outside the lines of normal, as something people should have great worries about stepping out in.

I feel that people should embrace dresses, suits and pieces of clothing which are eye-catching, and just enjoy them and enjoy wearing them. Wearing that sequined burgundy suit, knowing that there was a high chance that no other boy was going to be wearing anything similar and I was going to stand out, gave me such a thrill, excitement and energy, that I literally hopped out of the car when I arrived. I think that, if I had just worn a normal suit, I would have stepped out of the car as opposed to hopping out of it as I did, instinctively. For proms that take place in the UK, boys usually wear plain suits such as a black tux, navy coloured suit, or a grey suit. You normally find the girls wearing all sorts of different colours. I knew, prior to this, that would be the normal trend and I had no intentions of following it whatsoever. I didn't want to arrive at the prom looking pretty much the same as the rest of my classmates. I believe that my 'wear what I want' attitude had been developing over time while I was in my last year at school and being crowned as Prom King in such a suit confirmed that my decisions about my clothing were working well for me. If I had become self-conscious about wearing the suit and it drawing too much attention, it would have potentially resulted in someone else being crowned as King. For me, it was the suit that gave me the push to receive such an award, but it was the 'wear what I want' attitude that stemmed the entire idea.

So, as I made my transition from secondary school to becoming a sixth form student at BGN, a lot changed in regard to my usual school routine, how often I had lessons, the privileges and the freedom I was now given. One of the things that changed the most, however, was my school dress code. Being a sixth former at BGN, you are entitled to choose your own clothing and wear smart business attire. The uniform comes off as soon as you reach year 12. However, my school was quite strict on the dress code. Boys always had to be wearing collars and, on Mondays, we were assigned to wear ties and a blazer or a suit if possible, while the girls wore dresses. We were not allowed to wear clothing that had large logos across them and blue jeans were prohibited as well as sneakers and jumpers. The week or two before I started my first year as a sixth former, I went shopping for clothes that fitted my newly assigned dress code. I knew from the get-go which impression I was going for; I wanted to be the guy who was always dressed smart and presentable. The guy who wore ties on other days of the week too, not just on Mondays. I wanted to be the guy who made the most of being able to choose his own clothes for the school day and make looking smart look good. After I collected my shopping prior to beginning school, I was ready for my new start and approach to sixth form life.

As the first few weeks of school passed, I noticed how, initially, everyone dressed extremely smartly, especially peers in my year who were the new sixth formers, but then by week two or three people started becoming more relaxed with their dress code. The sneakers, the round necked shirts and t-shirts and jumpers all began to slowly creep in, as they do yearly. However, I continued to stick to my way of dressing in smart business attire, due to the fact that it was school protocol as well as the fact that I did not find dressing less smartly and being too causal that enticing or presentable. In regard to my wardrobe, I felt it was complete, apart from the fact that I did not have a suit I could wear during the week, or especially on Mondays. Instead, I was changing my combinations of clothing and colours of ties to keep my look refreshed each Monday. My dad kindly gave me the allowance to purchase a suit online and I went searching for something which I felt best expressed me as a person. I was initially thinking of purchasing a chequered suit and I was mostly interested in colours such as grey or navy blue. I, for sure, did not want a plain old suit similar to those worn by two or three classmates of mine. I came across a suit which most people would not even look twice at. It was a three-piece, forest green, chequered suit with white checks. Immediately I saw it, I knew it was the one. So, I purchased it within minutes and, as it was quite early in the year, I said I would save it until picture day.

Picture day soon came around in November and my hair had recently been trimmed and styled completely differently. I had gone from long hair on top to short hair once again. My green chequered three-piece was a perfect fit, along with a white shirt, and my recently purchased green bow tie finished off the entire outfit, accompanied by the same tight-fitted black loafers that I had worn to my prom. I was ready to wow pupils at my school with my suit and certainly ready to wow for the pictures too. However, before I even managed to get to my classroom for morning registration, a classmate of mine notified me that the pictures were not going ahead on that day due to the absence of a teacher. I was in such a deeply distraught state after hearing those words – most importantly because now, I would have to wear the suit once again for picture day and it was not going to have the same effect on the human eye after a second look at it.

I have this view with all clothing and outfits. To me, an outfit, dress or suit never looks as good again as it does the first time it is seen being worn. As I went on throughout the day, my walk was not as glamorous as I normally try to make it when wearing such clothing, due to my disappointment. People who saw me still stared and complimented me on my suit, but it just wasn't the same, having the photos cancelled on that day. It was a saddening day for my classmates too; girls had puffed their hair and made an extra effort with their make-up and outfits. We had all gotten dolled up for what turned out to be a normal day in school. I even decided to try and sit indoors and alone, away from people, so that fewer people would see my suit for the first time and its first-time effect would still be as powerful when I wore it the second time around for picture day. So, during lunchtime on that day I only sat with two of my friends in a closed classroom, helping them with something, and remained there until just before the end of our lunch break, so I could walk to my last class when there were smaller crowds of people. I had told my friends during lunchtime about the problem I had faced that day, but one of them told me it did not matter that I would have to wear it again for the second time, she said it would still look just as smashing. That had lifted my mood slightly but still, that day was quite a disappointment for me. However, one of my friends who had seen pictures of my prom suit did say that the green chequered suit was above it, and it was from that day that people at sixth form began to start associating my name with wild and smashing suits. Our picture day was rescheduled to January when we came back after our Christmas holidays and I had to wait until then to put the suit back on. Throughout this time, I continued to keep to smart business attire, but did not once wear the green suit again, nor any of its separate components.

Soon, January arrived and it was our rescheduled picture day. I underwent the same procedure as I had in November; I got my hair trimmed to refresh the short, smart cut, and the green suit was back out on show. This time the pictures did go ahead and I had a spring in my step too. I hoped that people's memories of when I wore the suit in November had faded. I received kind comments from my peers, other year groups, and my teachers too. A lot of people were just as wowed as the time I was seen wearing my prom suit. It was truly a good feeling. As we headed into later months, in the new year of

2019, I had a conversation with Sean. At the time, Sean was in the year above me, so was an upper sixth former in year 13. Usually, year 13s broke the sixth form dress code and Sean was among the people who did so. So, I had asked him one time, "How come you like to wear round necks, trainers and jumpers and simply not dress smart at times?". He replied saying that he did not feel the need to impress anyone in his dress. I understood his reasoning at the time and still do. However, I see dressing smart from a different perspective. How you decide to clothe yourself and present yourself says a lot about your nature. It's an expression of yourself.

When Sean told me what he did about impressing people, I thought, Well you shouldn't necessarily dress for others on any level, whether you're trying to impress people or not trying to impress people. You should simply dress for yourself. You should wear the clothes you wish to wear and the colours which represent you best. Not those that you think others will like, take notice of, or not take notice of. The reason why I dressed smartly in comparison to my friends and a lot of the sixth form cohort, is that I wanted to give an impression of myself that showed I was punctual, business-like and simply because I viewed dressing smart as more attractive as opposed to being casual. I would never wear either the same shirt or same trousers in the same week, let alone the following day. I would always change the combination of my outfits to make it look renewed, day in, day out. I actually only had five pairs of smart trousers, one for each day of the week, but because of the number of times I changed the colours of my outfit, it may have looked like I had ten. I remember one day, one of the girls in the upper sixth form had just seen me walk into our sixth form common room and bellowed at me, "Neo, how big is your wardrobe!" I stood there in shock, not knowing what to respond, and just smiled back.

A little secret, which I only let one or two people in on, was that I had actually increased the size of my wardrobe by picking different items of clothing from each member of my household. I began doing this very early on in the year once, when I realised that I was running scarce of different outfits throughout the week. I wanted to wear something different each day. I began with my dad's wardrobe, where I would pick different coloured ties which would go best with my shirt for the day. I then moved to my sister's wardrobe, which displayed various unisex jackets and coats that I could put on top of my own clothes. It has only ever been once that I have borrowed from my mother's wardrobe. It was for a Monday at school when I intended to borrow my mother's oversized black furry coat. I wore it with a white shirt, black bow tie, black blazer and black trousers. Coincidentally, I chose to wear it on a day that the Oscars were being held and my PE teacher jokingly asked me whether I was heading to the Oscars later that evening. With the help of my family members' wardrobes, it looked as if I had such a wide spectrum and variety of clothes. Whenever anyone complimented me on my sister's, mother's or father's clothing that I was wearing, I would always take the compliment and move on. I would never tell my peers that the clothing was not mine. I felt as if this added a certain dullness to the outfit and reduced its effectiveness.

Meanwhile, throughout my time in year 12, many of my peers would ask me how I had the confidence to wear some of the clothing I wore, such as the green suit, or my mother's long, oversized black furry coat. My classmates also thought that only I could rock such clothing. However, I disagreed with them. The reason they thought I was the only person who could wear such clothing, or make a certain colour work, was because I was the only one who attempted to do it and made it work, not all of time, but most of the time. I do not think that, in the seven years that I was at BGN, and maybe a few years before this, there has been a sixth former who showed up in a green suit for picture day, let alone on any other day. I was among the minority who did something as extreme as that and, when I did it, people admired it and were attracted by it. However, although they believe that I am the only person who can make a green suit look good, that's not the case. A lot of people could have made my green suit look good, they just may not have had the confidence to dress in such a suit, or felt it was too attention grabbing to wear. I always encouraged peers of mine, and still do, to wear whatever clothes they wish, as their clothes are their clothes and they should have the confidence to just wear them, regardless of whether they thought that their outfit was too smart, too eye-catching, or too bright! I encouraged them to wear what they liked because I truly think, as long as it is respectable, a person should wear what they want. Often, people would tell me that they thought about wearing a certain dress, or a certain suit, but just felt as if it was too much or too flashy; but I would tell them, forget the views and opinions of others. Some people may like it, some people may not. Wear as you wish. It is fine to be different or not fit in with the crowd.

One Tuesday, Champhe had asked me why I was wearing a tie since it wasn't Monday and I replied, "I wear ties on Tuesdays because nobody else does." This urge to be different at times can inspire others and birth a new way of doing things. I can recall the night of the BGN prize giving award ceremony, held in September 2019, when my Principal had come over to the table where I was sitting with other members of the student council and our guest of honour for the evening. Comments about my green suit were being shared and my Headteacher said to our guest of honour that I was probably the best dressed person in the whole of my town. Now, I don't believe this, personally, and I'm quite sure my Principal did not mean this in literal terms, but this comment authenticated to me that my idea of dressing how I liked for myself appealed to other people. Clothes and dressing are something which I have always truly had a great interest in and I have been fortunate enough to develop an attitude where I can casually wear whichever clothing I feel like wearing, and not get bothered by people's opinions or the norms of my environment. It is this attitude which has led to my peers and teachers describing me as the most dapper student in the entire sixth form, a person who should get into modelling and a great asset to the school. I encourage anyone who feels anxious about the opinions of others on what they wear to free themselves from these anxieties and wear clothing that truly represents who you are as a person.

Reader Exercises:

- Do you care about other people's opinions on the way you dress?
- When you dress yourself for different occasions, do you dress for you or the people who you are going to see?
- Do the clothes that you wear each day represent you and your personality, or something and someone else?

With Maddy on the red carpet

With Queen Molly soon after being crowned

Prom day, June 29th 2018

The day I wore my chequered forest green suit to school for picture day (for the second time) in January 2019

22. Run Before You Walk

Some of you may read the title of this chapter and think that I got the words 'run' and 'walk' the wrong way round. They are exactly where they are meant to be. When a new baby is born, in its early months and stages of life, every single thing they do for the first time is exciting and new to them. Everything they see, the skills they learn, it is all a thrill because they have never ever done it before. Learning a skill such as how to walk is fascinating for a baby or toddler, once they finally crack how to take their first steps. Firstly, a baby will learn how to roll, sit, then crawl, stand and, finally, walk. These are usually the stages a baby will move through in learning to take their first steps. However, a baby may not follow this exact procedure each time.

I was greatly shocked when my parents told me the story of how I took my first steps on this earth. I was informed that I was able to sit and crawl, but I had not begun to stand or walk at all between eight and nine months. One day, however, my eight to nine-month self decided that I was going to shock everyone who was present. In a room filled with my parents, sister and Aunt Esther, all watching television, I decided to first stand, and then hold onto a table that was close to me, and I started walking while holding on to the table. Everyone in the room was completely gobsmacked and began chanting, "He's walking! He's walking!" Soon after a few of my first steps, I let go of the table and began to walk using only my two legs. My parents were completely stunned as they had not even seen me stand before, let alone take my first steps. That day was not only an extremely special day for me, but also for my family who were present. I can picture baby me looking at my parents, sister and other people who were in the room, realising that they could walk and thinking to myself that I wanted to be able to behave the same way they did and walk like them. So, when that day came, I guess I decided it was the time to give it a try. The need to practise standing and testing the strength in my legs didn't seem too important at the time, for I was only interested in walking before I knew how to stand firmly and I did just that.

On the first day of the academic year at my new primary school, St Johns, something within my year 4 self, aged eight, decided that I was able to run before I had walked. Literally. Growing up, I was very passionate about running and racing and winning races and being praised as the fastest in the year group. At my previous school, St Joseph's, I was considered among the top three fastest and, along with one or two others, it seemed that I wanted to take this position and see if I could maintain it while being in a new school with new classmates. So, on my first day of getting to know my new classmates during our first lesson, which was mostly just an introduction to year 4 and how the year was going to be planned, I asked the classmate I was placed next to, "Who is the fastest kid in the year?" I was told that it was a boy called Jake Kelly and my classmate pointed towards him. I knew what I had to do to confirm to myself and my new peers who truly was the fastest child among our year group. I then asked for a message to be passed along to the table he was sitting at, saying that I would like to race him at the upcoming break time.

Break time soon arrived and both of us were laced up, ready to see who was the faster kid. One of our classmates called "Three...two...one go!" We both set off as fast as we could across the playground and back to the start line. I was taking quick breaths, in and out, in and out and, by the time we had both reached one side of the playground and were returning, Jake was slowly coming out of my view. The race had finally ended after I managed to meet the finish line first and came out victorious. I do not have the greatest recall of what I may have said after the race, but I presume it was along the lines of glorifying and proclaiming that I was now the fastest kid in the whole of year 4 at St John's because, soon after the race was complete, Mr Kelly was very upset. He insisted that I race his older brother who was in year 6 at the time, but was also the fastest child in the entire school. Not being one to back down from a challenge and having confidence from my previous win to prove I was the quickest in my year group, I agreed to race his elder brother within the same break time. In this race, I saw Jake's older brother at the start line, then quickly run past me to make his way towards the finish line. I was not so victorious that time around and lost quite terribly to Jake's older brother. This was some consolation to Jake and slightly humbling for myself too.

Years later, as I remember this story, I am shocked by the confidence I had at the time to make such a proposal, without first even ever conversing with Jake and getting to know him, let alone the people who I was asking to pass messages to him. I see this as a time in my life where I literally ran before I walked because the average child who may want to be recognised as one of the fastest in their year group would usually make a few friends first and then ask them whether they wanted to race. They would then continue to keep racing different people, until several classmates requested that the new, upcoming runner races against the child who is known to be the fastest in the year – in this case Jake. In my situation, however, these thoughts never came to mind and all I was interested in doing was finding out who was deemed as the quickest kid in order to beat them and make my mark. It was as if I had such complete faith in the speed I had within me and was bringing to the start line, that I did not think even the fastest child my age at a new school could match me. In that moment, I truly decided to run before I walked.

Another occasion that I experienced running before walking was when my mother was a part of a group of African women who took petitions that had been signed for 'Making Poverty History' to number 10 Downing Street, in 2005. The people who were attending the campaign were given the option of whether they wanted to bring their children with them or not, and my mum decided that she would bring me along. Once we arrived at Downing Street, we were greeted by the then Prime Minister, Mr Tony Blair, with a handshake. It was an extremely memorable moment for me because, after Mr Blair shook my hand, I continuously exclaimed to my mother that Tony Blair shook my hand while showing her the hand he shook. I also stated that I would resist washing it for the rest of my life, but that intention lasted for a very little time. Immediately after entering number 10, I noticed the enticing toys and toy cars of Mr Blair's five-year-old son, Leo, who was going to have his birthday party over the weekend. I could not help but ask my mother whether I could play with the toys that were set up and ready, she checked with Mr Blair whether it was fine and he gave the green light. I remained downstairs in Downing Street, playing with the toys belonging to the son of Tony Blair, while my mother went upstairs with the Prime Minister for her campaign.

Being so young, I cannot recall the exact feeling I had while at number 10 Downing Street, but that day must have definitely been an enjoyable one with the privilege of meeting Mr Blair and having the opportunity to play with such cool toys. Usually a person only gets the opportunity to meet the Prime Minister or be invited to 10 Downing Street for doing something that deserved considerable recognition. However, I did not fall into this category. I was just fortunate enough to have a mother who had been invited there for work purposes. It was simply a case of being in the right place at the right time and it was definitely an encounter that some people could wait a lifetime for, but again, I had the opportunity to ran before I could walk.

Overall, each time that I have ran before I walked, on the occasions I have just described, this strategy worked in my favour. However, there have also been many times in my life where running before I was able to walk did not work out, and led to me learning a lesson from that experience. For example, when I initially got into the process of writing a book for the first time – this book – I decided to tell my entire list of Snapchat contacts that I was going to have a book completed within one month and it was going to be released later in 2020. Having never written a book before, I was completely unaware of how long the process actually takes and the timescale it can require for different stages of book publishing. So, having not fulfilled this claim, I looked slightly silly to those people who remembered what I'd said and I learned a hard lesson early on during my writing.

People say that you should always learn to walk before you can run, because it is commonly believed that you should learn the basics of whatever you are doing in life before you start attempting the intermediate things. This is how most people progress in something, and it is a theory with which I agree. Nonetheless, you can see from my experiences that attempting to run before you walk isn't all bad, when attempted correctly. I only decided to challenge Jake to a race on my first day at school to prove I was the quickest kid in my year because I truly believed in my ability to run fast. I must have decided, early on when I took my first steps, that I was able to walk without going through the process of learning to stand by believing that my legs and body were strong enough to help me take my first steps. Running before you walk is an uncommon phrase and is not carried out by many people, but it is not unheard of. So, whether you wish to start your own business, Instagram page, company, or new career, don't be afraid to take actions that could be interpreted as running before you are able to walk if you truly believe you are capable of doing so. You never know, it may be you who ends up taking the first steps that lead to great things.

23. Reflections on Social Media

I was introduced to social media by peers of mine at quite a young age. I had downloaded Facebook and created an account by the time I was nine years old. I used Facebook for entertainment through the posts and videos that came up on my news feed. I also used it as a social platform to interact with my friends and other people who had the app. At that young age, whenever I posted statuses, they would be full of complete nonsense. People of my generation would post statuses such as 'like for a like', which meant that if you liked that status, the person who uploaded that status would tell you something that they liked about you. Lastly, I also used Facebook to play games – a game called miniplanet™ in particular.

Miniplanet™ was a virtual game where you could create your own avatar and connect with people all across the world. You could earn virtual money, buy virtual clothes, form virtual relationships with people and do most of the things that you could do on earth, albeit virtually. It was very similar to games such as 'The Sims'. I adored miniplanet™ and loved logging on to my friend Sean's computer and playing the game. It intrigued me greatly at that age. Nevertheless, despite how much fun I had using miniplanet™ and connecting with people through Facebook, I don't think it was in my best interest to have the app at such a young age. Neither of my parents knew that I had it as I never mentioned it around them, nor did I have my parents as friends on Facebook. I even decided to block them as I had heard that a few of my friends and cousins had done the same, so they could feel free while using Facebook as opposed to worrying that their parents might be monitoring their activities. I don't think it was a good idea to have Facebook at that age because I was still lacking in knowledge about the implications of social media, such as privacy and keeping safe while using the internet. It is most likely true that none of my friends and people who I connected with over Facebook were aware of these implications either at the time, which meant that we were all the more vulnerable. Fortunately, no incidences ever happened between Facebook and me in regard to any breaches of my privacy or meeting complete strangers who intended to do harm. However, the point is that I could have, and I was just fortunate in happening to avoid any situations like that.

Today, social media is at a peak and continues to expand and achieve larger peaks, with the fast-growing rate of technology and science. Social media platforms such as TikTok, Snapchat, Instagram and many others are thriving, because such a large percentage of the human population is constantly using them. These three app companies all managed to get thousands of millions of downloads each in 2020 alone, with Snapchat receiving 281 million downloads, Instagram 503 million, and TikTok a storming 850 million downloads, practically thumping any other platforms competing with it. Due to the fact that usage increased because people were spending more time at home during the lockdowns, all of these app companies were getting large sums of money in their bank accounts.

The age range of younger people who are using these social platforms is slowly increasing. More and more young children are beginning to have social apps such as Snapchat, Instagram and TikTok. There is no issue in regard to children having these apps for entertainment. However, just like myself, if they have no knowledge about the implications of social media it leaves them in a very vulnerable position, especially young children between the ages of five and 13 years old. So, it is in the best interest of parents, siblings and other close contacts of children to be aware of what apps your child or younger sibling are using, and ensure they are kept safe and well away from harm. Social media doesn't just harm people, adolescents especially, in regard to a stranger posing as someone they are not, but it also affects people's self-esteem, self-confidence and general views of themselves. It is very easy to be going through a rough patch in life, end up scrolling through the media on your phone and seeing that some of your friends, or people who you look up to, are living their best lives and having a blast. These same people may have just heard great news in regard to how they scored in a test at school; they may have just bought the coolest pair of shoes and showed them on their Snapchat, or they may just be posting a picture or status of themselves working and telling their followers and peers how hard they are working and how well they are doing. It could be a variety of things.

While you are sitting there seeing this good news and the great things that seem to be going on for everyone apart from yourself, it will undoubtedly put you in an even worse mindset and you may begin to start questioning whether you are good enough, or whether what you're doing is good enough in life compared to these other people – but you shouldn't. Every single person on earth is running their own individual race and experience different things and see different things each second and minute that they breathe. A comparison with the person sat next to you, or on the other side of your phone screen, simply isn't fair on yourself. No other person would have been in the exact same position as you and experienced the exact same things that you have experienced and the way that you experienced them. This applies from the different times people wake up, to the times they sleep, eat, rest and work. It is all completely different for each person and each person has their own way of doing certain activities.

Now, not all comparisons are bad, they are only bad in this sense. When you are comparing yourself with another person who has your best interest in mind, you are making a healthy comparison. For example, you may compare yourself to a friend of yours or someone you know that works very well and efficiently and gets things done. You may ask this person what they do with their time on a daily basis and how they manage it to ensure they complete their work but also find time to rest, relax and live their life. After that person tells you how they do that, you may compare how they go about their day to how you go about your own day, and you may try implementing some of the techniques that the person you're asking uses to have a more efficient way of working. You may even make a comparison with your work, schoolwork or university assignments with a friend or colleague, to see whether they may have done something that you could input into your own work. These comparisons are healthy and good because they are in the interest of helping you. So, while making comparisons, always bear in mind and be aware of your intention for making it in the first place. Is it to bring yourself down and say that somebody else has used their day more efficiently than you, when you may have sat and watched television all day? Maybe you were tired and needed a rest day. The person you may be comparing yourself with may have just gone back to work after three days of rest. You simply never know at times, especially with people you don't know personally, so why bother with the malicious comparison to yourself in the first place?

24. My Relationship with Social Media

I have mentioned how my relationship with social media started off, but now I am going to tell you how it developed and grew. I used Facebook as my main form of social media up until 2012. Once Instagram, which people now call 'Insta', was invented in 2010, it took me two years to download it but, like many other children my age, I began to use Insta a lot more. I posted pictures that I thought I looked cool and nice in and used all the hashtags I could think of while trying to gain as many likes as I possibly could. For me, this was validation that the picture I had taken looked cool and was a good picture. For many people today it is still validation that the picture they have taken is cool and looks nice. I continued using Instagram all the way up until I was in year 7. By then, Snapchat had been invented (in 2011) and I also downloaded that app later on. As Instagram and Snapchat made their way onto the social media scene, my use of Facebook gradually decreased. Among most millennials, Facebook is seen as a social media platform for the older generations, due to its inadequateness in comparison to fast-moving and attention-grabbing apps such as Snapchat and Instagram. I tended to use Instagram a lot more than I did Snapchat, simply because I was more familiar with Instagram and found it much easier to use. I soon got to grips with Snapchat and understood the whole process of taking a picture, writing a message or caption on it, and sending it to a friend, or creating your own personal story where all of your Snapchat contacts could view the post.

As I progressed throughout BGN, I began to use Snapchat more and became more experienced with the process. I used it quite frequently throughout years seven, eight and nine as a means of communicating with people and friends. It was definitely very handy for that. I also continued to use Instagram and post pictures here and there on my account. With Snapchat, however, I didn't post many things to my story. This may have been due to the fact that the app was still new to me and I was not sure what I could post about. Over time, I became a lot more familiar with the app and began to post slightly more, while I was able to see the type of things my friends were posting. By the time I was in year 9, I would mostly just post about things such as the scores of my football matches for Banbury Irish, or any cool places that I visited over the weekend. I also posted any moments either at school or at home that were unmissable and just had to be rewatched, either because they were funny or just uncommonly seen. It was during my time in year 10 that I really began to use both Snapchat and Instagram a lot more frequently.

In year 10, I was playing for both Brackley and Banbury Irish and it felt as if I had started my journey to becoming a professional footballer. I felt the need to share this with my Snapchat contacts and, at times, Instagram followers, each time I had a training session for Brackley or whenever I had match days on Saturday mornings or Sunday afternoons for both teams. I always used to love posting my Saturday morning Snapchat stories, as I was always up early, ready to travel to matches by 7am or 8am. I would post things such as a black screen with the caption 'Game Day', as well as the time that I posted it, which would normally be around 6am. I would post the scores of the matches, whether we lost or won, with a caption such as 'Good game lads, didn't get the win today but we continue on' and all sorts of other things. The reason I may have done this is because, at the time, I followed many academy footballers for professional clubs, such as West Bromwich Albion and Chelsea, and I noticed that they were doing the exact same thing. So, it was from them that I was learning this behaviour of posting my football life and letting my contacts and followers know how things were with football and what the latest scores and updates were. The only difference between those academy players and myself, was that they were academy footballers and I was still just a Saturday league player, playing just below academy football level. Those players had signed proper contracts which prevented them from representing their school for school football matches at times, in case they got injured. I, on the other hand, would sometimes complete a school football match and train later in the evening for Brackley, which was not an issue or something that Brackley worried about. A lot of them may have also had football agents at the time, who may have encouraged them to grow their social media following through posting things such as match scores and videos of some of their best plays.

Brackley Town U15s was a development team which aimed to help young aspiring footballers, such as myself, to get to higher levels of football. It was not an academy. Despite my knowledge that some of the people I followed on social media were academy footballers, whereas I was only aspiring to be an academy footballer, I still continued with my posting on social media for the entire season. Even after I was released from Brackley the following season and went to play for Chesterton Juniors, the posting continued. It was maybe a little less frequent, as I felt discouragement after getting released, but it was still relatively frequent. I would still post the scores of matches on Saturdays, where we were playing if we played at a nice pitch or a stadium, and many other things. I remember, vividly, one home game for Chesterton where I was sitting on the bench and unconsciously thought about what I was going to post on my story as the score and the caption, while we were currently losing. I had captions in mind such as 'Unlucky today lads, next week we come back stronger.' These were all good intentions and thoughts in regard to coming back stronger the following week, the only problem was that the match was still going on...

So, during a match that my team was losing and I was sitting on the bench towards the remaining quarter of the game, I unconsciously started thinking about what caption I was going to post on my Snapchat story, as opposed to completely focusing on the game and seeing what impact I could make if I was to be brought back into the game. At the time, I was even disappointed with myself when this involuntary thought came to mind. I knew that it wasn't necessarily a thought that I consciously had, it was one of those thoughts that you have while you're listening to something important that somebody is saying and your mind slowly drifts off to think about what you're going to eat for dinner later. Despite it being an unconscious thought, I was not pleased with the way my mind was thinking and working in regard to social media. I knew, at the time, that the only reason I uploaded Snapchat and Instagram stories was to show my followers that I was on my way to playing professional football and that I was taking steps through training and playing for two teams to make it come true. Little did I know that what I was doing wasn't actually in my best interest but, rather, in the best interest of letting people know about my business and life in regard to football. Doing everything I did with social media only added pressure and expectations on and of myself.

Since I was posting that I was up at 6am on Saturdays and training three times a week, whenever people may have come to watch my matches at either of the two clubs I played for, or when I represented my school, they would have probably been expecting me to be a wonderkid due to how much I always put out on social media about myself. In reality, I wasn't even among the top five best players at Brackley, let alone in the entire MJPL. I didn't know it at the time, but using social media in the way I did while I was at Brackley and Chesterton was a big mistake that I soon learned from. None of my teammates at either Brackley or Chesterton, who were seen as some of the best players in the team, posted about match days, training or anything like that. They were completely focused on playing football and improving as footballers. I also had these intentions, but I also had the intentions of letting the rest of the world know that these were my intentions. Even when I used to go and train by myself, either after matchdays or on a day I wasn't training or playing during the week, I felt the need to let my Snapchat contacts know this was what I was doing. No one really said anything to me, not my teammates or Snapchat contacts, or anyone, as this wasn't an uncommon thing. My teammate Warren also did it at the time and pretty much to the same degree that I was doing it, but he was also one of the top five players who played at Brackley when we played for them that season. Yet, we were clueless to know that what we were doing wasn't actually helping us improve as footballers as much as we may have thought it was – it was only giving our followers and contacts more knowledge about our lives. Soon, these activities all changed once I entered my first year of sixth form.

In the summer that I was sitting my GCSEs, I even felt the need to post and show people that I was revising, which I was, but there was something in me that felt everyone needed to know this information. This didn't add as much pressure as it may have done for football, but it still added the expectation that I would have been scoring extremely highly in my GCSEs when, in fact, I ended up achieving less than what was expected of me. Once I began year 12, however, I decided to see social media in a different light and used it very differently. Throughout years 10 and 11, I didn't only post about when I was playing football or revising, but I also used to upload videos of myself dancing or goofing around to music, with the intention to make people laugh and give them entertainment. This was especially true during my time in year 11, when I was preparing to write my GCSEs, which I knew was a stressful process for every student. After posting these dancing videos I would normally receive feedback and messages from my contacts, saying how funny it was or how I had made their day. This was a nice feeling which I received on my end and I wanted to continue bringing laughter and joy to people's screens and faces.

During years 10 and 11, I also didn't message people as often as I used to during my lower years in school. School and football took up way too much of my time to find the time to start messaging friends and other people. I even decided, during this period, that I was not going to get into any situations or relationships with girls at all. I had been in an entanglement with a girl that I had fallen for very early on in my school days, while I was in year 8, and I found it very difficult to suppress any feelings I had towards her during the years leading up to year 11. It was always me who was pushing to be with this girl, who had also formed a deep connection with me, but she was unable to see the two of us as a couple. We managed to stay friends and keep talking, using apps such as Snapchat, but soon after the new year in 2017, I decided that I no longer wanted to talk to her or anyone else for that matter. The situation with this girl was already consuming too much of my time, mind and life, and I was becoming too stretched across my school life, sport life and social life. Something had to give. The thing I decided I cared about least was my social life and I stopped using social media for communicating purposes from then on. The intention was to put my studies first and then my football career.

I carried on with this behaviour and mindset all the way up until I was in my first year of sixth form. I still posted on my social media as mentioned earlier, but that was mostly all I did when it came to social media. By the time sixth form had started, I was playing a lot of football still, but now for Banbury United U17s and U18s. I never posted Snapchat stories about this, the reason being that I didn't feel the need to. Throughout year 12, I had a conversation with Mr Bell that really opened up my eyes. I was sat in his chair having a haircut when we were discussing social media and how people used it. I informed Mr Bell how I used to use social media and how most people tend to use it, and it was he who first introduced me to the idea that posting in the manner I was only added unnecessary pressure and expectations. He gave the example of someone who goes to the gym. This person may one day post on their Snapchat story that they are at the gym. Once viewed by their contacts and friends, an expectation is developed that this person is going to have nice toned muscles, legs and arms in real-life. That's a natural expectation to develop of a person who posted that they were at the gym. If the person who made the post is seen in real-life and doesn't necessarily look like that toned or muscly and just looks like any other person, that same person would look like a fool. They would have made people believe they were going to the gym and getting into great shape over time when, in reality, that was the first time they were returning to the gym from a long break and decided to take a picture and post it. It was once I heard these words and thought about it deeply that I reflected back to the way I used to post myself and realised that I was simply adding pressure and high expectations onto and of myself that were completely unnecessary. I used this thinking and theory to guide the way that I used social media during my time in sixth form.

I rarely posted about my activities, whereabouts, or anything that I was doing during my first year in sixth form, because I knew that doing so only added expectations about myself in people's minds and placed extra pressure on me for no reason at all. I knew this was the case because these are the feelings I had from time to time during the periods that I was a lot more active on social media. Each time I posted a story, I would look on my phone to see who had seen it and who hadn't seen it, think about how other people may have thought about viewing my post, and many other unnecessary things that most people tend to do after they post things on social media. I continued with the behaviour of not sharing anything at all that I was doing or getting up to with my time, both inside and outside of school, throughout my two years in sixth form. It almost felt as if I was living on a different planet to everyone else. I even stopped posting my dancing videos and times when I was messing about to music, because I simply didn't want to have anything about my life on social media. I would see many classmates of mine, and children from both the younger and older years, post what they got up to, what was going on in their life, who they hung out with and many other things, but I refused to engage in this activity again.

Don't get me wrong, there is nothing wrong with posting your activities and parts of your life that you experience on social media. It is completely your choice what you wish to share and not share with the public. I just felt that, from my past experience and what I had learned about social media from Mr Bell, it was something I didn't really want to engage with as much anymore. I was still doing things such as playing football five times a week and studying, but this time, I was simply just doing it in silence and, as they say, 'minding my own business'. I found this way of using social media much more healthy, free and easy-going. Nobody was able to comment on things I was doing, the clothes I decided to wear, or anything at all, because I simply didn't give anyone any room to do this. Using social media in this way during my time in sixth form gave me so much peace of mind. I wasn't thinking about what picture I was going to upload next on my Instagram, or the caption it would have. Nor was I thinking about how I was going to tell my Snapchat story that I was playing in an U18s FA cup match for Banbury United. My mind was free. This also helped me to live more in the moment, as opposed to thinking in the future regarding what I was going to upload or post. It was truly a blissful and peaceful year of my life. I even decided that I did not need an Instagram account during my time in year 12, in 2019, and decided that the app was not worth my time, effort or mind. I personally saw Instagram and still see it as a platform on which people upload pictures and videos of great memories for other people to see. I also saw Instagram as a platform for people to spend two continuous hours of their lives watching other people's lives and see what was going on elsewhere around the world. It was for this reason that I thought Instagram didn't really serve much purpose to me as an individual, apart from consuming my time and I decided, during that time, it wasn't necessary for me to have the app. It didn't exactly add anything to my life apart from keeping me entertained, which many other healthier activities were also able to do at the time. So, I decided to deactivate my account and had finally freed myself from Instagram after eight years' total usage. It was a decision that I was very happy about.

Now, I do know that people also use Instagram for marketing purposes to sell their products – celebrities in particular- – but since I was not marketing anything and did not intend to for the meantime, I realised that if I was not the marketer and salesman, I must have been the product. This is exactly what I was and this is what millions of people around the world are. Those of us who use Instagram, Snapchat, TikTok and other apps solely for entertainment purposes, are simply the products from which these apps make money and which other people and entrepreneurs around the world use to prompt people to buy their products and make money. This isn't a problem if you think about it logically, as every single human being needs to buy products and things to help them survive and remain entertained. For example, if nobody could buy a Netflix subscription and Netflix was completely scrapped for whatever reason, people wouldn't really have that much to keep them chilled and entertained during periods of relaxation, or lockdowns for that matter. However, the state that I was in at that time did not require me to have Instagram and I definitely did not want to allocate time in my life to being a product to help these big apps and companies make more money. There were many more things that I could have done with my time, things that were truly in my best interests.

Overall, I do not view social media as a bad place per se. Social media has helped people to communicate far more quickly, and it has helped people to get their small or large businesses going and grow due to its wide reach. It has even helped in finding criminals around the world through the sharing of one profile picture. However, it also has its disadvantages. As mentioned earlier, it can lower one's self-esteem and confidence if not used and viewed correctly. It can add unnecessary pressure that one does not need to entertain in their life. It has pros and cons. I have learned the way that I like to use social media through my past experiences; I hope these experiences I have shared can help guide you on how you would like to use it too.

Reader Exercises:

- What type of relationship do you have with social media?
- Are you personally happy with the way that you use social media?
- Does time spent on social media bring you joy, or have negative impacts in your life?

25. Shakespeare for Schools

At one point in time or another, each and every single one of us has been a child. During our early childhood, we are more than likely to have been asked the question: "What do you want to be when you grow up?". Typical responses to this question are a doctor, lawyer, footballer, musician, and all sorts of other careers. My typical responses to this question usually involved career paths such as acting or becoming an athlete and performing at the Olympics. I hadn't developed a love for football and returned to playing it by the time I was being asked those questions. At young ages, however, we are extremely aspirational in what we would like to do once we are grown up and, at those ages, we never put any limits on ourselves or in our minds regarding what we could achieve in life. My acting career never took flight and is yet to take flight. I also soon realised that becoming an Olympic athlete, a sprinter in particular, was also most likely not going to happen after I arrived in year 7 at BGN and saw that my speed, which was viewed as the quickest in my primary school, did not even come close to at least three other boys in my year group. I only ran at a speed that was just above average and a speed at which a few of my new classmates could run too.

As I grew older and gradually learned more about myself and the world, I decided that the dreams I may have had while I was younger were not ones I wanted to pursue in my later years of life. This is most likely true for many people. People develop new interests, have a lack of exposure to what it is they wanted to do and dreamt about, so find new interests and, at times, people simply lose interest in what it is they thought they truly enjoyed. It is simply the way life goes. I soon realised that I did not have an interest in and love for acting when I transitioned into secondary school. From the start of year 7, all the way up until year 11, there were countless opportunities to be a part of school plays, productions and musicals. Not once, throughout my first five years at BGN, did I decide to put myself forward to be a part of any of these school showcases. This may have been due to the influence of my environment. I usually hung around the 'cool kids' in school, as my group of friends and I were seen as the popular set of students. It was like this throughout the five years – a group of us boys always having each other's backs, sticking up for each other when it came to disputes with the older and younger years. We all represented the school in sports, either through rugby or being a part of the school football team. It was through activities such as this that our bond as a group of friends was built. We were the group of boys who were always invited to parties by other pupils from our school, or we would receive invitations from pupils, popular ones in particular, at other local schools. None of my friends were interested in things such as musicals, the choir, school plays or the arts generally when it came to school. We were a typical set of schoolboys only interested in two things: sport and girls. I don't believe that my friends influenced my lack of interest in performance arts. I was just not interested in these activities at my school and, if I truly wanted to be involved in any of the school productions, I wouldn't have allowed the influence of my friends' opinions stop me from doing this. I was also already preoccupied with football throughout my time at BGN. Six years down the line I was into my first year of sixth form and that is where things slightly changed.

When I started sixth form, I was literally the only person from my group of friends at school who decided to stay at BGN to complete my further education. All of my friends decided it was their time to part ways with BGN and chose other pathways. Some went to study at football colleges, others attended normal colleges, and a minority went on to do A-levels at other institutions. This was truly a difficult time for me as it felt as if I had to create completely new relationships and friendships with the remaining students in my year group. I was friends with a few people from the sixth form, but this was mostly the group of girls that my friends and I used to hang out with. If I were to hang out with them, I would have been the only boy as all of my friends had fled to other schools. I did, however, manage to build bonds and find new friendships with the people I had not really got the chance to know over the five years I had previously spent at BGN. It was early into the school term that another school play was being produced. Each year, the school did at least two plays and, at times, did a proper production of a musical that involved shows night after night. In September 2018, it was announced in an assembly, early on in the school term, that the school was doing another play. I allowed the thought of it to sit with me for some time. The announcement was made on a Monday and the first rehearsals and meeting were going to take place on the upcoming Wednesday. The play was open to students from years 8 to 13. I didn't really have anyone to discuss this with, as I was still building friendships that early on in the school term. I also knew that many individuals were not going to be interested in being part of the play, as students in the upper sixth were preparing for their A-level exams in the summer and most students in my year were just not keen on things such as musical productions. There were only one or two pupils who had involved themselves in productions over the years at BGN and were most likely going to put themselves forward for this play.

The play that was going to be showcased was 'King Lear' as it was a Shakespeare for Schools production, which is a part of the Coram Shakespeare Schools Foundation. The Shakespeare for Schools production is where schools, local and regional, would act out a play that Shakespeare had written, and perform in front of each other and a live audience. The organisation is the largest youth drama festival in the UK. While I thought about whether it was the best decision for me to put myself forward for this play, I weighed up how much time I had in a week. At the time, as mentioned earlier, I was still playing a lot of football. I had training sessions on Mondays, Tuesdays and Wednesdays, and attended matches on Saturday mornings and Sunday afternoons. Training sessions on Tuesdays required me to go by train to the local town of Bicester, and this journey consumed a lot of my time on Tuesday evenings. After I calculated how much time I was devoting to playing football, I tried figuring out how many hours of studying I would need to be doing each night to keep on top of my A-level work. I was fortunate enough to be in year 12 at the time Shakespeare for Schools had come around, and I knew that if I devoted time to other activities it would not affect my overall A-level grades too badly as I still had two years until I was going to write my exams. After weighing up these factors and talking to the music teacher about how much time would be required of cast members for rehearsals, I made the decision that it would be best to challenge myself and see what the experience of taking part in a school production would give me. I was not completely buzzing or full of excitement to be embarking on this new experience, I was more on the side of waiting to see what the experience was going to be like.

It came to the first rehearsal and I attended by myself. I saw three other sixth form students out of a total of 90. Two of them were in the same year as me and the other was in year 13. The majority of students were those in the lower school, from years eight to 11. I was familiar with most of the faces from the lower school, but I didn't really know them personally. The only person that I knew and would refer to as a distanced friend was a boy in the year below me called Bradley. Brad and I had always seen each other around as he also played for Banbury Irish in the age group below me. At least knowing one person gave me some comfort as I stepped into an environment out of my comfort zone. The teachers organising the production did not require us to audition, they simply gave us the scripts to look at and asked who wanted a large, medium or small role. I knew that I had wanted a medium-to-large role, but was hesitant in putting myself out there as this was the first time I had tried acting and I wanted to allow the experienced people to make the correct decision. Our music teacher, Mr Wilson, then suggested that I have quite a large role and play Edmund, the bastard son of King Lear. I guess the teachers knew the type of people we were, our characters and personalities, and so were able to place us in roles they thought we could thrive in. This was especially true for students from years 10 and above, who had been at the school for a lot longer. A lot of the people at the rehearsal had also already featured and been part of many school productions over the years, depending on which year group they were in. I am pretty sure I was the only new face they had seen present for a school production, or I was at least in the small minority who were doing a play for the first time. When I received my role, I took it on happily and was slowly starting to get excited about what was to come. During that first session, all of the roles were given out and we began reading through the script and saying our lines. It came to the end of the rehearsal and us cast members were told that rehearsals would be running weekly on Wednesday afternoons immediately after school. It was the best day of the week to run rehearsals, as we finished school early on Wednesdays.

Weeks and weeks passed and, over time, the play started coming together. People felt comfortable in their roles, were coming to know their lines by heart, and the play was progressing. As an individual I wasn't doing too badly – I learned my lines as often and well as I could and gave my best when it came to rehearsals. Any advice given to me by my teachers was taken on board and I tried implementing it into my acting. One of the things I truly enjoyed and treasure from those weeks of practising was the bonds and friendships I was able to build during this time. Most of them were with students from the lower school and it was just amazing that this environment enabled me to know people much better, build friendships, and laugh with them. This was only possible because I was open enough to allow it to happen. My mindset at the time was not, 'I am older than you, therefore I am superior.' I saw each and every cast member as equal to myself and better at times when it came to overall acting skills. At times, the children in the lower school would be misbehaving slightly and may have had the odd conversation to a friend when they shouldn't have, but those of us who were higher up in the school would kindly tell them that we needed to get on with the play. By the time it came to the end of October, I was truly enjoying myself and having so much fun. We went to the Royal & Derngate theatre in Northampton to complete a workshop on skills in acting and roleplaying. Here, we were able to learn many more skills from people and theatre actors who had good knowledge of the industry. This was also something which led to the stronger bond between us as a group and the friendships between people. Soon, however, it came to the time that we were preparing to perform in front of an audience.

We were told that we would be heading back to Royal & Derngate to perform the play in front of a live audience, as well as in front of the entire school on BGN Day. Now things had

gotten a lot more serious. There was less messing about during rehearsals from everyone and we were all focused on the common goal of putting on a performance for our two audiences. We first performed in front of the entire school on BGN Day on 9th November 2018. I personally felt that performing in front of my peers and people who knew me was a lot more challenging than performing in front of an audience who did not know me. Each of our friends were about to see another side to us and see us in a different light. This was especially true for my friends, who had never seen me act before. The show went ahead and ended up being a success. Edmund's character had a distinct scene within the play that I was required to execute. It involved him talking to himself about the fact that he was a bastard son of Lear and felt less of a son in comparison to his legitimate brother Edgar, and he plotted to harm Edgar. The scene gradually got more intense, line by line, with Edmund becoming angrier about being the bastard son, and ended with him standing on top of a stage prop box screaming the line "Stand up for bastaaards!" This was the most challenging scene I was required to execute, but I was more than grateful for being given the opportunity to do it. When it came to the end of the play, we all got together backstage and congratulated each other, filling the room with good energy and excitement after our performance. When I got the chance, I went up to my friends from year 13, Champ and Sean, and asked them whether, while I was performing, they saw me as Neo or as the character, Edmund. They told me that they saw me as Edmund and that was all the validation I needed.

Four days later at the Royal & Derngate theatre, on 13th November 2018, we had our second performance of the play 'King Lear', this time in an actual professional theatre. The atmosphere was electrifying, from the time we sat on the school minibus heading for Northampton, until our dress rehearsal. By then, we all had our props we were going to be using in the play, as we did for the show in front of the entire school. Each cast member wore all black apart from King Lear himself. The character I was playing, Edmund, wore a black leather jacket. At the time we were rehearsing for the play, I wore magnet earrings to school as I had wanted my ears pierced at the time but my mother and grandmother were always against the idea of men having piercings due to their traditional upbringing which did not involve men wearing jewellery such as earrings. However, my teacher who was organising the play insisted that I wore my large diamond magnet earrings on the day of the show. This was because Edmund was quite a cool character in the play, who ended up having two women fall for him. The dress rehearsals acted as a warm up for all of us before the theatre was filled with eyes. When it came to performing in front of the live audience, which many of our family members were part of, including one of my older sisters, the only goal we had in mind was to remember our lines and put on a performance. Each time any of us were backstage it was a moment of thrill, knowing that we were about to step out on stage. I continuously looked at the script to ensure I said my lines perfectly, word for word. After you had completed your part on stage and went behind the curtains, it was almost a sigh of relief that you had done what you were supposed to do and executed it correctly. The transition of props on and off the stage was adequate and I cannot recall a single significant error during the performance.

It soon came to the end of the play, which involved the majority of us being on stage and a few cast members around me as Edmund's character died at the end. The experience of receiving applause, whistles and reactions from the crowd was truly comforting on stage. There was complete excitement after we returned to the dressing room after taking our bows, at the fact that we were able to pull off and produce a shortened version of the play 'King Lear'. It was a feeling and environment I was not familiar with but I deeply enjoyed every second of it. At the end of the evening, all the local schools who were a part of the Shakespeare for Schools production and had performed that evening sat on stage to be congratulated and talked to about our performances.

This experience of being a part of the Shakespeare for Schools production with BGN is one that I will hold closely with me until I grow old. By the time that I was laughing with my newly made friends and enjoying the rehearsals, I knew I had made the correct decision to put myself forward as part of the production. I even reflected and pondered upon why I hadn't put myself forward for previous productions over the five years I had already spent at BGN, if this was the amount of fun that I could have been enjoying while being a part of it. I came to the conclusion that I simply didn't know I was going to enjoy performance arts as much as I did while performing in 'King Lear'. During the first rehearsal described earlier, I wasn't sure what I was in for or what was coming along the path of making that production. It just happened. Yes, I could have made this decision five years earlier, or somewhere throughout those five years, but the thing is, I didn't. I don't feel regret for my decision of not ever putting myself forward for school plays, but I do acknowledge that I could have missed out on a lot of free fun, new friendships and experiences. Maybe it wasn't the right time for me to start doing performance art, maybe it was. No one will ever know. It is for this reason that I encourage people of all ages to simply put themselves forward for things. Throw yourself in at the deep end. Rather than stepping out of your comfort zone, leap out of it into a field for which you have no knowledge or experience. Maybe even explore a field you have no interest in, for who knows, you may discover an interest you have been longing for. I didn't know that school productions could be such fun as 'King Lear' was until I decided to go there, put myself forward and see how it went. A lot of us don't know all the things in life that truly fulfil us, things that make us laugh until our stomachs hurt, or things that feed our souls. We just need to have the confidence to go out there, have the experiences and find these things.

Quote from Sean Williams:

> I've known Neo for the majority of my lifetime. Within that period of time there have been numerous occasions that I've been inspired by Neo's abilities, such as his dedication towards his education and his drive towards pursuing his dreams of becoming a professional footballer. But there is one moment in particular that I've reflected upon that Neo really inspired me, and this moment occurred during our time in sixth form. If you know Neo, you'll also know he is man of many talents, but one thing that I've always told him that he can't do is dance. In sixth form, me and a few other friends of ours were always on his case about his dance moves. We had repeatedly told him that he is not a great dancer. It was fair to say he was slightly offended by some of the comments made, but this did not prevent him from continuing to dance. A few months after this conversation, the annual school Christmas talent show was slowly approaching. Neo had proposed to me and a few

of our other friends that we all come together and perform a dance routine. We all declined the proposal for different reasons. However, although we had all said no, Neo was still keen to perform a dance routine, so he auditioned for the Christmas talent show by himself and, in fact, did end up performing in front of the whole school – which was approximately at least 900 students. As we all cheered Neo on from the audience, that's when I felt most inspired by him. After all the jokes and criticism that Neo had taken from us, he still had the confidence and self-belief to perform in front of all those people. He didn't care what other people thought, he just did what he enjoyed doing. Just from that three-minute and 27-second performance, Neo had inspired me to always believe in myself.

Reader Exercises:

- How often do you put yourself forward for things you have never tried before?
- Are there activities or things in life which you have thought about getting into or trying out, but have simply dismissed due to your environment?
- How often do you stand alone and follow through on something you aimed to do, even if you have to do it alone?

On stage at the Royal and Derngate theatre in November 2018

26. Starting University

Ever since I was quite young, I dreamt about attending university but, at the time, I used to call it 'college' due to the influence of American television. Watching American TV programmes such as 'Drake and Josh', 'The Suite Life of Zack & Cody', and 'Wizards of Waverley Place' influenced me to have the desire to study at Yale University in America. Between the ages of seven and 11 years old, I had this hidden dream that I never shared with anyone, not even my parents or my siblings. I may have since shared the dream during conversation with my close friends, but I am sure this is as far as the dream went. At those ages I knew nothing about Yale University, other than the fact that it was viewed as one of the top two universities in America, or maybe even the best. I thought this principle applied worldwide and that Yale was seen as the best university in the world. I did not consider or even know about highly ranked British universities such as Cambridge or Oxford. I guess I never felt the need to share my dreams about what I desired for my future because I was never viewed as being the best student during my primary school years, or at least among the group who were seen as high flyers. I more or less sat closer to the average set of pupils. Despite this, I always wished to achieve good grades and be seen as a clever student, regardless of whether my behaviour at the time did or did not match this intention. As I began secondary school, the thought of university as a whole was foreign to me, as I focused on experiencing school in another light and was in a new environment. I rarely thought about how my life was going to look after my five years were complete at BGN, both generally and in regard to academia.

As I approached the end of year 9, I began to grow a bigger desire and hunger towards improving as a football player. My good friend Warren also played football at the time and he and I had just finished a football season together with Banbury Irish. During that time, Warren was improving rapidly as a footballer and played a big role in helping our team to become champions of the second division in our local area. Warren told me he began training by himself, either in his garden or at a close-by field, to help him improve his football ability and it sure seemed to have worked. He did this because Banbury Irish only trained once a week on Friday nights and played matches on Sundays, meaning he still had five other days free where he was not doing much after school. He recommended that I do the same and simply get a ball, my boots, and begin practicing my ability to dribble, juggle the ball, and use the ball as I would during a match. I did just that. I began training in my back garden on nights I had free to improve my own skills and ability in the same way I had witnessed Warren improve his. I used objects such as punctured or old balls I had in my garden and used them to train my dribbling. I also tried juggling the ball a lot more, as that was something which I needed to improve. Soon, I began to see an improvement in my game.

I vividly remember one PE lesson in the summer term of 2016, where we were playing small-sided football matches on our school field. The way I was able to dribble against my classmates that day was slightly above what I had been doing for the past season, and I felt a bit more dominant than them and comfortable when the ball was at my feet. At the time, I was already viewed as someone who could play football well among my peers at school and I was also a member of the football 'A-team' which represented BGN for my year group. Two classmates of mine, who were also two of the best footballers in our year group, said to me during the match that I was playing well and that I had 'come on' which, in football terms, means I had improved. After receiving this positive reinforcement, all I wanted to do was continue to 'come on' and get better as a footballer. This simply meant doing more and keep practising in my garden. That same summer is when I decided to attend trials for an u15s squad at a semi-professional club called Brackley Town. A few of the local boys who also played football for Brackley but who went to Banbury school, which was next door to BGN at the time, suggested that Warren go and try out at their club. Warren decided to do this and asked me whether I also wanted to attend. At the time, I was aspiring to be a professional footballer, but the thought of trying to attempt, for the first time, to make this dream a reality was slightly daunting. Having had some time to consider this before the trials began, I decided I would go ahead and see whether I had what it takes.

As the trial period progressed, I thought I was definitely going to make the Brackley U15s squad, due to the way I was performing and my ability compared to other trialists. I also thought that Warren was going to make it for the same reasons. I even thought that, if only one of us were going to make it out of Warren and I, it would have been me. Warren later revealed to me, after the trials were complete, that he also thought I was going to make the team if only one of us were going to do so. However, as you may have already read before, I did not make the trial whereas Warren did. This left me devastated and in tears, but it did not prevent me from trying to pursue professional football. Later that summer, it was to my fortune that a player who had been picked to play for Brackley had gone to another team, and there was now a space available. I was at the top of the shortlist and received a call from Warren during the summer of 2016, stating that the Brackley U15s manager wanted to speak to me. I soon received a phone call from the manager and was truly happy to hear what had happened and that they wanted me to sign for the U15s. I ended up playing an entire season for Brackley Town, starting 16 games out of 20 and scoring a total of two goals as a defender and, occasionally, as a midfielder. Unfortunately, that was my first and last season at Brackley Town, as I was released during the preseason of the upcoming season. Again, I was truly devastated and found myself crying in Warren's mother's arms as I got dropped off at home on the night I was released.

However, I soon found another team that played in the same league as Brackley and continued playing football there. Over time, I managed to keep my football ability and level I was playing to a high standard. I maintained this all the way up until I started my first year of A-levels, when I even managed to play a year up against Brackley Town U18s for local club Banbury United U18s. In this same season, I also had the privilege of featuring for 30 minutes in an U18s FA Cup match against Kidlington U18s. It was during this period that I was still playing high-level football, and with the age group above, for the first time, that I reflected on my life and my future and asked myself a life-changing question: "Given the option to either play for a professional academy after A-levels are complete, or go to university, which would you prefer?". It was a question I did not want to answer, as I knew that one option would result in my dream of making it as a professional footballer reach its end. It was something I gave a good set of hours and days reflecting upon and my answer was: "I want to experience life at university." After this, I knew that professional football was not what God intended me to pursue and I managed to put that dream and chapter to rest.

Now that football did not take up so much of my time as it had done since I started playing for Brackley, I was now able to give a lot more attention to my studies and where I could see myself after I had completed my A-levels. By then, realising how difficult it would be to study at Yale in America, I also managed to lay that dream to rest.

After receiving average scores in my GCSEs, I still managed to study Biology, Psychology and Physical Education and complete an extended project during my A-levels at BGN. I think the reason I received average scores in most of my GCSEs was due to my revision technique, stubbornness and naivety. I would read the content of my subjects, twice, but that was all I would do. I disliked writing things down, making notes, using flash cards, or doing anything that involved writing and real effort. I also did not like change and still do not like change when it comes to studying. While I was scoring the highest in my science class for the end of unit tests, all I would do was read my notes from class and the revision guide and I managed to do extremely well in a test. However, I guess what I did not realise is that the content during those small end of unit tests was a lot more limited than the entire content of two years' worth of GCSE material, which required a much more active revision technique. I did not even do as many practice questions as I potentially could have done during the GCSE revision period. Mostly, all I did was read what I had learned and use the revision materials available. I was passively revising.

Despite how much I read around my subjects, the fact that I did not actively do anything with this knowledge is the reason I only manged to score mostly grade 5s and a few grade 6s, with the aim of scoring grade 7s and above. A grade 5 is equivalent to a C grade and grade 6 is equivalent to a B grade. Take it from my experience, passively revising or trying to get around productively revising, which is much harder work, may potentially not get you the grades you hope to achieve. Despite this, my teachers at BGN saw my potential and efforts throughout my GCSEs and were more than happy to allow me to take my A-levels at the BGN sixth form.

From the start of my A-levels, I always hoped to attend Loughborough University due to its sporting background, with the hope of still pursing professional football. Even after I gave up the idea of professional football, I still desired to attend Loughborough University due to its attractiveness on the open day that I attended in year 12 and the fact that I would at least be around professional athletes who truly have good mindsets when it comes to both sport and life. Throughout my A-levels, however, I was not performing as well as I would have wished, scoring mostly D grades, occasionally C grades and rarely B grades. Initially, I thought it was just due to the increase in the amount of content I was now being taught, but there were also technical problems in my ability to answer questions. I continued receiving similar grades across all three subjects, with Biology being the worst graded subject and PE being my strongest subject. By the end of year 12 I managed to average a D in Biology and Psychology, and a C in Physical Education, which truly were not great grades, but I aimed to work hard over the summer, get myself together and be ready for my last year of A-levels; I knew I simply had to pick it up and mean business this time. It was not a case of not trying during my A-levels, or passively revising most of the time, I was receiving low grades due to the fact that my ability to answer questions directly was poor and the fact that I, as well as many others of my classmates, found A-levels darn hard!

Over the summer holidays in 2018, I mostly focused on completing my 5,000-word extended project, which I truly took by a storm and managed to gain some good ground on. This allowed for a lot more timetable time to be available for me, which could be used to dedicate time to improve my grades in my A-levels. It was probably the wisest investment I made during my A-levels. By the early days of year 13, teachers were asking us students which universities we were planning on heading to, when we were planning to apply, and whether we knew what we would like to study. It was all becoming real now, my time at BGN was slowly coming to an end. I had thought about taking either a Sports degree or a Psychology degree throughout year 12 and got to learn more about both subjects. By year 13, I had decided that Psychology was the correct path for me. This may have slightly been influenced by my experience of mentoring younger students in the lower school while I was in year 12. So, I had my mind set on studying Psychology at Loughborough University, my plans were in place, and now all I had to do was work for the grades to get there.

However, I soon realised that due to Loughborough's status in the university rankings, I may have not been eligible to even be considered there because of my average performance throughout year 12. My predicted grades from my GCSEs, averaged at CCC and that was nowhere near what

Loughborough University was interested in. So, I was stuck at a standpoint between whether it was even worth applying to Loughborough, which required me to achieve a minimum of ABB in my A-levels, with a high grade in my extended project and high-graded GCSEs, which I did not have, or whether it would simply be a waste of an application out of the five I had available. In the end, I let the situation get the better of me and decided that I would not apply to Loughborough University. I allowed the thoughts of my teachers, as well as myself, to prevent me from applying to my new, dream university. This was a mistake that I wish I had not allowed myself to commit. In the end, I only applied to one Russell Group university, which was the University of Liverpool. Unfortunately, Liverpool also turned me down because they wanted higher maths and English GCSE grades, and the only other places that I applied to and had a chance of attending were Leicester, Huddersfield, Bath of Spa and Essex universities. I attended the applicant days of both Essex and Leicester universities and was more impressed with Leicester, due to its modern style in comparison to Essex. My mother preferred Essex as she felt the course was a lot better than Leicester's, but this was not one of my worries as courses across all universities do not vary too drastically. After the open day at Leicester University, I had made a decision that, if given a place, I was going to attend there. The University of Essex had even given me a lower offer of CCC after an interview at the university; all I had to do was register the university as my first choice among the rest of my offers.

It was when travelling back from Leicester in February 2020 with my parents, that my father asked me a question which made me reconsider my university choices. After a few discussions about Leicester, as well as Essex, my father boldly asked me the question: "If you could attend any university, which would it be?" I plainly answered, saying "Loughborough." Nothing was said after I gave my answer and there was a moment of silence among the three of us in the car. During this moment's silence, I asked myself the question: "If you wanted to go to Loughborough University so badly, why on earth did you not apply there?" Despite the reasons I gave earlier for not applying to Loughborough, at that moment, I refused to allow these to be reasons and excuses as for not even sending through my application to the university. It was in that moment that I realised the reason that I did not apply to Loughborough was because of self-doubt. It wasn't the doubt from my teachers who helped us with our university applications, nor was it the doubt from the entry grades that were staring at me from the Loughborough University website, but it was my own self-doubt that allowed to me to believe that Loughborough would not take me anyway, after they saw my GCSEs and predicted A-level grades. I also had self-doubt in my capability of achieving the grades they required from me. I do not know whether it was my father's intention to cause this reflection and rewiring in my thinking, but this surely did happen. I flipped the way that I was approaching going to study at university and decided, there and then, during that car journey, that I was going to work like I have never worked in my life before, and sacrifice and slave to achieve the highest grades I possibly could in my A-levels.

After receiving my, hopefully, new and improved grades on results day, I intended to call Loughborough University on the day, inform them of my good grades, and hope to be granted a place through clearing. The idea of limiting myself to the grades I could achieve and the university I could attend was scrapped. I had mentally transformed into an animal and was hungrier than ever to prove myself wrong about my self-doubt through my own ability and capacity. I was even hungrier to prove my teachers, who had already began lowering their expectations of my capacity after year 12, wrong too. By the remaining three months of 2019, my parents and I had agreed that I should have tutors for Biology and Psychology to deal with my problem in answering exam questions. I informed my tutors about my newly organised plan and goals and they were more than on board to help in making the dream come true for me.

From the end of 2019 all the way through to March 2020, I was revising and doing all I could to make my dreams a reality.

The extended project was complete by February 2020, and I was seeing both my tutors twice a week. In March, I had mock exams coming up that I only managed to achieve grades BDD. I had made improvements in PE, yet Psychology and Biology still needed a lot of work. My parents had contemplated on whether it would have been best for me to have had tutors throughout my time in year 12, as it would have given me more time to improve on my question-answering skills and the tutors would have been able pick up on any other skills I was struggling with. I also reflected and thought that this probably would have been the best decision, as I would potentially have been improving a lot quicker and much earlier on with the help of my tutors. The reason I initially denied the help of tutors, early on, was my own pride, and not wanting to accept that I could not complete my A-levels by myself and required external assistance, as well as the internal help of extra revision sessions from my teachers. This was another mistake that I had made during my A-levels. Never allow your pride or personal ego to refuse help when help is truly what you need to take you to the next level. There was no time to worry about this, however, I had scored badly in two of my A-levels once again and needed to continue to tap into another gear to achieve the goal I had set for myself.

During this intense period of my life came COVID-19, towards the end of March 2020 to completely disrupt all that I had planned and prepared to work for. I say disrupt, but when I heard from my Psychology tutor during an online session that Boris Johnson had cancelled the 2020 exam period for A-level and GCSE students, it was like being told that I had just won the lottery. I was truly happy to hear that I would no longer be sitting A-level exams and that my time at BGN had abruptly come to a much earlier end. As much as it may seem that I wanted to do well in my A-levels and attend Loughborough University, I knew myself that the type of hours I was going to have to devote to studying and working hard was going to be the most difficult thing I had ever attempted in my life. So, once I heard this was no longer necessary, or even an option at all, it felt as if I was a freed prisoner. I am not a scholar who genuinely enjoys the process of having to revise hard to prepare for and sit an exam, but I am one who enjoys receiving good grades. Therefore, in February, I ultimately knew what was required of me in the months leading up to my A-levels, but I was not over the moon and full of joy about it.

The coronavirus pandemic resulted in all secondary educational students taking public exams in 2020 receiving centre-assessed grades from their schools. It was the first time that such an event had ever happened in UK educational history since the two forms of educational assessments were introduced in 1988 and 1951. Some people did not know what to do or how to react. I, on the other hand, danced myself away on the last day of school on 20th March 2020, two days prior to when the lockdown began in the UK, and told all my Snapchat contacts that I was not sure about the rest of them, but I saw cancellation of the exams as a three-month extension to our two-month summer holiday, while the government provided grades for us to attend universities. In my eyes, as a student, you couldn't have really asked for much more than that. The pandemic did have its pros and cons in terms of exam grades, however. Many students received the grades they achieved in their most recent examinations. If they were high, those students would be in a good position for university places; if they were slightly low, as mine were, those students were at a disadvantage when it came to university places. I was not too worried about the grades I received and was sure that universities were going to be lenient that year in giving out places to applicants. Throughout the UK lockdown, I reconsidered my plans and decided to put the University of Leicester as my first choice, despite the lower offer from Essex. I felt that Leicester represented me much better than Essex did, mostly in a modern sense. I still desired to attend Loughborough University, however, and decided to email the university to explain my plans and goals which had been disrupted by COVID-19. They responded and requested to view my GCSE results and predicted grades and, after they saw these, they stated that I did not meet the entry requirements and practically said that my application would be discredited. From then, I knew that Loughborough was out of the picture for university choices, as well as the fact that I knew I was not going to receive a grade A in any of my A-level subjects. So, Leicester was now the new prospect!

It came to results day and I was awarded my March mock grades, BDD, in my A-level subjects. I was fortunate enough to not have been graded even lower by my teachers, especially in Biology and Psychology. I technically did manage to receive one of the As I intended to achieve in my A-levels, through my extended project which answered the question: "What does it really take to make it as a professional footballer?". On results day, my results did not meet the entry requirements that Leicester required of me either, which was BBC, as long as I achieved a B in my extended project. I was so worried on results day, after not receiving an offer from Leicester, thinking that I might have also been rejected from there too. I began to get a bit agitated and informed my mother of the situation. I contemplated on whether university was the route I am supposed to take at all, as I was running out of choices to attend a university I was interested in. My mother called BGN, informed them of the situation and explained the plans I had made for myself in February, that would have all led to that exact day where I was in need of a university to accept me. As I thought, my school stated there was nothing they could do, as the results were based solely on how I was performing at the time. There was still plenty of time for me to improve my grades and I am sure I could, but assumptions and predictions such as that were serving no purpose while a mass of students received grades B and above. After calling Leicester University and explaining the situation, they did not have any desire to offer me a place and this is when I really started rethinking whether I was meant for university.

My mother then called Leicester University herself and managed to speak to one of the first year Psychology tutors. She explained the situation once again and, this time around, there was some hope. The tutor looked at my grades and was very convinced by my extended project, but was also doubtful of my D in Psychology. My mother stood there, in her prayers, as the tutor thought about this decision and whether the university was going to give me a place or not. I sat their thinking: God this is in your hands now, I have no control over this decision and I just hope that it is the best one for my future. Moments passed and the tutor said these exact words, "I think we'll give you a shot." I was immediately so grateful and praised him as if he had just rescued me from poverty. I was extremely happy and felt comfortable to be heading to Leicester University and, overall, making my way to university! It was the next chapter of my life that I was about to write. I wasn't the happiest about the process of having to go through a system and plead to get where I wanted to be. However, this time it was not entirely my own fault.

In hindsight, some of these things could have easily been avoided, all the way from starting with my GCSEs. If I had been less stubborn about changing my revision technique and trying out other ones, this could have resulted in better grades, which universities do actually take into consideration, for anyone who believes GCSEs do not matter in the 'real world'. Likewise, if I had decided to not allow my pride to get in the way of seeking help early on in my A-level courses, potentially, my grades might have improved a lot earlier too, which would have positively affected my mock grades. Despite this, these are not mistakes, or things that I regret and look back on with sadness, but simple learning curves in life that I need to take with me during my next lessons and experiences. I hope that that they can be learning curves for you too.

Quote from Warren Byfield:

> During my football days, Neo and I attended the Brackley Town U15s trials. We wanted to get in so bad after coming from a lower standard of football to a higher standard at Brackley Town Football Club. At the time, we were both pursuing a career in

football. We attended every trial session from the first to the last and, to be truthful, we smashed the trials from what I witnessed. I think Neo and I played so well because the pressure was on like never before. Everything we had ever trained for was coming into place on the pitch, everything the coaches wanted us to do it would be done with quality and consistency. Every time we left the pitch I would pray and thank God for the opportunity we had been given and I would pray for both of us to get in; we truly wanted it so bad.

The final day of the trials arrived, and it was the final session. I could feel the tension more than ever, as I believe Neo also did. So, we were on the main pitch, St James Park, giving it our all one last time. We smashed it once again and it soon came to the end of the session. Neo and I were both looking at each other knowing we did well and were proud of each other, ready to go home and wait for the results, which were going to be sent to us by email. Suddenly, the coach that was taking the trial called out for every one of the players to go and sit in the stands of the stadium. Neo and I slowly walked up to the stands and took a seat, fearing what they were about to say. First of all, they said thank you to everyone who came to the trials and mentioned that whoever did not get picked did not mean that they weren't good enough, they were just not what they were looking for at the club. Soon they started to read out random names and asked the people that got called out to stand over the other side of the stadium. Now, after the first few names I heard I was thinking, 'What is actually going on right now?', as I believe everyone else did. By the tenth name I think everyone knew what was going on, because they called out all the old players that had been at the club before and some new players that were very outstanding in the trials. Now I was panicking, sitting there thinking I haven't got picked and, in that very moment, my name was called. I had never felt so humble but yet so excited in my life. As I was walking over to the stands I didn't look back because in my head I was thinking that if I got in my brother had got in too, because I felt like we matched the same energy and style of play in the trials. As I got over to the stands and took a seat, I looked up and there was no one else walking towards our direction, all the others who got picked were talking amongst themselves, saying how all the people sat on the other side of the stadium didn't get in. Suddenly I didn't feel that joy anymore, I was upset. Through that whole time of thinking Neo didn't get in with me and at grief knowing that we wouldn't be able to make it together, Neo remained strong and positive. Also, not only did he maintain his consistent training, he also trained a lot more harder and effectively than he was doing before. Seeing that after I saw how badly he got treated at the trials inspired me; it taught me that no matter how bad the situation is, you always have to get up and still fight for what you desire. Soon after the trials, a player chosen during the trials decided not to take up their place in the team and this left a big hole in the squad. The coaches decided that they wanted Neo to come in and Neo was soon a member of the team.

Time passed by and we had a few training sessions together. One session, our coaches came up to me and said, 'We had made a big mistake with your friend Neo' and they then went on to say that to him directly too. That story played through my head the whole season and we went out to smash teams in different matches. Winning various man of the matches, Neo, for me, was a warrior in football as well as a big inspiration.

Reader Exercises:

- Do you find yourself refusing help from time to time when that same help is something you could really benefit from and, if so, why?
- Do you allow the doubts and thoughts of others to affect the way that you see yourself and your capabilities?
- When you truly want to achieve something, to what lengths are you prepared to stretch to reach that goal?

End of Section Reader Exercises:

- Do you take the time to reflect upon moments where you have been your own source of inspiration?
- What are some of the things that you have managed to accomplish in your life that inspire you about yourself?
- What qualities do you possess that inspires you about yourself?

SECTION THREE

PLACES WHICH HAVE INSPIRED ME

27. Africa

In the summer of 2017, I was blessed to have the opportunity to go travelling with my mother across Africa, visiting five different countries. In the beginning I was quite reluctant to the idea of going on holiday and being away from home for the entire six weeks of my summer holidays. Soon it came to the last day of school, 21st July. The bags had already been packed, and we were ready to go as soon as I got home from my last day as a year 10 student. By then I was thrilled with excitement at the thought of travelling the two-hour car journey from home to the airport and that I would be mid-flight later that same evening. Once we were on the plane, we were surrounded by many people of a similar ethnic background to us and this already felt like home. I was around similar people to myself and we were all heading to a common home, Africa.

Our first country that we were visiting was Tanzania and we had to make a connection through Kigali in Rwanda. My mother was astonished to see the modernness, cleanliness and simple beauty of Rwanda's newly built airport. Meanwhile, we soon landed in Dar es Salaam and were welcomed by family friends, the Christians. Each time I returned to Africa and saw people each time I returned and saw people selling things on the road where cars were moving and stuck in traffic, it always made me feel that I was truly home. For me, being home is not being in my home country, but being around a common culture and a way of living – and that is simply what I felt while visiting Tanzania for the first time. We stayed in a range of homes while visiting Dar es Salaam. For the first couple of days we stayed in a hotel, and for the last few we stayed with the Christians.

At the time, I was aspiring to be a professional footballer so, wherever I was, I tried to ensure that I could either go running or play football. At the hotel we were staying in, we were fortunate enough to find that it had a beach. Seeing as I rarely had the opportunity and access to surfaces such as sand in England, I saw the opportunity and was inspired to train on the sand. I had seen many athletes undergo beach training sessions and I wanted to try it out for the first time. I requested a ball from the office at the hotel and spaced out the seating chairs that were by the pool to set up a drill. I then experienced my first exercise of the holiday. We spent a total of nine days in Tanzania and, on one of the remaining days, we travelled across water on a boat to Zanzibar to spend one night. By then my father had joined us on our travels.

In Zanzibar, we first went to see a spice museum where there were all types of foods, spices, and vegetables. I was shocked to discover that the earth has so many natural and organic substances that can help with all sorts of problems, illnesses and bugs. Who would have thought one could use turmeric alone to help with several body ailments. Throughout our day in Zanzibar, we visited various tourist sites such as Zanzibar's Salve Market Memorial. We were driven around by an extremely kind driver, Mwaba. One of the things I found truly inspiring about our time with Mwaba was his infinite kindness and genuineness to us visitors. His helpfulness and simple willingness to serve us and give us the best experience of our time in Zanzibar was truly admirable. We even ended up sharing a meal with Mwaba in a local restaurant, as opposed to him just waiting in the car for us to finish. This is something of which I took great notice, both from my parents and Mwaba. This act and nature of valuing individuals and seeing them as not less or more to oneself, but equal, was heart-warming. It was not the type of experience and environment I was used to in the UK. By the end of the day, Mwaba felt as good as a brother to me, not just a friend. Soon, the next day arrived and it was time for us to head back to Dar es Salaam. It wasn't too long after returning from Zanzibar that we were waving Tanzania goodbye. Our next stop was Kenya!

Just before we headed to Kenya, we spent one night and an entire day in Kigali. Even though we were only in the city for hours, my mother and I had lunch together at the Rooftop Rendezvous restaurant and went to visit the Kigali Genocide Memorial for some hours. At the time, the experience was more of an informative moment for me, that involved a lot of reading of the displays of information that encapsulated so much pain and horror the country experienced. It was also a shock to me that this was really something that had happened before I arrived on earth. Later in the day, we met with my mum's friend, Liberal, who lives in Kigali. Liberal is not a blood relative but in Africa it is common to call anyone who is significantly older than you aunty or uncle, followed by their first name, to show respect. It also builds a sense of unity and community on the continent. Uncle Liberal took us to a few sites and showed us around his home city. As Rwanda had undergone so much progression, from building a new airport to new roads, it looked like a country on its own, away from the continent, due to its lead in beauty and overall development. We spent the evening having dinner on the roof of another restaurant with Uncle Liberal. The late-night view was exceptional. That night my mother and I stayed in a hotel for the evening.

The following day we were heading back to the airport for our connecting flight to Nairobi. After arriving in Kenya, we were picked up from the airport by a great friend to my mother, Aunty Lillian. It was only my mum and me who travelled to Kenya as my dad had to travel elsewhere for work. Aunty Lillian had been kind enough to accommodate us during our four nights in Nairobi. As we travelled from the airport to home, my mind and eyes were solely focused on seeing the city and country for the first time ever. The woodlands, forests and overall landscape was simply eye-catching. On the day we arrived, I asked my aunty whether there was anywhere that I was able to either run or play football and, to my fortune, she told me that there was a local playing field nearby where many people went to play football.

On day two we spent the day at home and, in the evening, both Aunty Lillian and my mother escorted me to the playing field. When we arrived, we found one gentleman sitting in an area just outside the playing area. We asked him whereabouts we could find a place I could play football and whether there was going to be any football where we were anytime soon. Luckily, he told us his football team were coming to train there that very night. My mother and aunt, knowing I was going to be occupied for the evening, went on a walk, so it was just the gentleman and me. We began to get to know each other and I explained how I was visiting during my summer holiday. Soon, other members of the team arrived and we got into practice. Just before we started training, we formed a circle as a group and said a prayer and blessing, then commenced training. There were no goal posts present in the field and I am not sure whether the club could not afford small goals at all, but instead, the men improvised and put large stones there instead and used those as mini goals. After training, once again, we said a final prayer of thanks for the session.

From this one crazy experience that I have never had before, of training in a different country with players from another part of the world, I experienced a few moments of inspiration. Firstly, being a man of faith, I found it truly warming when we prayed before training. This was something I had never been able to experience in England; I only used to say my prayers by myself at home before training sessions. For me, this act was a moment that the team spent together and was a time to simply be as one and bond for the few seconds we had our arms across each other's backs. Secondly, I was inspired by the encouragement that each player had for another. While doing some conditioning throughout the training session, it was my turn to undergo a very tough abdominal exercise that I did not do regularly. One of the gentlemen helping me carry out the exercise couldn't have been more encouraging. Again, this is something that I had never experienced back in Britain while training and playing at both high and regular levels of football. Everyone was either too shy, or too focused on themselves to really give somebody else true and compassionate encouragement during training. Overall, that one experience I got from that evening of playing in the field near to my Aunt Lillian's home in Kenya will remain in my memory for a long time. It was truly a great experience that I hope to keep forever.

On day three, my mum, aunt and I all went to The Sheldrick Wildlife Trust (SWT) elephant orphanage in Nairobi. This trust in Kenya was founded in 1977 by Daphne Sheldrick and the organisation was created to rescue and hand rear elephant and rhino orphans, along with other species. The animals that I recall us seeing were both adult and baby elephants and giraffes. My mum and I even had the opportunity to feed a giraffe. These experiences, from this day, left me feeling content and happy with what I had seen and been exposed to. By the end of day three our Kenya detour had come to an end. On the last day, we were preparing for our travels to our next destination. However, in the short time that I spent in Kenya, it was truly an amazing experience and one I will not forget. I was very grateful and blessed to have received such an experience.

Our next stop was my birth country, South Africa! Although I was born in South Africa, my family and I left there while I was just one years old, which resulted in me never having the opportunity to develop a connection with the country. We were spending three nights in Johannesburg as my dad was doing some work there. Due to our extremely short period in South Africa, we did not go sightseeing or visit anywhere during our time in Jo'burg. Therefore, my experiences of being in South Africa for the second time since my birth mostly comprised enjoying the luxuries of a nice hotel room, the gym, and the swimming pool. By the end of the three nights, we had four weeks remaining of our travels and had one last destination to visit. Our home country, Zambia.

I always experience a bubbly feeling while travelling to Zambia. It begins on the plane journey from England, all the way up until I exit the plane and see the advertisement on the walls of the Zambia airport. I think this feeling comes from the fact that, here in England, I do not have many extended family members. Most of my family members live in Zambia. Each time any of our family from England arrives in Zambia, we are always received by at least four to eight different family members – whoever was simply available to go and receive the incoming visitors at the time. It is a cultural thing that has occurred in my family for decades now. After being received from the airport by my mum's immediate young sister, Aunty Cecilia, and her husband and daughter, we travelled back to their home. The good thing about truly being home is that, due to the amount of family around from both my parents' sides, there are several different homes that we can stay at during our time in Zambia. We spent the first couple of nights at Aunty Cecilia's and, throughout this time, I was constantly pestering my parents to find me a playing field where I could play football, due to my previous experiences in Nairobi.

Later, we went to visit and stay at the home of my dad's younger brother, Uncle Joe, which wasn't too far from Aunty Cecilia's home. One evening, my father told me that he had managed to get hold of coach Willie, one of the head coaches of a professional football club in Zambia called Zanaco FC. He told me that I was going to be able to train with them the following week. I was full of complete excitement at the opportunity and experience I was going to have, and the idea of training with professional Zambian footballers truly fulfilled my aspirations of wanting to become a professional footballer to some degree. Meanwhile, it came to our second week in Zambia and training with Zanaco was going to commence on the Monday morning at 7:30am. We had to train extremely early due to the hot climate in Zambia. Once I arrived at the stadium, I found many players there and it was during a time just before the season was beginning that players were able to come and trial for one of the teams that were going to be playing in the different divisions in the upcoming season. As in Kenya, we began our session with a prayer and started training. It isn't something I find difficult, but I formed friendships and bonds immediately after the session while I had the opportunity to talk to some of the boys. Again, the environment there was very different to that of England. Players were introducing themselves to each other and it was a warm and communal environment. A few of the friends I had made were intrigued by my British accent and would continuously emphasise the fact that I had such a great opportunity and chance in Britain to play professional football, as that was where all the big clubs were. I continued attending training with Zanaco during our stay, and we would train three times a week, on Monday, Tuesday and Wednesday mornings.

As our time spent visiting various family members and places, and just being home, slowly ran out as the weeks passed us by, I managed to get a lot of exposure and learn multiple things. On the football field, I had learned new methods of training and how to interact with my teammates. Also, in Zambia and in many countries in Africa, a household usually has a maid who helps around the house; usually it is a female who takes up this role, whereas men usually do outside and field work. I discovered that, despite the position that the maid may have in society, in Zambia it is your duty, especially as a person who is younger than they are, to treat them with the utmost respect and as a family member as opposed to an employee. In Zambia, you even refer to the maid using the 'aunty' prefix followed by their forename, as a sign of respect. Also, respect doesn't end there in Zambia; I learnt that whenever a child or someone of youthful age greets a person or a group of people older than them, they either squat completely to the ground as a sign of respect, or bend their knees and put their hands together in front of the person or people they are greeting', you also do this while shaking hands with someone you meet. All of these things were completely new to me. I witnessed these acts carried out by friends, cousins and other family members. As I was experiencing all of these different behaviours, which you don't find in the UK, my brain was slowly transitioning and learning to carry out the same behaviours I was seeing and attracted to.

In my last week of being in Zambia, through my father's connections, which he had once again pulled through for me, he managed to get me the opportunity to meet football legend Kalusha Bwalya, also known as the 'Great Kalu'. Mr Bwalya was a born and bred Zambian footballer, who had made it to play professional football and also had the opportunity of playing alongside Brazilian dynasty Romário and against Cameroon star, Roger Miller. Kalusha was also the first player to be nominated for FIFA World Player of the Year in 1996, where he was voted 12th best player in the world. In 1988, the Great Kalu was said to have made his mark when he participated in the 1988 Olympic Games, scoring a famous hat trick in a 4-0 victory against Italy. In 1998, Great Kalu was also crowned as African Footballer of the Year. In my hour spent with Mr Bwalya, I had a Q&A with him, asking for as many tips as I could have in my attempt to become a professional footballer and, hopefully, represent my home nation. The knowledge this great legend shared with me was something I tried to implement into my game and training as I returned to the field, and I was fortunate enough to receive the Zambian National home jersey as a gift from Mr Bwalya. This had truly been the cherry on the cake of my wonderful adventures.

I had learnt a lot by the end of my holiday and I experienced several inspiring moments throughout the journey. My parents and aunt vividly remember me telling them that I was going to always greet my teachers and ask them how they are, and that I finally saw them as people as opposed to 'just teachers' for the first time, and it was completely true. My time spent in Africa, Zambia especially, taught me that you have to be respectful to each person you meet along the way and especially people you have relationships with, such as coaches and teachers. As a whole, one thing which truly inspired me was the welcoming and warm nature of the people of Africa, and I was determined to introduce this into my own behaviour and life. Over there, there's no such thing as 'second cousin', 'step-brother, dad, mum or sister' or anything like that. There is only brotherhood, sisterhood and family. No matter whether you share the same blood as the person next to you, or the player in front of you, in Africa you are one.

With the elephants at the Sheldrick Wildlife Trust in August 2017

At the Sheldrick Wildlife Trust

With the tour guide on a spice farm in Zanzibar in July 2017

With my sisters Katepe and Bobo

Kalusha Bwalya kindly gifting me with a Zambian National football jersey in September 2017

With my friends Derrick and Limpo, after training, at Zanaco Football Club's Sunset Stadium in Zambia, August 2017

28. The Pitch

The football pitch has been a place where I have experienced multiple events. This goes from certain tackles I have won while helping my team to defend, to the advice and encouragement from my coaches and teammates, all the way through to watching a star on the opposing team cause trouble against my own. Initially, however, the beginning of my football journey was not the most pleasant, nor was it the most inspiring. I mentioned earlier how I started to kick a ball at age three and that I had a kick so strong that it convinced my father I could be a professional football player for England. However, after attending a few practices from the age of three, I decided to put my football career on hold. My parents told me that, one day, all of a sudden, I just decided to stop playing and kicking a ball. From then, my father thought that was it for me. He still believes that, if I had carried on playing, kicking and practising from that young age, I would have been exceptionally good once I grew older but, because I decided to take such a long break, all of the motor neurones and memory cells I used for football had reduced significantly and making any return after the time I had spent away would be like trying to learn a new language.

When I did return, that was exactly what it was like. After playing during lunchtimes throughout my primary school days, I really developed a love for it when I moved primary schools at the beginning of year 4, from a school in Danbury called St Joseph's, to another primary school called St John's. My good friend at the time, Sonny, invited me to train with his team of which his dad was the manager, namely, a local football club called Azad Hill. Azad Hill was a club that was founded by Nic Weir in 2002 and had been running for ten years prior to when I joined the club. The club aimed to bring together ethnic communities, predominantly from two council estates where there had been racial tensions over the years. The name Azad, being an area in Pakistan, represented the Asian community, and the name Hill represented the community of people who lived in an estate in Banbury called Bretch Hill. The only strength I brought to the pitch at that time was how fast I could run. Other than that, my technical skills, how I hit the ball, how far I could hit the ball and how well I could move with the ball, were poor compared to the other kids who were the same age as me.

As soon as I was signed up for Azad Hill, I began to play my first football matches ever, at the age of eight. My manager at the time, Nic, remembered my first game for Azad Hill extremely well and still remembered it ten years after it had passed. Nic also told me later that, having run Azad Hill for ten years prior to when I joined the club, and before I was born, he had worked with thousands of young people through football and found it difficult to remember each one. However, the first match I ever played was one that he remembered quite vividly. I don't have any recollection of my first football match ever and my first match for Azad Hill, but Nic stated that it occurred on the field next to my home, NOA playing fields, and it was a sunny day. The match was being played against the top team in the town, Banbury United. Those days, in our town, two league matches were usually played. The first match involved the best players from each team, while the second match involved the newcomers to football and was more of a development match for young players who still hadn't advanced completely as footballers and didn't feature that much during matches. Nic stated that I was playing in defence. He also stated that he clearly remembers me looking like a rabbit caught in headlights, meaning that while I was playing, I simply froze. He also went on to add that I had no spatial awareness or game awareness and, when he saw my facial expression, he read, "What the hell was going on around me?" Nic also stated that both my parents attended the match and were on the side line encouraging their son. My dad was said to be very proud, even though he could see that I was completely lost on the pitch. Nic added that my father's humour and energy was a great example of how you would want your parents to be, whether the child is succeeding or failing miserably.

Throughout that season, Nic decided to hand over the role of manager to another helping hand at the club with football knowledge, Mr Sanders, as he was overseeing all of the other teams in the club at the time. Whenever it came to match days on Saturday mornings, I would always be the last one to be introduced to the pitch and the player who played the least minutes among everyone. Week in, week out. This was purely due to my ability and what I was able to bring and do for the team which wasn't, at the time, all that much. Now, usually while kids are at such a young age, it is crucial to give them a fair amount of time and opportunity to play, grow and develop in any sport or activity that they take part in, especially team games. However, this was not the case for me. The two coaches who were in charge of running the team, Mr Sanders and Mr Frenchie, but predominantly Mr Sanders, were not interested in my personal development – only in winning. Therefore, I would consistently be the player who played the least, every week. My parents had monitored this behaviour by the coaches, but did not give it too much attention or feel the need to speak to either of them. Instead, they wanted to wait and see how things went and whether I would be given more playing time.

Meanwhile, two seasons had passed and we had transitioned into year 6. After my first season at Azad Hill, the club changed its name to Hanwell United. Usually, at the end of a football season, there are tournaments you can enter. One day, we had a tournament in Oxford. My mother and I travelled together, just the two of us. After arriving and registering, the tournament soon began. The first two games were played and

I did not get a single minute out of the two of them. After this, my mother mentioned to one of the coaches that I should be getting at least some minutes on the pitch. However, the two coaches who were there on the day, Mr Sanders and Mr Frenchie, still denied me any minutes. Our previous manager, Nic Weir, was not present that day. Frenchie said that I should have been put on for at least a bit of time in one of the two opening games, but Mr Sanders was still dismissive of this. After the third game I still hadn't featured in a match, or any of the games after that. My mother and another mum of a good friend of mine at the time, Sid, were discussing this and saying that I needed to receive equal or at least similar time on the pitch to everyone else. Then it came to our last game, where I was expected to finally receive some of my first minutes of the tournament. Mr Sanders and Frenchie did decide to start me at the beginning of the match, but it wasn't too long until I was taken out once again and played just about the same number of minutes as another teammate of mine who had featured in previous matches. So, overall, I once again played minimal minutes compared to my teammates and this time my mother and I travelled all the way to Oxford for me to play a total of seven to ten minutes out of an available 90 minutes.

My mother was completely furious and told me that I was not going to play for Hanwell any longer. She was livid about the fact that we had travelled one hour to Oxford, starting off around 7am, for me to receive an unfair amount of time on the pitch compared to my teammates. I, on the other hand, just felt a certain numbness about the situation and about my treatment during my time at the club. I had almost become used to being the player who played the least and who was viewed as the weakest link. She said to me, that day in the car ride, that I would never be returning to Hanwell United and that she would find me another club where the playing time is fairly shared among the players. Soon after we arrived home, my mum sent a text to our manager, Mr Weir, that we had not been happy with our treatment at the club, especially on the day of the tournament, and that I should have received a lot more time on the pitch over the entire two years, let alone the day of the tournament. Mr Weir sincerely apologised for this. My mother told him that, after this, I was not going to return to play in Hanwell again. During Nic Weir's discussion with my mother after this tournament, he actually tried convincing my mother to allow me to remain at the club, as he believed that I could develop under the team and saw potential in me. Despite this, he couldn't change my mother's mind in that she was determined I was not going to return to the club due to the potential risk of continuing to receive the unfair treatment I had experienced already. Nic felt upset about the fact that a child had experienced such a negative day of football and felt even worse due to the fact that his son, Sonny, and I were extremely close friends, as well as the fact that he had a lot of respect for my parents. Nic felt obliged to at least recommend a new football club to us, as a result of the events that had occurred over the two seasons, and especially on the day of the tournament. The club Mr Weir recommended was called Banbury Irish Football Club and the manager looking after my age group was called Mr Graham McCallum.

My mother soon got in touch with Mr McCallum and explained our past experiences with Hanwell United. Graham told us that, at Banbury Irish, each player plays the same amount of time and is given an equal opportunity on the pitch. It wasn't too long until I was invited for my first training session, which was going to take place on the field of my primary school at the time. As I sat in the car with my kit on, ready to meet my potential new coach, teammates and friends, I simply wanted to perform my best and train my hardest to make the best first impression in my new environment. During the session, my mother had talked to one of the parents of the team and explained, once again, our past experiences at Hanwell. The parent replied, mentioning that at Banbury Irish, every player got an opportunity to play and received similar time on the pitch. My mother also mentioned that she felt the parents at Banbury Irish were a lot more friendly and welcoming than those at Hanwell. My experience of my first session was a good one, the abilities and talent at Hanwell may have just been slightly higher than those at Banbury Irish, but those at Banbury Irish were still to a good level. At the time, for me, it was probably the better environment out the two teams and gave me an opportunity to really get some time to play. I felt welcomed already by my soon-to-be teammates. The atmosphere and energy there was a lot warmer and more easy-going, compared to Hanwell. Soon after, I was positive that I wanted to play for Banbury Irish and was signed up and playing the following weekend.

My first ever match for 'The Greens', as we were called, gave me the chance to start the game and I was playing in the left side of defence as a fullback. I was given the opportunity to play the entire match and managed to play well enough to receive the Man of the Match accolade. I remember, vividly, the words Graham used in saying why I was awarded the Man of the Match and it was simply because I continued battling through the match and through tackles the entire time. That experience and exposure I received, for the first time really, was one I will never forget. I noticed, from that match, that my strength was another of my strong points regarding my abilities, and I intended to use that as fully as I could, going forward. So, during my final year of primary school, I played for Banbury Irish in the 2012/13 season and enjoyed most of the moments I spent there with my team. We were not the greatest of teams and would lose to some of the good local clubs, such as our rivals Banbury United, by 10-11 goals at times but, as a team, we had one of the strongest bonds. We would rarely argue with one another; each player would fight for themselves and win their individual battles which helped in the fight we fought for each other and our overall contributions to the team. We were building and moving truly as a group, and this is something I had not experienced before during my time at Hanwell. The bonds I formed with my teammates at Banbury Irish were a lot stronger. This is something that inspired me deeply about football and the club during my first year there – the ability for 15 to 16 boys to work together, week in and week out, and support one another without making it all about one person or all about winning, but just to be together and work together, for each other and for the collective team, in a healthy manner too.

Seasons and seasons passed by and, year by year, we grew stronger and improved as a team through the recruitment of better players. Throughout this time, some of the original players who I had played with for the first time in 2012 had left and each year, the team would change ever so slightly. I went on my first football tour ever with the team in 2014, to Pontins Pakefield, which is located in the east of the UK. We didn't manage to elongate our stay for too long, due to the ability level of the teams we played against . Nevertheless, all in all, I had one of the most fun and memorable times there with my teammates, who I had come to call friends. It was a bonding experience which only brought us closer together as people, and gelled us more and more as a team.

During my time with Banbury Irish, we won our local league in four different seasons in the third, second and first divisions and were soon seen as one of the dominant teams in our local area during our years of growth. As an individual, I was gradually improving in my footballing ability and overall confidence. After getting the opportunity to play for much longer, I naturally improved due to the fact I was practising and gaining experience. Throughout my time at Banbury Irish, beginning from when I first joined, I was labelled as the kid 'made of steel' because of my natural strength, which the majority of my teammates and opponents could not match. Slowly, I was making a name for myself in the team and was growing as a footballer. Experiencing success, and finally being viewed as one of the best teams in the area and a threat to opponents when we turned up on Sunday afternoons, were all things that made us, as players, happy and motivated to simply continue doing what we were doing. Even as I was growing and improving in my football ability and was gradually moving to higher levels, I had never experienced a more inspiring and dominant season than my 2016/17 season with the Banbury

Irish under 15s squad.

Throughout all of my seasons at Banbury Irish, starting from the 2012/13 season, we had one manager and one coach. Mr Graham McCallum was the manager and Mr Ian Val Poole was the assistant coach. In our pre-season of the 2016/17 season, Mr O'Neil Bell was asked by Graham and Ian whether he could come and help our team to improve on our defending. O'Neil was initially reluctant to get involved with our team, as he had only just given up coaching another team a year younger than us during the previous season. O'Neil's intention was to start coaching a younger set of children between the ages of five and six. Soon after taking a few training sessions with us, O'Neil told me that his passion took over. In addition to this, some of our new players who joined us later in the pre-season were boys who he had been watching play football from age nine onwards and he stated that this made the group very special. The way that we responded to O'Neil as a team was also very positive, in his view, and he was happy to be with us throughout the entire 2016/17 football season. Mr Bell had also coached a couple of other teammates and me in his Sunday football each time we decided to attend. At the time we were receiving him as a coach, those of us who had known him from before were pretty excited and happy to have him on board.

Mr Bell wasn't the only addition we had that season either. As well as the fact that we had recruited some boys who were familiar faces to O'Neil, we also recruited several different players that season and two of them were playing in the MJPL for Brackley Town. In total, there were four players including myself and Warren from our Banbury Irish squad playing for Saturday league side, Brackley Town. Because the team had undergone quite drastic changes, Graham continuously told us that it was now time to gel and form bonds within the team. With the signings we had made and the quality we already had in the team, on paper this looked like one of the strongest teams Graham had managed to pull together in his years of being a football coach. Six of us from that team all went to the same school, BGN, so we were now going to be seeing a lot more of each other, especially the two others who I was playing with at Brackley. During some of our first sessions of the season, Mr Bell, especially, and Mr McCallum would continuously look at us and tell us that we were the best team in the county of Oxfordshire. Most of us and the older players in the team had never heard such bold words from our managers and coaches before and it really took some time for it to sink in. However, with their knowledge of all our individual abilities and what could be achieved if used co-operatively to the best level, they truly believed we were the best U15s team in not just the Witney district, or our local league, but the whole of Oxfordshire.

A few things changed with Mr Bell's addition. One evening at training he asked us all whether we swore and most players put their hands up. He told us that from then on, we were not allowed to swear in his presence, during our training sessions or on match days, because whenever we were training or playing matches, we were not just representing our teammates and coaches, but we were representing our entire club. Additionally, our discipline as players and people also changed throughout that season with him. As time passed and as we won more and more games and progressed throughout the cup competitions, we were gradually becoming more of a disciplined team and coachable group of players. In the beginning there were one or two anomalies who would not take training seriously, not follow training rules and have their own way of doing things, but over time each one of them conformed to the expected standards. We got off to a very successful start, annihilating each team we came across and continued to progress well in our biggest competition of them all, the County Cup. By February 2017, we were first in our local league and were still contenders for the League Cup as well as the County Cup. During this reign, the four of us who were currently playing for two teams, both 'The Greens' and Brackley, were completely consumed by football. We had to train on Mondays and Wednesdays for Brackley and on Fridays for Banbury. We played games on Saturday mornings for

Brackley and on Sunday afternoons for Banbury. Since all of us were aspiring footballers, we enjoyed it and got used to it, as it wasn't too different from the schedule professional football academies had at the time.

Soon, we managed to make it to the final of the League Cup and were going to be facing another one of our local rivals, Hook Norton. The match was to be played at the only stadium in Banbury, owned by Banbury United football club. Masses and masses of people came to watch and support both teams. The atmosphere was truly electrifying on the big stage. Most of us were playing the biggest game of our lives yet. Early on in the game we managed to score one goal and, later in the match, the second and third goals resulted in a 3-0 victory for us. It was a glorious evening and one that I believe will remain close to each one of us. As I reflected on that evening, three years later, I was inspired by the fact that, six years prior to that moment I was playing in a team where I could not even get a few minutes on the pitch. However, six years down the line I had found managers, coaches and teammates who believed in my abilities and efforts and gave me the entire 90 minutes during one of the biggest games for them and the rest of the team. Furthermore, now that we had become League Cup champions, we had gained even more confidence and were aiming to achieve the treble by winning the League and the County Cup to complete a fully successful and dominant seasin. With a few months left of the season still to play, we were very much promising campaigners to be crowned as champions of the first division in the Witney and District league and we now focused our attention to our County Cup campaign. No other team in Banbury Irish's history had ever won the league, the first division League Cup and had managed to get to the final of the County Cup or win it. We were going to become history makers if we qualified for the final of the County Cup and won the league.

As the season continued, my team and I managed to get to the County Cup semi-final against, who would have guessed it, Hook Norton once again. We managed to come out on top again and secured a victorious win. We were met in the final by MJPL side, Chesterton Juniors, who played in the same league as Brackley Town. A lot of us were familiar with the players there, as we had either played with them before at Banbury Irish, or we went to school with them. They were also another local team full of good players. They were playing in a league that was completely out of our district and county, Northamptonshire and Birmingham, but had still managed to qualify to play in our Oxfordshire County Cup. The final was played on 7th May 2017, at a stadium in Kiddlington owned by Kidlington Football Club, where masses of people came to spectate once again. One of our most dominant players at the time, Warren Byfield, was suffering from an injury at the time and that reduced the power of our attack. After committing an early foul in the box, not too long into the game, we found ourselves 0-1 down. The end result was Banbury Irish 0-2 Chesterton Juniors. It was truly a sad and demoralising day for each one of us, especially the likes of Warren who didn't even get to play more than 15 minutes on the pitch. As we watched Chesterton Juniors lift the County Cup and celebrate, in a fashion, a part of our successful run halted and remained there that afternoon in Kidlington. Despite winning the double and making it to the final, as players, having the chance to prove we were the best U15s team in Oxfordshire by claiming that trophy would have been all the validation we needed. However, as time moved forward, we successfully finished the season as league champions. We had completed a truly successful season and made history in the club.

That season was extremely special to me and my favourite one yet, due to the fact that we won so many accolades and matches and had achieved so much. I had never played with such a dominant football team before in my life or been so involved. The managing and coaching we underwent by both Mr McCallum and Mr Bell were to some of the best standards I had ever received and I learnt such a lot about the game in that one season. It was inspiring to be relentlessly told how strong and powerful we were as a team and go out, week in and week out, to prove it. It was inspiring to have played alongside teammates who would fight every corner for me, both on the pitch and off it. It was a season that I hold dearly to my heart.

After the 2016/17 season, we were heading into our last season of youth football with Banbury Irish and our last season of being eligible to play in the Witney District. As mentioned earlier, in the pre-season of 2017/18, I was released by Brackley Town so was in search for another club. Our Banbury Irish team had also suffered two losses. Mr Bell decided that he wanted to leave and Warren was not allowed to play due to new rules Brackley was placing on certain players. Our captain also decided that he was going to leave at the end of the 2016/17 season, having served the club greatly for one season. We were slightly bare boned and were currently in the process of looking for one or two new players. A new captain was also needed for the forthcoming season. Since we had two months' notice of all these changes, we had some time to start looking for players and an assistant coach, if possible, now that Graham was on his own.

During my holiday and travels in Africa, I received a message from Graham asking whether I would like to be the new captain for the upcoming season. I was in slight shock and immensely happy as this was something I'd had my eyes on for the past two seasons and I had hoped the role would soon come before me. I happily accepted and was looking forward to returning to England to serve my first and potentially final year at Banbury Irish, now as captain. Soon, some players from the team tried persuading our previous captain, Lewis, to come back to the team because of his strong presence in defence. In the end, he did so. When this happened, I was unsure about what I wanted to do while sitting in my new role, now that Lewis, who had helped in serving one of the club's most successful and historical seasons, had returned. Initially I thought, let me just give it back to Lewis, as I thought he would serve as a better captain than me, due to his experience of football generally and of being captain not only to our team the previous season, but also other local clubs he had previously played for, and our school football team. Graham and I even had a long discussion about this issue as I informed Graham, after he gave the captaincy to me, that I was debating whether I wanted to take up his offer or whether I should hand it back to Lewis. Graham told me that he didn't want me to even consider handing the armband back as he felt I had earned my place as captain. I was very grateful to Graham, but I still wasn't keen on the idea and told Graham that I would make a decision about the captaincy once I returned to England from my travels.

Graham tried persuading me to see his point of view by asking me if our previous captain, who served the club before Lewis and had led our team to a successful season, returned to Banbury Irish that current upcoming season, would I still feel the need to return the captain's armband to him. I replied to him stating that I wouldn't, because that player had been gone for two seasons but Lewis had only briefly left the club after the season had finished and then made a return during the pre-season. Plus, I argued that Lewis managed to achieve a lot more than the captain who was before him did. Graham then told me that it wasn't just Lewis who achieved what the team achieved the previous season and that he was still able to lead by example on the pitch. Graham then followed up by saying that, ultimately, it was my decision and he felt it didn't make a difference whether Lewis was captain or not –he was coming back, no matter what. He also stated that he had told Lewis I was now the team captain as soon as he asked to rejoin. I later informed Graham there was another contributing factor influencing my decision whether to accept the captaincy. A minority of my teammates had even told me that I should hand the captaincy back to Lewis and that I could become vice-captain while Lewis was the full-time captain once again. I informed Graham that this mindset and behaviour from my own teammates wasn't encouraging me to serve the club and had even put self-doubt in my mind about my ability to lead. Graham replied that he understood where I was coming from, but that it was his decision who he chose as captain and not the minority of my teammates, who were also the ones who had persuaded Lewis to return. Graham even went as far as to say that he would remove the minority who had these thoughts about the captaincy if they didn't follow his protocol.

I told Graham that I also understood him and that I had one last question for him. I asked, "Who would you want as your captain next season, me or Lewis?". He replied, "You." I thanked him and, after this, he said that if Lewis had stayed with the team, he wouldn't have taken the captaincy off him and I would, indeed, have been the vice-captain. However, Lewis had left, and he saw me as a perfect replacement, stating that my positivity throughout the previous season was second to none and when he realised he was losing Lewis it was a blow, but he knew he had someone to step into his leadership shoes for the upcoming season. We left the discussion there and, despite my thoughts, I held onto the role until I arrived back in England in September and the season was soon starting.

At this time, I was also still in search of another team to play with on a Saturday, to fulfil my week with more training and playing, as I was still aspiring to play professional football. I still wanted to play in the MJPL due to the level of football and competition in that league. Scouts and big clubs were also known to spectate different matches that were played in the league. During this period, I knew that Chesterton was playing in the Midlands, as well as Brackley, which was close to my town. Therefore, I got in touch with some of the players I knew at Chesterton. I gained contact with the manager and informed him of my intentions, and I was invited to go and train with them once the season had begun. I knew each one of the players, either through playing with them at Banbury Irish, or playing against them in our local league or for our school teams. I began attending training sessions with Chesterton during the week and was really giving it my all, as I knew this was most likely my last opportunity of playing in the Midlands. After three or four sessions the manager, Mr Kernan, pulled me aside as he had made his decision about me. Now, after facing two consecutive rejections from Brackley over the past two years, drawing tears each time, I was not emotionally ready to face failure once again from Mr Kernan. I vividly remember him telling me that he was pleased with my ability and told me I was a very good player. He knew I was a defender and said that adding me would mean the team would then have six defenders and that was quite a lot of defenders. However, he soon told me that the team was very impressed with my efforts and that they would be happy to have me at the club! I was thrilled with complete excitement as soon as I heard those words. My racing heart began to slow down. I was so relieved to finally be accepted, fully, after trialling for a team, and not having to face rejection or be called back.

By then, Banbury Irish's season had commenced and we had made two new signings. As mentioned earlier, we signed back our previous captain and another Brackley player who I had played with at Brackley the previous season. Once the season had begun, I served my first game as captain, but still had a few doubts about myself serving as the captain for the season. A minority of my own teammates still held the same belief, stating that Lewis was more natural for the role. One day that all changed though.

The week we began school for the new academic year in September 2017, after the first day back, I went to get my hair cut by Mr Bell. He knew about the situation in regard to the captaincy and had actually recommended me to Graham while he was searching for a captain. However, he was deeply disappointed with my unenthusiastic attitude to serve and my doubting nature that I would not fill the boots of our previous leader. He told me that he thought I had more about myself than I was showing. In that moment, he inspired me to believe that I was capable of serving the team and doing the job I was being assigned to complete. His belief in me alone had inspired me to think and know that I had what it would take to captain the team successfully and, after that day, my thought process changed about the entire situation and I began to step up to my role.

During the 2017/18 season I only trained twice a week, as opposed to three times, but I still played on Saturday mornings and Sunday afternoons. I managed to gel with my new teammates at Chesterton and had managed to leave any grudges or negative feelings at the stadium in Kidlington. Banbury Irish were doing pretty well in the league and the cups, but we were nowhere near as dominant as the previous season. We didn't manage to make it that far into either of the cups, only making the semi-final in the League Cup competition, losing to Hook Norton, and the quarter-final of the County Cup. This was quite a low moment during the season, because of what we had achieved the previous year. We were not that emotionally distraught from this though, as we knew that it was our final season together at the club. Despite our short cup campaigns, we did manage to retain our title as league champions of division one.

Once both seasons had finished, my time at Banbury was up as not many players were interested in carrying on into another league; it was the same case for Chesterton Juniors. I had just finished my GCSEs at the time as well, so options in regard to both school and football were quite open. I had still wanted to play in the Midlands, as I made my steps into studying A-levels, but my options had become even narrower due to the folding of Chesterton. I decided to go and trial for Brackley's u18s squad but once again, I was turned away. My parents had advised me to never return to Brackley after being rejected three times. So, the pre-season I went to train with local club Banbury United U17s, as well as a team in the age group above, Kidlington U18s. I was offered the opportunity to be a part of the Kidlington U18s team, where several Chesterton players had now transferred to, and I took up the offer. Due to the number of players present and it being a mixture of U17 players and U18 players, I did not have to pay for training fees or match fees and was more of a reserve player for them. I did not play a single game throughout the season, but travelled on Tuesday evenings each week to go and train with them. During pre-season, I decided to sign with Banbury

United U17s. I was now playing in a league in Oxford for the first time, where the level was just above that of the Witney District. The level of football in Oxford was not that elite or comparable to that of the Midlands. I soon discovered, while at Banbury United, that the age group above us, the U18s, were playing in the MJPL. I immediately set myself the goal to get a call up from them, after hearing that it was a possibility if players in my team were training and playing well.

A certain event, which occurred a few weeks before the season began, also helped me try to achieve this goal during the pre-season. Towards the end of my two-month summer break after completing my GCSEs in summer 2018, I met former professional footballer and Nigerian superstar, Augustine Azuka Okocha, also known as Jay-Jay Okocha, at a birthday party thrown for my uncle. Jay-Jay was invited to my uncle's party as he is a big football fan and he and his family are Nigerian. So, Jay-Jay showed up to the party late in the evening with his wife Mrs Nkechi Okocha. Many of the children present at the party, including myself, were extremely shocked to see the African football legend in such close proximity to us. Jay-Jay Okocha was a footballer who I had looked up to and watched YouTube videos of during the time that I was pushing myself to become a professional footballer. He was one of the footballers who I wanted to play like, and truly had high admiration for. I wanted to fake kicking the ball the way Jay-Jay did when he tricked goal keepers during matches; I wanted to be able to use a football in such a way as Okocha did during his days of playing, which brought so much excitement and entertainment to spectators. Okocha was the second professional footballer I had ever met in my life, along with The Great Kalu, and was one who I knew a lot more about.

So, after digesting the fact that Jay-Jay Okocha was literally standing in the same garden as me, I knew immediately that I needed proof that this moment happened and went to take a picture with him. My parents were one step ahead and managed to get a few photos with him, along with other people who had attended the party. I had the opportunity to sit and have a conversation with Jay-Jay after the photo of the two of us was captured on my phone. Being an aspiring footballer at the time, I asked Jay-Jay as many questions as I could about what he did in order to make it as a professional footballer and any advice he had for me as an aspiring one. He gave me tips similar to those that Kalusha Bwalya had given me in regard to working hard and staying focused. I then also had the opportunity to talk to Mr Okocha about his son, who is the same age as me, regarding his football. He told me that his son, Ajay Okocha, did play football at the time but, Mr Okocha said that, above all, his son's schoolwork came first and football came second. This was quite a shock to me, coming from an individual who was crowned African Footballer of The Year and had won the 1994 Africa Cup of Nations with the Nigerian national football team during his time as a footballer. Soon, my minutes were up with Mr Okocha and I left him, his wife and the other guests at the party to enjoy the rest of the celebrations. The time that I was able to spend with Jay-Jay Okocha, let alone get a photo with him, is a time that I will cherish and remember for the rest of my days.

The football season soon commenced for the Banbury United U17s, where five of us from Banbury Irish were now playing. One day, while studying after school in the early weeks of my time in sixth form, I received a call from my new manager, Mr Jones. He told me that the manager from the U18s had seen me train in the pre-season and wanted me to join them for training on Monday evenings. I was very grateful and very happy, once again, to have the opportunity to play and train at a higher level. The following week I began training with the Banbury United U18s and continued with them on Monday evenings until the end of the season. It wasn't too long after a few training sessions with the U18s and featuring in one match for them, that I played another huge football game. The U18s were playing in a U18s FA cup match against, who would've guessed, Kidlington. I technically played for Kidlington, even though I didn't feature in matches. Therefore, I had a choice as to who I wanted play for. I knew I was going to get far more minutes playing for Banbury so I decided to choose them. The match took place in the evening on a weekday and we were beaten 0-3 by the Kidlington team so were out of the competition. I was fortunate enough to play a total 30 minutes at, most probably, the highest level of football I have ever played. It was all due to my new manager, Mr Ben Lovatt, that I had managed to feature in one of the biggest games of my life and the only ever FA cup match that I played in as a footballer. I was inspired to perform at my best due to Ben's belief that I could make a difference, when he decided to put me in for the 30 minutes that I played. Furthermore, as we got more into the season with me now training on Mondays with the U18s, Tuesdays with Kidlington and Wednesdays with the U17s, I began to receive less time and call ups with the U18s for matches. I was slightly disappointed, but could see there was a lot of talent and good players in that team.

Soon, after being the first U17s player to be called up to the U18s, two more of my teammates in the U17s were called up separately to play. One of them even managed to gain more minutes than I had received in total in just to one match. I could see that my value had gone down since I first joined the U18s and, during this time, my passion for the sport of football was slowly fading away. As mentioned earlier, at one point during the season, I asked myself whether, given the opportunity, I would rather go to university or play professional football in an academy team. As you already know, I chose to attend university. It was from then onwards that I knew I no longer had dreams or interest in getting scouted or becoming a professional footballer. I still had a passion for sport, playing it and winning, but also I just didn't want it as a career anymore. Soon, it came to the end of the season and the U17s team managed to win the second division of the Oxford invitation league. It was my third and most likely final year of playing in the MJPL, as I was about to enter year 13 – the most important and significant year of my entire school career. After that season, Banbury United folded and the options to play for different teams became even narrower.

For my last season of football before I headed off to university the following September, I decided to join my first men's team at local club Hardwick United for the 2019/20 season. By then I had lost even more passion for the game and, instead of playing it to become a professional footballer, I was now playing simply to keep fit as well as for my A-level PE course. Throughout the period that I was deciding between university or professional football, and just thinking about the idea of giving up on my dreams of football, it felt like a weight on my shoulders ready to be lifted. While playing for Hardwick, I was nowhere near as concentrated, focused and stimulated to perform at my level best and didn't feel the same pressure I had put on myself to excel above others, as I had while aspiring to become a professional footballer. It was during this time and with these reflections, that I realised I may have actually been aspiring to become a professional footballer for the wrong reasons. Ever since I joined Brackley Town I got extremely excited about pursuing professional football, as I made steps closer to that goal. However, I got a bit lost in being a 'Brackley player' as opposed to just being a player who now played at a higher level. I consciously and unconsciously began to think about things such as what life was going to be like when I became a professional footballer, the salary I earned and many other material things, rather than the actual playing of football. I even recall a journey to Brackley training with Warren one time, when he asked me a question that is commonly asked when it comes to sport, especially football, "Why do you want to make it as a professional footballer, is it for the love of the game or for the money?" I boldly replied to him, "Oh I play for the money." Immediately, we both began to laugh, but at the time I didn't think much of it in regard to how this goal was going to affect my raw desire and reasoning to pursue professional football.

Now, there's nothing wrong with pursuing a certain career for its monetary value – millions of people do it. They normally tend to dislike the process but enjoy the money when it starts coming in. There are many professional footballers who thought the same as me at one point and only pursued a career in football to bring money home to their families, especially those who suffered from poverty. For me, however, running around my school field until my lungs hurt and sprinting up hills until I was breathless were things that I sometimes questioned were worth doing, just to become a professional footballer, due to the difficulty of those tasks. The reason I felt the need to ask those questions was because, deep down, I knew that I did not desire to play professional football for the complete love of the sport alone, but also for what the sport could add to my pockets and lifestyle. If I had had true, unconditional love for the sport, those questions would have not crossed my mind. So, it was for some years that I thought I wanted to become a professional footballer, train like one and play like one, which was correct, but it was also true that I wanted the luxurious lifestyle that goes with it. It was for this reason, I think, that when I decided to let the idea of professional football go, after putting in so much hard work, training and sweat, it felt as if a weight had been lifted off my shoulders. Take it from my experience, whenever you are putting a lot of hours into something that means a lot to you, whether this may be a future job, an activity you like doing or anything else, always check in with yourself that you are doing it because you want to do it and for reasons that make sense.

Overall, my experiences of football and the pitch have truly been huge and inspiring moments throughout my life. I experienced many different events and have many memories to keep. The pitch inspired me in so many different ways, from methods of being and feeling free, to being happy and part of something. In all of my experiences, matches played, goals scored and tears shared, there were two distinct inspiring moments that I underwent while being a player on the pitch. The first was when Mr McCallum believed in me that time when he took me in after my experiences at Hanwell and gave me the opportunity to play for his team. The second was the time my teammates and I made history at our local club during the 2016/17 season. Due to the fact that Banbury Irish played in the local league in Banbury, we came across my old team Hanwell United on several occasions. After managing to get in touch with my old manager, Nic Weir, he informed me of how he viewed me as a footballer after I moved on to Banbury Irish. Mr Weir stated that, when he witnessed me playing for Banbury Irish, he saw a player who got stuck in, learned and studied the game and developed into a promising young footballer. The attributes he had seen in me before were said to have come to fruition and I was seen as a strong and determined defender who played fairly and honestly. Mr Weir also stated that I probably wouldn't have developed into the footballer I became at his club under the newly appointed manager at the time, but that I would have probably developed under his guidance. He finished by saying that he was just pleased to see me enjoying the game and playing with a smile on my face, as opposed to being that same rabbit caught in headlights.

Quote from Graham McCallum:

> When I first met Neo around a decade ago, he was a very shy, quiet lad. After a couple of training sessions, I noticed that Neo tried his hardest to be better every single time he trained or played. That had an inspirational effect on the other players around him. I began to use Neo as an example of what hard work, dedication and always trying your best could achieve. All that hard work bore fruit with the evolution of our football team.

On tour with my teammates from Banbury Irish, Will and Nathan, in Pakefield in May 2014

Brackley Town u15s at the end of the 16/17 Season in 2017
(Warren is stood directly behind the person on my right)

Oxfordshire County Cup u15s final played against Chesterton Juniors, in May 2017

Banbury Irish u15s team photo on the day of the league cup final, April 26th 2017. Coaches Ian and Garreth on the far left. Manager Graham and coach O'Neil on the far right.

With my teammates on the night we won the league cup 3-0
against Hook Norton at Banbury United stadium

With Jay-Jay Okocha at my uncle's birthday party in September 2018

At Banbury United Stadium during the 18/19 season in October 2018

29. Lourdes

In May 2019, I was fortunate enough to go on a religious pilgrimage with classmates while I was studying as a sixth form student in year 12 at BGN. The annual pilgrimage to Lourdes is a trip that has been part of BGN's history for a long while. The majority of the year 12 cohort at BGN decided to go on the trip and, through this decision, a lot of responsibilities were required from each individual. First of all, each of us were required to contribute and help in raising money to fund our trip to Lourdes, to help lower the cost of the trip for the 46 of us attending. For those of you who are not familiar with Lourdes or have never heard of it, Lourdes is a city in France. It is a sacred place for the Roman Catholic Church because it is a place where Marian apparitions of Mary, the mother of Jesus Christ, were said to of have occurred. These sightings are said to have happened 18 different times with a 14-year-old girl called Bernadette, taking place between February and July in 1858.

Bernadette was a young girl who had contracted cholera when she was a toddler and suffered from this illness throughout her short life. She was fetching firewood one day, on 11th February 1858, with her sister Tionette and a friend of theirs. They were near the grotto of Massabielle, which is simply rock. This is where Mary was said to have first appeared to Bernadette. Bernadette was sitting down ready to take off her shoes and socks to cross some water, which her sister and their friend had already crossed and continued ahead of Bernadette. While Bernadette was lowering her stocking, she reported that she heard the sound of wind rushing, yet nothing moved. A wild rose in a natural niche in the grotto, the cave, did move, however. From this same spot, "came a dazzling light and a white figure." This was the first sighting and, after this, Bernadette had another 17 apparitions of this same figure who she declared was "a small young lady." In her sixteenth apparition, Mary is said to have revealed to Bernadette that she was the Immaculate Conception. The Immaculate Conception means Mary was born without sin, whereas Christians believe that each individual is born with sin and has to undergo baptism to cleanse oneself of this born sin. This belief is said to have begun in the creation story of Adam and Eve, where Adam and Eve were said to have gone against God by eating a forbidden fruit from a tree which God told Adam and Eve not to eat from.

Now, it is believed that this story is true, as it was very unlikely for words and phrases such as 'Immaculate Conception' to be around at those times. In addition, Bernadette was only 14 at the time she reported these apparitions and was very unlikely to have had such knowledge about the Catholic church. Once priests and religious leaders were informed of what had happened to Bernadette each time an apparition happened, they knew that it must have been true as there was no way that she could have made it up in her head. Picture somebody from the 19th century, the same period that Bernadette experienced these apparitions, telling another person that they discovered what the internet was through a genie who appeared to them. Without that genie, no one would have had a clue what the internet was, how it worked or could be built, and this was the same idea for the Immaculate Conception. Moments throughout history, such as the invention of the internet in the 1980s, are not likely to have happened earlier due to the fact that people just didn't have the knowledge of how to make the internet work prior to this, including the technological advancements to make it happen. In the same way that there was no knowledge about the internet 100 years before it came, there was no knowledge about Mary being the Immaculate Conception until she is said to have told Bernadette on her sixteenth Marian apparition on 25th March 1858.

After the apparition of Mary to Bernadette, Bernadette was declared a Saint in the Catholic church, on 14th June 1921, and became Saint Bernadette. Because of this, Lourdes is one of the very special places in the world for Catholics, among many other religious places where a special event in Catholic history has occurred, such as the apparitions of Fatima in Portugal.

BGN pupils go on a pilgrimage to Lourdes each year to do many things, such as grow their faith and learn more about another country and city. However, the main goal is to go and serve. The students help look after people, predominantly older people, who have been in care homes for the most part of the year due to illness, disability or loneliness. These people are called pilgrims. For the week they at Lourdes, BGN students are required to help feed the pilgrims, clean the rooms at the Accueil Notre-Dame (Acci), where the pilgrims stay, take them to different events going on in Lourdes throughout that week and, ultimately, serve and help them. Everyone was very excited about going to Lourdes. Some were excited to learn more about their own faith and what type of impact an environment like Lourdes was going to have on their faith, others were excited about simply going to another country and being able to spend time with their friends in a place outside of the UK, and some were just happy to have the opportunity to get time away from school. I personally was looking forward to having the opportunity to let my hair down, get time away from A-level books and relax but, most importantly, I was looking forward to what effect the pilgrimage was going to have on my faith.

We travelled by bus and by ferry to Lourdes on Saturday 25th May. In Lourdes we encountered a significant number of experiences. We met masses of new people from different schools and Catholic churches in the same diocese as us, the archdiocese of Birmingham. We experienced various events, such as the underground Basilica Mass which is said in different languages and takes place in an underground carpark that was converted into a massive church that can hold up to 25,000 people. We experienced different religious processions, such as the Marian Procession which is usually conducted later in the evening as the sun begins to set, and involves over 15,000 people walking around in the grounds inside the gates of St Michael, the sacred part of Lourdes where the apparition of Mary was said to have occurred. We managed to go and visit holy buildings, such as the chapel that Saint Bernadette used to visit for prayer, as well as the church where she used to attend mass. On our fourth day in Lourdes, we also had the opportunity to go to a place called Gavarnie and spent some hours at the Cirque de Gavarnie, a valley with a mountainous glacier. There were many experiences that we were able to receive from the trip to Lourdes and it was truly a trip that made people see things in a much broader perspective. I know that it definitely made me view things in a different light. There were two particular aspects of the trip that truly made me feel so inspired while I was in Lourdes. The first was the spiritual revelation that I experienced, and the second was the togetherness and bond that I experienced and shared with my fellow classmates.

Before we set off for Lourdes, teachers at my school had mentioned to us that Lourdes was truly a special and sacred place where we may encounter an experience that past students had also encountered, called a 'Lourdes moment.' This was a moment described as some sort of spiritual uplifting or epiphany, through which your life changed for the better. Teachers informed students of this as it had commonly happened among the previous year groups of students who attended the pilgrimage in past years. They also informed us that it didn't happen to everybody and that it was ok if it didn't happen; we shouldn't be in search of it but instead, simply focus on enjoying the trip. I feel that I encountered two 'Lourdes moments' during my time there.

The first was when I went into one of the chapels for the blessed sacrament, which is where Jesus is taken out of the tabernacle and placed in a case on the altar for people to encounter deep prayer. I decided to attend the blessed sacrament because I made a pledge to myself to attend every single event and procession that I could, in order to get a full and complete experience of my time in Lourdes and ensure that I didn't feel I missed anything whatsoever. As I entered the chapel there was complete silence, as there always is during the blessed sacrament, in order to establish a prayerful mood and environment. I went to find a place near the front, closer to the altar. After finding my place near the front, I kneeled and entered a period of prayer. At the time I had gone for my trip to Lourdes, my family and I were suffering from some family troubles. It was an extremely difficult time for all of us and was a type of issue that we had never experienced handling together. So, this was on my mind during my time of prayer, and I soon remembered what I had witnessed earlier on in the day during a very early morning shift helping the pilgrims at the Acci. I had witnessed and helped to serve a mother, who seemed to be no more than 40 years of age, feeding her disabled child, and I began to cry heavily as I remembered this moment. I didn't cry in a loud manner that caused disruption to those also in prayer around me, but I cried silently as tears rapidly ran down my cheeks one after another. I was crying because I realised that, although the issues I had at home were difficult, they were nowhere near as difficult as the severe task this mother was given in looking after her son, because his physical and mental challenges did not permit him to feed himself. I realised after this that my situation at home could be a lot worse than it was and, in a way, I was fortunate to be given the task of dealing with the problems I was having at home, compared to the huge task that the mother at the Acci was having to fulfil and complete every day. This gave me the energy to deal with what was going on at home and have the strength to do my best with the situation presented to both my family and me.

The second time I encountered a 'Lourdes moment' was when we had just finished attending the multicultural underground Basilica Mass in the underground Basilica and I had shared a few words with the Principal at my school, Mr Long. He said something meaningful and kind to me, which I cannot recall word for word, but I do remember him earnestly telling me that I was simply a good guy. This made me feel certain types of emotions and I began to cry once again. I think it was the mixture of experiencing such a mass service spoken in different languages, which I had not experienced before, as well as the nice words Mr Long had shared with me. I tried to turn away from my teachers and classmates so they couldn't see my sobbing, but one teacher called Mrs Hart came over to me, realised I was weeping, and asked how come I was shedding tears. I informed her that they were tears of joy due to the experience of the mass and my tears had begun to flow after Mr Long shared some meaningful words with me. She totally understood my state and reasoning.

Lourdes was a place that I truly experienced different spiritual revelations and managed to gain new experiences and ways of praying and experiencing God, Jesus Christ, the Holy Spirit, Mary, and faith as a whole. It is commonly said that the veil between Lourdes and Heaven is very thin, meaning that in some form, being at Lourdes can make you feel the positive feelings that you would experience once you enter into heaven. It was an experience during which, as I described to my parents, I felt closer to God than ever. Indeed, it was the true pinnacle moment of my spiritual journey as a believer in God so far.

Another time when I felt truly inspired during my trip to Lourdes was when I was simply able to bond and strengthen my relationships with peers from my year group. Before we had left for Lourdes, each of us students were working extremely hard towards our A-levels as we began to make the transition into our last year, year 13, and we knew that our exams were now in just under a year's time. Therefore, there was not much time for real deep conversations with one another while we were at school and so most of the time small talk would be the main topic of conversation. So, as the Lourdes trip was approaching, we all realised that we were going to have much more time to converse with one another and finally spend some quality time together. I had even stepped out of my comfort zone by requesting to share a hotel room with two other classmates of mine called Ben and Luca, who were not classmates that I was particularly close to or that familiar with, but they were the boys who I had the most in common with among my peers in sixth form. We managed to create some of my greatest memories sharing a room together and strengthening our friendships throughout our time in Lourdes.

The bonding between the group of students who were attending the Lourdes trip actually started months in advance, during the time that we were fundraising for the cost of the trip. So, we had already started our bonding and relationship strengthening by the time the day of departure came around, and we were now in a much more open and able space to really bond well as a group. From the time that we left our school gates on the coach, to the time on the ferry to France and again on the coach to Lourdes, this was all time during which we were able to bond. On the coach we watched movies, sang songs, chatted a lot and laughed until our stomachs ached. We were able to do all of the things that being inside our school building, classrooms and common room did not permit us to do fully. The best thing was that we were able to do this together and, in this, we learned so much more about one another.

When we arrived in Lourdes on the morning of the second day, after our 24-hour journey, we went sightseeing to different parts of Lourdes and explored the local part of the city where our hotel was. Over the days we spent at Lourdes, we bonded and strengthened relationships with one another through working at the Acci in our dedicated groups, which truly helped us build the skills of teamwork. We gave our shoulders for others to cry on, during happy, sad and spiritually uplifting moments throughout the trip. This was especially true one evening when we went down to the grotto in Lourdes and lit candles for all those who had passed away from us, whether this was family members or family friends, and the evening ended with many students crying with and beside one another in remembrance of their loved ones.

Our trip to Gavarnie was also simply amazing, due to the sights we were able to see. The weather was completely on our side, as the scorching sun blazed down on our skin. My roommate Luca and me, together with a friend of ours called Emily decided to go to the end of the valley and reach the point close to the start of the glacier in Cirque de Gavarnie. We had limited hours with our school and were told to report back to the bus in two hours, giving us time to explore. So, the three of us headed there with the aim of reaching the end of the valley and seeing the glacier. Throughout our journey, we looked at our watches and realised that time was not on our side and that we were potentially going to return to the bus and everyone else slightly later than permitted. Luca began to run towards the end of the valley. Due to the fact that Luca was a professional swimmer for his local club and his country, Seychelles, he had no issues with running. Emily wasn't much of a runner at the time and I had just come off the back of a football season and I wasn't really training much. Despite this, we had no choice but to join Luca in his actions and we also began to run. At last, we managed to reach the end of the valley and see the glacier. On the way back, as Luca continued to jog to get back in time, I travelled at a more comfortable speed so I could witness and reflect on the sheer beauty of planet earth. I even had to capture the moment on my phone and commentate the belief of whether there was a God or not after I had seen such mountainous beauty and creation. Fortunately, the three of us did manage to get back to the bus in time and found out, later that evening, that we were the only students in BGN history who had managed to reach the end of the valley on a school trip to Gavarnie.

There was one particular moment that truly fulfilled the trip for me and it was during the time we were travelling back to England from Lourdes. Evening was soon coming into play as the sun was slowly setting. We were all watching 'High School

Musical 2' on the coach as we cruised our way out of Lourdes. The coach was quite silent because we were all watching the movie, but I also think it was because people were just in a deep moment of reflection on what we had all experienced, what we had witnessed, and what we had felt and been a part of throughout the past week. There had just been so many amazing experiences. Then, while a few people were taking pictures and videos of the sun setting over the city of Lourdes, the song from 'High School Musical' that goes 'Na na na na, na na na na, yeah, you are the music in me...' began to play and this, in one single second, really felt like a 'High School Musical' moment for me. The movie trilogy 'High School Musical' portrays a fictional school that each of its students from a particular year group work together and as best as they can to produce musical shows. This behaviour and action displayed in each of the three movies of students from a school working together, helping each other and building relationships with others, all in mind of a common goal, was what I felt my classmates and I had managed to do during our stay in Lourdes. Not for the aim of producing a musical, but in the aim of helping the pilgrims who we served and helping each other to have an amazing experience. It was at this moment, when the music from 'High School Musical 2' was playing, sitting there not just as group of schoolchildren but as a team on the coach, that I truly felt complete and in a state of total peace. It was a moment I will remember and cherish for the rest of my life.

Overall, my experience of Lourdes was truly an inspiring, spiritually uplifting and liberating encounter. Learning more about my faith and beliefs and having these strengthened was an experience I would like to frequently recreate with return visits to Lourdes. Having the opportunity to be closer than ever with my fellow peers in sixth form is an experience that I would encourage anybody who has the opportunity to most definitely take up. Being in Lourdes simply showed me the benefits and lessons that I am able to learn when I put myself forward, give things a go, and decide to step out of my comfort zone. There were many people who attended that Lourdes trip who were slightly anxious about what they were going to get out of it, as they were not practicing Christians and did not attend church every Sunday. Despite this, they were still able to gain a great experience from going on the trip and learned so much about their peers from school, Christianity, and themselves. So, whenever given the chance, don't be afraid to visit a place that you have never been to before, or learn more about practices that are completely foreign to you. Who knows, you may end up learning a thing or two or encountering a 'Lourdes moment' of your own.

With Luca in Lourdes at the end of the Mariam Procession. We were a part of the Mariam Procession and carried the flags of different countries

The Mariam Procession in Lourdes

With Emily at end of the valley in Gavarnie in May 2019

End of Section Reader Exercises:

- Which places in the world inspire you and for what reasons?
- What are some of the memorable stories and moments you have from different places you have visited?
- Have any of the places you have visited throughout your life impacted the way that you live and perceive the world?
- Among the places around the world that you have seen, have the populations of people there taught you any life lessons?

SECTION FOUR

HOW TIME IN LOCKDOWN INSPIRED ME

30. My First Week of Lockdown

At the start of the year 2020, I did not expect to find myself locked down towards the end of March while I was still studying and living in the UK. I don't think many of us around the world thought that we were going to be locked down and in the midst of a pandemic a quarter of the way into the new year. My A-level exams were cancelled on the day this happened and I did not know how to react when the news was broke to students. At the time, I was finishing an online tuition session with my psychology tutor. Once I realised, in March, that I was no longer going to be sitting nine exams that would have greatly influenced my future and my university choices, I felt a slight relief, but I was mostly filled with shock as were the rest of my classmates, especially those who hoped to show their talents and hard work through sitting exams. Before I knew it, the remaining two days of the school week, 19th and 20th March, were my last days as a student at BGN. After schools were closed on Friday 20th March, lessons moved to online platforms and all students destined to graduate from primary and secondary school were to receive grades based on their past assessments and were, essentially, on holiday. However, unlike a normal holiday, things had changed and restrictions regarding what you could and could not do were in place.

Restaurants, pubs, cinemas, gyms, non-essential shops and many other places were all closed. You were only allowed outside once a day for exercise, either alone or with members of your immediate family who you lived with. In fact, mass gatherings of people were prohibited. You were only allowed to be in the presence of a few people and, even with them, you had to remain socially distanced. Despite all of these restrictions, a lot of people across the UK did not follow them and a lot of people around the world failed to conform too, myself included. On Sunday 22nd March 2020, I decided to meet up with my friends, Gilbert, Warren and Tyrell for the day and we did not maintain social distancing between us. We wanted to see each other for the last time before, as we put it, we "really went into lockdown." However, we were ignorant to the fact that any of us could have had the virus at the time and passed it on to each other due to its potentially asymptomatic nature. We were extremely fortunate that none of us had it at the time.

Lockdown officially began on 23rd March, after it was announced by Prime Minister Boris Johnson, but I began my lockdown by dancing in the evening on the day I returned from school on 20th March, and I posted a dance on social media, captioned: 'I don't know about everybody else...but my take on this is: A-levels without having to sit exams… [tick emoji] … Government provides grades for uni… [tick emoji]… 6-month summer…! [running emoji]'

I was extremely happy when it truly sank in that I had finished my A-levels three months ahead of schedule, that I was no longer going to be sitting exams and I would still receive A-levels out of it. I was quite certain that universities would be slightly more lenient in taking in students due to the destructive end to our school year, and so I felt as if my classmates and I had just avoided one of the most difficult and pressured three months of our lives, in preparing to sit those A-level exams. We were free! When we did hear the news, most students put their pens down immediately and closed their textbooks. Some even decided to throw them away. As my father said to me, the moment Prime Minister Boris Johnson cancelled the summer exams it was like releasing a prisoner. In the midst of all of this celebration, the first ten days of lockdown will be a time I will never forget.

Despite the sudden flip in my schedule, I was still waking

up at 6am every morning while in lockdown, due to the fact that I had trained my body clock to be up at this time, ready to set aside one hour to revise for my exams. Even without an alarm clock, my body was tuned to being awake at this hour. Most mornings, I wouldn't really do much other than go on my phone and flick through social media, or just lie in my bed listening to music. During the first couple of days of lockdown, I was mostly into watching news and learning more about how the virus was moving and how bad the situation was getting. Due to the reported aggressive nature of the coronavirus and the daily media updates on death rates, most days I would post something on my Snapchat account about it, or the latest death toll, to raise awareness in those not taking it seriously. My parents were busy trying to find different ways of working so they could still earn money, because travel was cancelled and most of their work involved travel. One of my older sisters was living in Manchester at the time and was locked down there, so for most of the days I was having to entertain myself. I was not that creative at the time, since I was still adjusting to this new way of life that had brought the entire world to a standstill. Therefore, my days were mostly filled with watching TV and news in the living room. I barely exercised, as I never really found the time to do this in the weeks leading up to the UK lockdown as I was so focused on studying at school, so I did not decide to schedule this into my days in the early stages of lockdown either. I also only ate two meals a day most days, which was the way I had been living while studying for my A-levels. The only thing I really did was attempt writing a book as Gilbert had proposed during the early days of the first lockdown.

During the first week of lockdown, on 26th March, I had a day which flicked a switch in my brain regarding how dangerous this virus truly was. The day wasn't too different to how I had been living the previous days, other than the fact that I had engaged in a discussion with one of my friends from school about scripture that was being shared around social media. The scripture stated how God would send sickness to his people for them to humble themselves and turn away from the evil ways of this earth. I thought quite deeply about this, being a believer in God and being in the midst of this pandemic which was already taking the lives of so many people each day. I was also watching the breakfast show 'This Morning' where Philip Schofield and Holly Willoughby were interviewing someone who had predicted that a time like this would come, where the world has to work together due to a global issue and come together for once, as opposed to being so divided. This concept that the person was describing was known as the 'blackout' and had occurred previously throughout history and, once again, involved uniting the nations of the world to fight a global issue. This gave me a lot to think about after the show had ended, while I headed into the late afternoon and evening.

The sun was shining that afternoon so I went to jump on my trampoline in the garden. As I was jumping up and down, I looked into the garden to my left and saw our neighbours, who are an elderly couple, doing things that I hadn't managed to often seen them do. I saw the woman doing some gardening and her husband was inside their conservatory, pedalling on an exercise bike. As I looked to the neighbours on my right, the garden had no one in it and I just saw the plants and their trampoline. There was no music playing, no noise other than the occasional passing of cars and the tweeting of birds. While I jumped on my trampoline, I felt a blissful moment of complete peace. I did not think much of it at the time, but I remember the moment very vividly. Later that evening, I decided to go and hang out with the children who lived next door, who were around about the same age as me. However, some of my Snapchat contacts did not approve when I posted videos of us hanging out, even though we were socially distanced. Some argued that it was not social distancing as I was with people outside of my household and so on.

Before I left, I spoke to the mother of my friends about the pandemic and what life was like for them now. She was telling me about the London riots she experienced in August 2011. During this conversation, I had shared with her my recent knowledge of the Spanish flu that occurred in 1918 and killed over 30 million people. Throughout that discussion, I was thinking back to the scripture my friend and I were discussing earlier and all of the events throughout the day that led up to that conversation. People at the time were still taking the pandemic and lockdown as a joke, especially young people. I had witnessed one guy lick the part of the toilet underneath the seat as part of a social media COVID-19 challenge. Within days he contracted the virus.

After my conversation with my neighbour, I went home in deep thought and said to my father, complacently, "I wouldn't be surprised if over one million people die from this virus." He replied with similar thoughts, because both he and I knew some people truly didn't fear it at all. Later that evening, I managed to discover the new Netflix series 'Tiger King' that was released a few days prior, on 20th March, and watched the first episode with my parents to discover the shocking actions and work of people such as Joe Exotic and what they do to animals. After I watched this first episode, I thought to myself that humans truly have come too far in our control over animals and the earth. From a religious perspective, I felt as if we had tarnished the beauty God had intended for the earth and we had overstepped how much authority we truly have over the planet, despite being its most dominant species. Throughout this overload of thoughts, I reflected back to what I had experienced throughout the day and thought that the blissful moment I had experienced while jumping on my trampoline is what this pandemic may have come to restore. Basic nature and finer things in life. I believed this was God's involvement in it all. I was not sure whether I believed it was something God had planned to put on the earth and had done so purposefully, but I did feel as if it was a time for us to stop in our tracks, good and bad, go back to basics and value what matters in life – loving our families and neighbours and respecting everyone.

During this evening, my survival instincts also kicked in. The thought of the virus killing many people made me fear that mass genocide was approaching us. My friends and I had already discussed how some people would simply not be able to cope with remaining at home and would begin to lose their sanity. I thought this would then lead to the death of even more people through domestic abuse, murder and suicide, and result in an exponential rate of death. I genuinely thought that it would turn into 'The Hunger Games', which is as a series of science fiction books and movies that display an imagined state of society where there is great suffering and a world where people have to eliminate one another through killing in order to survive. So, as I looked back at myself and my family, I realised that I would need to do all I could to protect myself and protect them too, from the virus as well as from any people who were beginning to struggle with the lockdown and, in my mind, might become opponents as in 'The Hunger Games'. I realised I was not as fit as I could be and, if it came to me attempting to outrun my killer, I would most likely have a 60 percent chance of surviving. As such, getting fit was on my immediate 'to do' list. I also did not know how to fight using proper skills other than just my survival instincts. So, if I was to get into combat with an outsider for whatever reason, I would need to be better trained on what to do and how to defend myself properly. So, my dad ordered some boxing equipment. I was going to ensure that I helped train my parents in getting fitter too. It was definitely safe to say, by then, I was truly scared. I had even decided that, if the situation was to get really bad, I would install Instagram and follow the likes of Will Smith, The Rock and Michael B. Jordan, as those were the people I looked up to and thought would step up and give advice in the middle of a crisis such as the one we were actually facing; along with the dystopian horror I believed was soon approaching.

Close to around midnight that night, after watching 'Tiger King', my parents called it a night. However, I remained downstairs watching television. I decided to put on the first episode of the sitcom 'The Fresh Prince of Bel-Air', as I had never really watched it in my teen years and wanted to understand the storyline and the jokes a lot better now that I had more knowledge. Throughout this first episode, 'The Fresh Prince Project', it was as if I was seeing it in a different light to anything else I had watched in my life. My eyes and ears were completely attentive to everything the characters were saying and picked up on every cue. Surprisingly, the 1990 series raised awareness through commenting on serious issues in a humorous manner. Those issues were still present, 30 years later, at the time that I was watching that episode. Problems such as climate change and discrimination were joked around, but it was clear they were just trying to raise awareness of those issues. So, when the episode came to an end and I realised that problems such as climate change were problems that humanity had still failed to solve, having been a part of conversations for the past 30 years, I felt quite sad.

Around this time, a video of Bill Gates had resurfaced and, on this same day I think, I had decided to watch it, show it to my parents and share it on my Snapchat account. The video was a TED Talk by Bill Gates that took place in 2014. In the talk, Mr Gates stated that the next war the human race would face would not be one that involved guns and nuclear bombs as we have experienced in the past, but it would be against a virus due to our poor health systems and how inadequately equipped we were at the time. As I sat in my living room, thinking and reflecting upon these things and the fact that Bill Gates had warned world leaders and the entire world that healthcare systems needed to improve, I felt that, as a human race, we had failed in our duties to prepare for global issues such as the ones that were becoming more apparent and visible to us in 2020. I reflected, thought and felt as if we had failed in taking care of the earth which we were so kindly and freely given and it had now come back to bite us. The only thing was, I felt this bite was going to leave a scar.

The next three days of the lockdown were among three of the worst days I have ever lived in my life. Moving from the 26th to 27th of March, I did not sleep for more than three hours throughout the night and had to entertain myself using my phone and music. I continued raising awareness of the seriousness of the virus and how it seemed as though we were going to be in this for the long run. I also tried encouraging people to get to know God slightly during their increased free time at home, as it was a difficult period for the entire world. I decided to intervene with people who were posting fake news about causes of the coronavirus, such as the 5G conspiracy theory, as it had the potential to really scare people and get them even more paranoid and searching for answers they may never find. Little did I know, my own paranoia had already begun. I was upset in the early hours of Friday 27th March when I discovered a close friend had gone to work, simply to keep his pockets healthy. I tried to persuade him to refrain from any more work due to the risk of contracting the virus in his workplace, which was a hotspot for the virus at the time, being a food shop. With barely any sleep and thoughts rushing around my head about the COVID-19 situation, it was around 9am or 10am when I began to get bad.

I knew I hadn't slept much and was therefore sleep deprived, so my parents insisted I take a hot, relaxing bath. However, because I knew that I was running on quite an empty tank, but I couldn't sleep again to refuel the tank throughout the day, I began to get worried about my health and just felt that my heart was beating slightly quicker than it usually does at rest. I really felt the contractions of it in my chest and in my head. As I soaked myself in the hot water, each time I put my head under I could hear my heart beat even louder and this simply made me feel more afraid. Despite this, I continued on with the day and got ready as I would if I had just woken from a usual night's sleep. At one point, however, as I still felt my heart rate was slightly raised above what it normally would be, I got on my knees in my living room and said a prayer to God, asking for protection. My mother and I had also been quarrelling that day, as she was also still adjusting to life in lockdown. Around 11am, the Prime Minister of England, Boris Johnson, had been showing symptoms for the virus and had tested positive for it. Due to my experiences of the previous day, and especially Thursday 26th, I had abstained from watching news and decided to head out for my first walk since the lockdown. My father asked if he could accompany me and I agreed.

We just walked around my street and towards the grounds of the school we live right next to and, in that moment, being outside felt completely different to how it had ever been before. We didn't see anyone and, on our way back, we realised that it was bin day and we had forgotten to take out the bins. I endured the remainder of the day with no sleep, hoping to get some as night came. Initially, I failed to do so once again and it was around 1am when I decided to pick up my phone and keep myself busy, as opposed to just lying there attempting to sleep when I was unable to. I engaged in a discussion with a friend of mine who I attended primary school with. We caught up for most of the conversation and laughed and joked about fake news that had been shared about lions being released in Russia to roam the streets and keep people indoors and under lockdown. As we jokingly saw it, maybe lions were the only feasible way of making people conform to the new restrictions, especially considering the rebellious way that the people of Britain were behaving. It was when my friend sent me a message around 4am, stating that the sun was going to rise soon, that I realised I had wasted my whole night's sleep and, as soon as the sun rose, it would be extremely hard for me to even attempt to sleep. Now I was pushing close to 30 hours without any sleep at all. After we had both decided to call it a night and realised we had been slightly foolish in our actions, especially myself with no sleep the previous night, I felt such disappointment in myself. I had once again put my health at great risk and went to my parents to seek help in what I should do. My father came to my bedroom and found me sobbing, as I told him what I had decided to do for most of the night. He came and sat with me in my bed as I continued sobbing in his arms, knowing that I was simply failing to fall asleep. We even considered whether I would need medication to help me sleep, but we also knew that visiting the hospital would be a great risk for all of us. Later that same morning, before 10am, my father gave me a full body massage to help relax my body and my mind and I managed to sleep for one hour, but soon woke and shot up again. I was pleased that I had managed to at least sleep for some small time, but my father knew when I came down to speak to him that it was still not enough and could see that I was off-key and talking a lot more than I usually do, and he began to worry slightly.

My mother suggested that I go on a long proper walk with her to tire myself out, but I felt that, if I went on that walk, I would potentially collapse along the way because I'd gone close to 30 hours without any sleep. I took 28th March easy, but did end up going for a stroll just to take some time away from being home and feeling trapped, as well as the fact I needed to let off some steam after another quarrel with my mother. I ended up calling my close friend Champhe, who helped me with my situation after I told him what had gone on and he told me that I simply needed to sleep. Within the first week of the lockdown, I had waited until Saturday, a full week, to go on my first walk and it seemed due as I had built up this idea in my head that I was trapped at home and the outside world and streets simply was not safe. After I returned home, I resolved the matter with my mother and began to eat some food to try and get my energy up in some way, as my eating habits had been quite poor ever since 26th March. During this time, I was fasting from meat due to the Christian period of Lent, but I had to break my fast in order to get protein into my system and give myself the energy I desperately needed, after being so deprived of sleep. On the night of 28th March, I finally managed to get some sleep. It was only around six hours or so, but it was a start. I was so relieved to have finally enjoyed sleeping again. From then on, I was solely focused on correcting my sleeping patterns and getting a minimum of eight hours a night. After the events of my sleeping problem, I jokingly named it 'Neo's 30-hour challenge'. That, in a nutshell, was essentially my experience of my first week in lockdown.

What I learnt throughout my first week in lockdown is that, when a crisis such as a global pandemic falls upon the earth, you truly need to monitor news and social media consumption as well as be aware of how the two are affecting your mental and physical health. I also learnt about the importance of sleep in being able to function during any period of life and especially when there is something as catastrophic as a global pandemic going on. My first week of lockdown wasn't the most pleasant of experiences to remember, but it was an experience from which I was able to learn a few things.

31. The Highlights of Lockdown

Many of us around the world have undergone lockdowns for periods of three to four weeks at a time, with some countries seeing even longer full lockdowns, with a year-and-a-half of varying restrictions at the time of publishing this book. Within this time, many of us have branched into finding new hobbies. Some people may have become gardeners and used this as a way of keeping their minds sane and a method to keep busy. Cutting your lawn once or twice a week doesn't sound too bad when everything else in the outside world is unavailable. Some may have become writers, athletes and artists. Many people will have found something to keep them busy and free from boredom during the unprecedented time of the coronavirus pandemic. In my case, after my initial floundering period at the start of lockdown, I began to exercise quite frequently and learn the skill of boxing. However, in my situation, exercising and boxing were the results of motivation as opposed to inspiration per se.

After I finally managed to start getting a good night's sleep again, the following mornings I would wake up early, around 6am to 7am, to train my body and condition it as much as I could, to prepare it well for combat, or any threats I was potentially going to face in the near future. Or so I thought. After some days, I realised that mass murders may not be descending upon us in the style of 'The Hunger Games' and I had probably allowed the overload of news social media, as well as my own imagination, to get the better of me. I then managed to enter into a different space with it all. I started exercising for up to two hours each morning of each day, just for the sake of wanting to increase my athletic ability. It was in the first two to three days of training that I realised I was actually more athletically gifted than I had given myself credit for. So, after this realisation, the time that I now had in lockdown inspired me to test my body and its athletic capacity, and train more often and at higher intensities.

During the first few days after I had recovered from my sleep deprivation, I also realised that before, while I was preparing for my exams, I was not living a balanced lifestyle. I was not exercising anywhere near as much I should have been, on a weekly basis, after the football season was completed in February 2020. I also realised that I was not eating three meals a day. I never used to skip meals just for the sake of skipping meals or not wanting to eat, it was because I used to wake up early, study, and not want to give time to find something to eat, as well as the fact that I wasn't that hungry early in the mornings. I ate my first proper meal at breaktime at school around 11am and then waited until after school to have dinner in the evening. I was mostly just skipping breakfast, had an early lunch, and ate in the evening. It was after this reflection that I made it a principle to ensure that I exercised at least once a day and ate three meals each day.

One evening, I looked out at my garden and thought that it needed some shaping up. So, I got my loppers and put on some old clothes and wellies and began to chop away at trees and branches that had overgrown and made the garden look untidy. After two to three hours of doing this, I realised this was physical labour that I could gain experience from. While never previously applying for a job or being employed, I saw this time as an opportunity to get some experience of doing physical labour and I set myself the task of working in the garden for a minimum of two hours a day, each day. I did this for three to four weeks, but was also quite flexible with myself regarding my hours at times and the days that I worked, but both my father and I were shocked to realise that I really enjoyed physical work. I had maintained, for the majority of my later years, that physical labour looked boring and I would rather study than just work eight hours for money.

Meanwhile, while we would have all come to a point when we had enough of being inside our homes and wished to go outside, my next-door neighbour, Rowan, introduced me to mountain biking and riding bikes over ramps. My neighbours kindly allowed me to use one of their bikes so Rowan and I could go riding. As we went for our first ride together, within minutes we were into mountainous land and I soon saw a side of my town that I had never seen before. Beautiful, adventure seeking and admirable sites. After the bike ride, I soon realised that there was so much of my town that I had not yet seen. Every two or three days I would ask Rowan whether he wanted to go riding with me again and, even if he was busy, I would go alone and explore different tracks, routes and trails, hoping to see more eye-catching landscapes the town of Banbury had to offer. Mountain biking was and is a new hobby of mine, one which I am grateful the lockdown enabled me to discover and enjoy.

Before the lockdown was initiated, I was having piano lessons with my teacher, Diego Sunga, who is three years below me but an extremely skilled pianist. I took up piano as I had to learn a new skill for my Gold Duke of Edinburgh award. At the beginning of March, I managed to finish the hours I was supposed to complete learning the skill of playing the piano, but we decided that we were going to carry on with lessons in order for me to finish learning the piece we had been working on. Lessons only took place when I requested one, as my exams, which were not yet cancelled, were drawing nearer. However, once the lockdown was in place, my piano lessons with Diego were no longer going to be possible. So, when my birthday came around in April I decided to invest in a keyboard and intended to finish the piece I had begun learning through online lessons with Mr Sunga. Since I knew, in April, that the UK would most likely still be under lockdown until late June at the earliest, I thought that improving my skill of playing the piano may be a wise thing to do with all the time that lockdown offered me. We managed to finish the piece and went on to learn several more pieces throughout lockdown.

One of the first things my time during lockdown inspired me to do was to write this book. If it was not for lockdown, my good friend Gilbert Healey would not have boldly said to me: "You should write a book!" in order to keep busy during lockdown. Funnily enough, the idea of writing, let alone writing this book, may have never come to mind if it wasn't for him. Therefore, in spite of the deep sadness that the coronavirus pandemic has brought to many people across the world, it also has its advantages. The various lockdowns have sparked opportunities for people to embark on new adventures, make new discoveries, find new interests and begin new hobbies. I believe we should at least recognise it for that and seize these opportunities whenever they become apparent to us.

32. A Ride with Gilbert

I have mentioned earlier that mountain biking is a hobby I picked up while in lockdown. On 13th June 2020, I went for a special ride with my friend that I will never forget. Gilbert and I organised to go on a bike ride together on Saturday in my local town. Gilbert lives in Brackley and was going to travel 15 minutes by car to my house. The Friday night before our ride, Gilbert gave me a call and said he had to cancel due to a last-minute studio session that was going to take place in London. I was slightly disappointed, but I wasn't too down about the situation. I stayed up past midnight watching movies, now that I knew I didn't have to be rested and ready for noon the following day. On the Saturday morning, I only decided to leave my bed at noon, after continuously dozing, falling asleep and waking back up. After freshening up a little and saying hello to my family, I looked at my phone and saw two missed calls from Gilbert. I called him back immediately and was fortunate to discover his studio session in London was cancelled and he was now available to go on the bike ride again. Gilbert and I both chuckled at the fact that I only left my bed at noon, which was one of the latest times I had managed to lie in during the entire lockdown. He had mentioned how, if I had answered either of his calls at 11am we would've been right on schedule to head out from my home at noon. I quickly contemplated whether I still wanted to ride, while I stood on the phone to him with an empty stomach and still yet to shower. However, I decided that I still wanted to go and told Gilbert that I would give him a call letting him know when to leave his home and drive down to

Banbury. I also still had to hoover the house as part of my Saturday chores. I estimated that I would probably end up calling him within the next hour or so. This would've resulted in him starting his journey at 1:30pm. So, I quickly got to work and finished hoovering within 20 minutes and hurriedly got ready to increase our riding time, which was originally going to be seven to eight hours. During this process, I nipped over to my next-door neighbours' house and asked whether I could use their bike for the day for Gilbert to ride. They kindly allowed me. After I finally finished eating, I was ready to give Gilbert the call. Soon after, I hopped in the shower and was almost ready to begin pedalling.

Gilbert arrived and had a quick catch up with my mother while I hurriedly prepared my last bits of packing. Within minutes we were on the road. We were both excited and happy to see each other once again, as we had not met up since the end of March, around the time the lockdown was announced. I was quite cautious to greet Gilbert with the newly developed elbow bump, due to his whereabouts after the UK slowly lifted and relaxed its restrictions. Despite this, within metres into the ride, Gilbert finally asked me to greet him properly with a fist bump, or at least an elbow bump, and so we stopped and bumped elbows.

Originally, I planned for us to tackle a route that I had discovered during my weekend retreat in 'My Locked-Down Expedition Adventure'. We were going to do the same route that I did on day two, which was a total of 20 kilometres. Initially, I thought that route would have been the beginning of our bike ride and it we would have finished cycling around Banbury, moving towards local villages just outside of Banbury. As we continued on the trail from day two, Gilbert and I had the opportunity to catch up and talk. We first rode into Shotteswell and, this time, I managed to follow the correct footpath that led us to towards the M40 and close to Great Bourton. Before, when I was walking, I missed this footpath and had to pave my own way through some stinging nettles and a grim dip in the ground. For someone who doesn't regularly go on bike rides and who doesn't go exploring often, Gilbert was doing very well. We finally reached the M40 as we prepared to leave Shotteswell, after taking one or two stops along the way. It was the second time I had walked over that bridge which goes over the M40, whereas it was Gilbert's first. He was quickly excited and thrilled with happiness as we watched and felt the energies of the fast-moving vehicles and wind. I then decided to stand in line with one of the lanes of cars driving towards Banbury and began to pump my arm up and down, signalling that I wanted the drivers to hoot their horns. Gilbert was not familiar with this action, but soon came to know its meaning once drivers, especially lorry drivers, began to hoot their horns. Gilbert soon joined me in the arm pumping, and we tried this on around 40 different cars. It really looked as if Gilbert was enjoying himself and he confirmed my thoughts when he pulled me aside in the midst of the fast-moving atmosphere and said, "Thank you". I replied, "For what?" and he said, "Showing me the way and this other side to life." I just smiled back at him and told him that we needed to get going as we had already lost two hours from starting off late.

Throughout our ride I was commentating on different places, fields and areas of land that we were passing through. I didn't want us to ride on normal paths and busy roads, as I felt that it was plain boring. I prefer mountain biking and riding through footpaths, trails, bridleways and tracks, as it is different to the traffic and busy roads I'm usually exposed to. When you get into fields and the heart of the countryside wherever you are, it is almost like another world and feels separate from the normal busy roads and loud car engines a lot of people experience in everyday life. It is quiet and peaceful in fields and they are places where I am able to literally hear my own inner voice and thoughts.

After leaving the bridge of the motorway, we were on our way to enter into Great Bourton village. Before we could do this, however, Gilbert and I had to ride up quite a steep hill. By then, hunger and fitness levels had really gotten to Gilbert, as well as the scorching heat that was present on the day. He also hadn't worn a hat, so his face was very exposed to the heat. He was quite far behind me as we approached the start of the hill and asked me whether we could take a break. So, we took a break and, coincidentally, we sat in the exact same spot that I had sat in when I went walking. Since we were sitting on a flat bump with a lot of wheat around us, Gilbert didn't feel as if it was the most comforting place to take a rest and suggested that we could rest at the top of the hill instead, after climbing it. So that's what we did. We didn't cycle up the hill due to its difficult terrain, so we carefully walked with our bicycles. Once we had reached the top, Gilbert looked back at where we had just come from and had the same look in his eyes and on his face that I'd had when I first climbed that same hill. A look of accomplishment and achievement. We decided to take our proper break in a shaded area along a small passageway to a main road. I thought that it would be a good time to replenish my energy stores, so I began to eat my usual meal which never fails to please me, cheese sandwiches. I asked Gilbert whether he had carried lunch with him but, even though I had repeatedly told him that he must carry food, he had not. He only carried his bank card, which was of no use as we were nowhere near any shops. So, he and I shared my cheese sandwiches, having one-and-a-half sandwiches each.

Soon after being fed, Gilbert's energy and spiritual levels increased and he was ready for the second half of our journey. We soon set off for Bourton and were once again riding through the countryside and through lots of wheat. During our time in Bourton, Gilbert caught his leg on my neighbour's bike and cut the skin on his calf muscle. While we took a short break to attend to his cut, Gilbert mentioned how the seat of the bike was making it hard for him to ride. I thought that he was just being difficult, as I had taken the bike he was using out for rides several times. However, after I suggested that we could swap bikes, I understood why he was in pain as the seat was slightly tilted upwards. As we continued on, just before turning into our next footpath, still in Bourton, I received a call from Champ. Champ said how he was currently around our local area with another friend of ours and wondered whether Gilbert and I wanted to meet up and hang out with them. I agreed, as I knew that Gilbert didn't come to our town often and that it would be good if he could spend some time with a couple of our other friends in addition to myself.

Meanwhile, we were making our way out of Bourton by approaching a track called Mill Lane, leading to the Oxford canal walkway, which led us all the way back into Banbury. This was the route I had ran along on my expedition previously, due to my phone being on a low battery and me needing to get to a certain point where my father was going to collect me before it ran out. However, just before we met the track, we came across a herd of sheep. They were standing on our right as we passed along the footpath. Suddenly, they all began to stare at both Gilbert and me. We stopped for a moment and looked back directly at them. For some reason they did not look afraid of us at all. It was more of a staring competition. Gilbert suddenly commented that he wanted to charge at the herd, because he was convinced that they were actually afraid of us, as well as the fact that he simply wanted to see this mass of over 150 sheep smoothly move as one. He said that he did not want to do it alone, but I was quite happy spectating from the other side of the fence. The farmer who owned the sheep was nowhere to be seen, so we thought we could flee the sheep, get out, and leave quickly. I soon agreed to join Gilbert and we set to charge at this massive herd of sheep. Once we got over the fence, I said to him that we needed to find the quickest escape routes in case the sheep actually began to charge back at us, or the owner of the sheep decided to come out. Once we located our best escape route, despite being massively outnumbered, we began to charge at the herd. The sheep immediately began to flee as one large group, but it was not as smooth or graceful as we imagined it, or would have preferred it to be. They also didn't run that far in the opposite direction to us. I wasn't going to allow us to try it again, due to the fact that we were trespassing.

So, we carried on along our route and, just before meeting the track, we stopped for another break near a lake where Gilbert suffered from his second nosebleed during the bike ride. He frequently gets nosebleeds so this wasn't too much of a concern for us. We also observed the behaviour of some ducks during this break. After Gilbert's nosebleed had stopped, we were on the track towards the canal. Soon, when we reached the train track that I had come across before, Gilbert was in shock that we were crossing a train track and immediately saw danger. I repeatedly told him that there was not as much danger as he thought there was, as long as we took precautions. Soon after crossing the track and cycling a couple of metres, Gilbert turned to me and said he wanted to experience the train go past. So, we turned back, left the bikes close to the track, and waited for a train to pass by. Gilbert still thought there was great danger and insisted that we stood 15 to 20 metres away from the track. On the other hand, I suggested that we stood five to ten metres from the track and he earnestly told me "No!" He believed that if we were too close to the track, the speed and energy of the train would be far too great and would suck us under it. However, I had different views to him and thought that the distance I suggested would be best for the type of experience we were now both in search of, and it was certainly safe.

So, as we waited for a train to go by, Gilbert stopped me from going to the position I thought we should stand at and, while trying to muscle past him, he held onto my rucksack and accidentally tore it. Gilbert apologised immediately, but said that he was only trying to do it for my own good and safety. I forgave him, knowing that his intentions were pure. We were like a pair of schoolboys disagreeing over which one of us had the correct answer to a maths question. As we both waited for this train, for at least 15 minutes, still quarrelling about how close we should stand, we both decided that, as it was unknown when this train was coming and that we could be waiting for a long while, we should forget the idea and continue towards the canal. However, within five minutes of our journey from the track, we began to hear the train approach the spot where we had just been standing. I looked at Gilbert and said, "That's the train!" I quickly began to cycle and, while I did this, Gilbert shouted to me, "You're too far Neo!" I stopped in my tracks with great disappointment. We began to quarrel once again about the fact that we missed the train for which we could have waited just five more minutes. I told Gilbert that we were going back immediately and that we would wait two whole hours if we needed to, just to get this experience. So, we headed back to the same spot and this time we began to get comfortable.

We found activities to do while we waited for a train and I agreed to stand at the distance that Gilbert had wanted us to stand at. I began to play a song by a rapper called Ice Cube, which goes by the name, 'It Was A Good Day'. We played games such as who could throw a rock the furthest and who could throw a rock over the distanced train line. We were also accompanied by a group of cows who were next to us in a field, which kept us entertained. It was during this moment, when the sun was still shining down on us as the evening began to set in, while we threw rocks to keep us entertained and listened to the soothing voice of Ice Cube, that I realised COVID-19 had changed matters for Gilbert and me, for the better. At that moment I knew this was how I wanted to spend my weekends and days that I had free. Out in nature and the outdoors, experiencing the warmth of the blazing sun and listening to 90s music. That moment in itself was simply perfect. There were no sounds from car engines, or from masses of different people's voices. Instead, all that our ears were attentive to was the sound of sweet music and the calming air. We even managed to play with the cows in the field next to us, by attracting them with rocks and making them think it was food.

Soon, 45 minutes had passed while we were enjoying ourselves and the moment we were both in. Shortly after, the train finally came. A train moving at a moderate pace travelled from our left and began hooting to signal to anyone approaching the crossing that there was a train coming. Gilbert and I were both excited and braced ourselves as the train passed. Despite all of the excitement and expectation of this experience, we soon felt disappointed. We did not feel any wind, current or energy from the train at all, and were deeply sad about this. Gilbert had blamed it on the fact that the train was on the track furthest away from us, but I didn't buy it. The train simply wasn't moving fast enough to give us the experience we had patiently waited for. As a result of this, we decided to wait for another train, hopefully one that was fast-moving. Now that Gilbert had his first experience of what it felt like as the train passed, he grew the bravery to stand at the distance I had originally suggested and we did so. Within minutes, another train came by and this time it was on the track closest to us. We once again braced ourselves, holding onto a wooden fence next to us. As the train passed, the wind and energy of that train was only slightly above that of the previous train. After this, we decided to call it a day and were happy with the experiences we were able to encounter.

We began to head towards the canal from the train track for the third time and were finally riding home on the walkway. We had to ride five to six kilometres along the canal back to Banbury, but those metres were covered quickly on bikes and we were soon back in Banbury after four hours outdoors. I realised very soon into our ride that the track I chose wasn't only going to be the beginning of our ride, but it was going to be the end too. I had clearly underestimated how much time it was going to take us to complete that route. We were also met with great rain showers shortly after entering Banbury. Nevertheless, we soon met up with Champ and Co at a playing court in Hanwell, after going into the local Co-op in Hanwell en-route to buy some food as replenishment after a long but memorable bike ride.

As I reflected upon our journey that day, I truly saw what kinds of benefits the coronavirus pandemic brought upon myself as well as Gilbert. If it was not for lockdown, I am not sure whether Gilbert and I would have thought about and been motivated enough to encounter the type of journey and experience we did, and we may have simply settled for an elongated Facetime call or a car trip out in Banbury. Times throughout history, like the coronavirus pandemic, brought a lot of negativity, sadness and pain into the world, but also opened quite a few doors for all of us. The real question is, during times like these are we prepared to walk through these same doors and explore what they have in store for us?

Quote from Gilbert Healey:

> I am pleased to say Neo has inspired me so many times in my life and has, in a way, been a mentor for me from a young age, starting around the age of 13 to 14 when I was playing for Brackley Town and he was playing for Banbury Irish. There was one significant event which stuck with me while the both of us played at Banbury Irish, and this is where I saw how hungry Neo was. It was a cold Friday night of training and everyone was playing a small game and, at the end of the session, our coach Graham said, "Look around boys, look at Neo, he is the only one sweating." Because it was so cold, steam was coming off of Neo's head and body, and this was a clear representation that Neo was working hard and Graham's words made me think I needed to be like Neo and work as hard as him. I think a lot of the boys went away with this thought as well, knowing that they needed to work hard throughout training. Seeing Neo play football and playing with him definitely inspired me to work harder, on and off the ball when playing, as just by watching him everyone could see how hungry he was; and that's one thing nobody could fault about Neo. Even though everyone has their good and bad days, he always gave it 100%. Even while we were at Brackley Town, when he was released from the trials, he came back to trial for the club a year later, stronger and better, knowing to never give up."

With Gilbert on a day out at Broughton Castle in July 2020

End of Section Reader Exercises:

- Do you capitalise on moments, where you suddenly have more time on your hands, to truly reflect and try new things?
- How do you react to times when you are faced with great adversity? Do you try and make the most of the situation you are in?
- What are some of your highlights from lockdown?

SECTION FIVE

EVENTS THAT HAVE INSPIRED ME

33. My Upbringing

The environment that an individual is brought up can have a profound effect on the way they see life. If an individual is brought up with parents who love them completely and wholly, it is most likely that this individual is going to grow into a decent human being with good values and respect for other people. On the other hand, an individual who may grow up with parents who didn't seem to care much about them will most likely will turn out to become a person who finds it hard to trust others and may not hold such good values after not being given the chance to learn such values throughout their upbringing.

The type of environment that you grow and develop as a child, especially, and as a person, will always have an effect on you – either positively or negatively. Your environment has an influence on the way you think, behave and, overall, live your life. Phrases such as 'Like father, like son' and 'Like mother, like daughter' are used whenever a child, female or male, displays behaviours that are similar to their same sex parent. These are phrases that are used because people know and understand that the way that parents behave and how they are as people can have an influence on the way their children behave and the people they turn out to be. My upbringing has had a significant effect on my life and the way that I behave and perceive life. It has inspired me to become the person I am today.

Both of my parents were born and grew up in Zambia, a country in southern Africa. My father, Martin Kalungu-Banda, grew up in a village in the city of Kasama in Zambia, and my mother, Agnes Kalungu-Banda, grew up on a farm in the capital city of Zambia, Lusaka. After my parents married and had my older sister, Bobo, they found work in the UK in Oxfordshire at an international development organisation called Oxfam, and they moved to Oxford after staying in South Africa for just one year after I was born. After one year of working at Oxfam, my parents decided to move to a town called Banbury, close to Oxford, which is where we have lived ever since. My parents were still working for Oxfam during the early days of living in Banbury, but they soon found other work elsewhere. In 2007, they decided to set up their own consultancy called Talent Africa Limited, which then underwent a name change to BBS Consulting in 2012. This involved my dad, individually, doing a lot of travelling ever since I was very young. I found it extremely tough at a young age to see my father walk out of our house with a suitcase, ready to get on a plane, and I would usually be crying heavily each time he left.

Over time, I soon got used to this as I grew older and the tears began to stop falling as quickly as they used to when I was slightly younger. I was usually home with my mother, my older sister, aunty Esther, and my mother's sister who stayed with us for a couple of years before she got married. As I got older and reached my teenage years, I began to gain more of an interest in what my parents actually did for a living. When I was in year 9, I had the chance to go to Austria with my mother, father and Bobo. The aim of the trip was to have some time to go on holiday during my Easter holidays, as well as go and see and learn more about my father's work. I attended on one of the days that my father was working and doing a workshop. My mother was helping facilitate the workshop and there were many other people, all of whom were adults, attending the workshop. I remember that one of the tasks throughout the session was to use different bits of material to sculpt out what your current situation in life was, what was important in your life, what needed to be removed and, overall, anything that was going on in your life. Mine wasn't too complex at the time, it involved God, my family, my education and football. After the sculpting exercise had passed and the session was coming near to an end, each member of the session shared something about how they felt about their own sculptures and how they felt the session had gone. Some people shared their views and feelings and one person ended up shedding tears because of the emotion she felt from the workshop. When I witnessed this, I saw just how much my dad's workshop had affected her; it also showed me how influential my father could be. During the discussion at the end of the workshop, I put my hand up to share my thoughts and feelings and that I was so shocked to see the influence my father had on people and the power of his work and teaching. However, before I could get this out, my emotions got the better of me and I began to cry heavily too, due to how proud I was of my father and what I had witnessed him do.

Another time when I experienced my father in action at work was when I was in year 10 at school. I had the opportunity to go to The Hague in the Netherlands with my mother and father for a couple of days, during the school term, to see how my parents worked once again. My father was teaching leadership skills to international students at the American School of The Hague. After sitting in on one of the sessions that my father was teaching, a student came up to him at the end, shook his hand and thanked him dearly. I hadn't been that attentive as to what he was teaching in that session, all I knew was that it was to do with leadership. After I saw the student thank my dad for the lesson, I viewed my dad differently to any way I had viewed him before. I saw the type of effect he had on people through his work and his teaching, and his influence in people's lives. In that moment, I was inspired by what he did and what he was able to do – giving to people and teaching people. Seeing both of these events had a huge effect on my life and taught me more about the type of person my father was and what he did for a living.

My mother and father have worked together for a lot of their lives since they first met and even more so when they started their consultancy company. Ever since I was in year 11 or so, it became increasingly apparent to me how hard my parents worked on a daily basis. I would see them on calls a lot of the time. They would either send me texts or call me from time to time and tell me that I needed to call a taxi to either travel to school or back from school, because they would be on a work call at the time that I needed a lift. During my time in year 11 and year 12, while it was apparent to me that they worked a lot, spent a lot of time on calls and were busy every day, I didn't really understand the extent of it. Due to the fact that I was at school for most of the day during the week, I rarely ever saw what they got up to whenever I was not at home. Both my parents worked from home if they were not travelling, as their type of work allowed them to do so. Despite not always being around them and seeing them work, things such as not being able to pick me up from school because they were busy, were slowly registering in my mind and I realised they were very busy people. At times, when we left for school in the mornings, they would tell me that we needed to leave ten minutes earlier because they had to get back in time for one of their calls.

This workstyle and work ethic that my parents displayed, on a daily basis, became a lot more apparent and vivid to me when I was in year 13 and my exams got cancelled due to the coronavirus pandemic. I was at home for a full 24 hours, as opposed to being at school for close to seven hours a day. In the early days of lockdown, my parents were still working as their work occurred virtually and not much changed in regard to their lives, apart from not being able to travel any more for work. While I didn't get up to much in the first week of lockdown, as I took some rest from revising for my exams which had then been cancelled, I witnessed fully what my parents did for most of the day and that was, simply put, work! They worked from close to 7am through until 7pm every day. At times, my father would have to get up early, around 6am, because he had a call with someone who was in a time zone with a difference of over eight hours. One day, I had witnessed my mother work close to a 12-hour shift, while I waited on the sofa for the two of them to close their laptops and come and watch 'Tiger King' with me.

One day I told them that now I was not at school and could see what they get up to all day, I saw how hard they worked. They responded to my comment by chuckling. I guess it wasn't too bad for them because the work they did, and still do, is something they like and are passionate about, so even when a ten to 12-hour shift may seem like a lot of hours to be working for the lay person, for a person who is doing exactly what they want to do and enjoy it, those hours may seem like nothing. It was after I had seen what my parents did and continued to do with their lives and time, that I knew I couldn't just be sitting around all day and doing nothing myself. I knew within myself that wasting my time during lockdown, by either complaining about it or just watching Netflix and TV all day, would have been of no use. When I saw my parents work relentlessly and keep busy as they did and continue to do, it inspired me to do the same. Being in that type of environment and around such people inspires you to act in a similar way and start doing things yourself.

It is like if you are in a classroom at school and see that everyone else around you is messing around and giving the teacher a hard time , nine times out of ten you are likely to follow suit and not do your school work. On the other hand, if you are sitting in a classroom where there is complete silence and everyone is studying, you are probably going to do the same – be quiet and study. This is exactly what happened to me during lockdown, especially, but also throughout my entire life. I have always grown up and been in environments where I have seen people try, work hard and put their all into whatever it was they were doing at the time. This is what I witnessed with my parents and their work and it is what I witnessed my sister Bobo do with her education.

Within Bobo's first year at BGN, when she was in year 7, she set the tone and expectations for me well before I had even got the chance to reach double digits in age. Bobo was invited to almost every prize giving award ceremony at BGN during her five years at the school, and the only one she missed out on was when she was in year 9. Prize giving at BGN was an award ceremony that not every student would be invited to. It was only to receive an award for exceptional academic achievements, or other achievements such as representing the school through sports, or being an overall good student and role model to others. I didn't know what prize giving was before I attended BGN, but I had an opportunity to go and see one award ceremony when I accompanied my sister and parents, when Bobo got invited to be awarded a prize for her achievements throughout year 10. Once I began BGN, as Bobo waved BGN goodbye, I had my parents jokingly tell me that they looked forward to receiving the invitation for my own award at the prize giving award ceremony but, as you may have read earlier, the only invitation that I granted them from my school was to come in and discuss my internal isolations with my Head of Year. In the end, however, I did manage to give them their request of being invited to a prize giving award ceremony, it just took me five years to do so.

Bobo went on to study at an International Baccalaureate (IB) school in Oxford called St Claire's. The IB was a lot tougher than studying A-levels or taking a course at college and required students, both internationally and from England, to take more subjects than the standard three at A-level. After scoring well in her IB results, Bobo was offered a place at King's College London University (KCL) to study neuroscience, and she went on to study the subject at university. Now, being five years younger than my sister, each time she was finishing something, I was most likely just beginning that same thing. When she had left BGN and left her mark at the school, all the teachers who knew her expected me to be similar to my older sister, who had made quite an impression through her exceptional academic achievements. Despite the way that I behaved during my early secondary school days, I was always inspired by my sister to do just as well as she did in all areas of my education. It was due to the fact that she had been invited for four prize giving ceremonies that I wished to even receive an invitation for one, even if it was just for having 100%

attendance throughout the entire academic year. It was from her exceptional GCSE grades, which were all A*s, As and one B, that I aimed to get as many As as I could in my GCSEs. As she attended a Russell Group university, by the time I had applied for university in the early months of year 13, despite what my mock grades showed at the time which were not too great at all, I wished to at least be offered a place by one Russell Group university. It was all of the actions, steps and ways that my sister handled her educational life that inspired me to attempt to do almost as well with my own.

Another way that my upbringing has inspired me, is the strong bonds within my family. The four of us who live together in Banbury – my mother, father, one of my sisters and me – all tend to spend quality time together. This has always been the case while we have grown as people and as a family. We usually eat each meal of the day together, whether that is sitting around our kitchen table or sitting in front of the television in the living room. As Catholics, we usually pray together before our meals. As my sister and I have grown older, we don't always eat at the same time as each other, or at the same time as my parents, and this led to us sharing fewer meals together. However, we often do still come together as a family for meals. Over the years that my sister and I have lived under the same roof together with our parents, we usually have family discussions every now and then, or just sit together as a family in our home, and bond. No phones, no laptops, just the presence of one another. We have never really exercised as a family over the years, due to our different ages and fitness levels, but we started walking together and doing exercise together when lockdown was introduced in 2020. During the time I have spent in lockdown with my parents, I have managed to have some of the deepest and most intellectual conversations with them. This is partially due to my capacity to reflect deeply upon situations, events and concepts, and also because I am born from deep thinkers too. Periods such as this, which I have shared with my parents, are truly heart-warming and have inspired me to want to incorporate some of the same activities and practices that I experienced with my family growing up, when I have the opportunity to start my own family later in life. The family bond and strong base that has been built in my family is a bond I will treasure for my entire life and it inspires me in its power and influence on one's life and well-being.

Overall, your environment is always going to have a huge influence on the way that you live your life, behave and do things on a day-to-day basis. Mine has definitely had a large influence on the way I decide to act in life and perceive life, and it continues to do so. Many other people's environments will also tend to do the same. However, not everyone's environment is one that they feel they can grow and learn many things from. Those people who have had much tougher upbringings and have experienced more hostile environments may find inspiration within themselves to be the difference they seek, or live a different life to the one they have been brought up in, and break the cycle. Quite a few musicians, rappers especially, have had very tough upbringings which has resulted in them either having to sell drugs or steal to put food on the table for themselves and their families, but they have found inspiration from within to make something of themselves and become musicians. This has been true for musicians such as 50 Cent, P. Diddy, Jay-Z and many others.

On the extreme other end, those who are brought up in a more stable type of environment, where money and food are never an issue, may believe that they don't need to work as hard and will probably just inherit the wealth of their parents. However, these same people who do not have to work for anything and who never experience true struggle, will never be able to look back upon their own life and say that they either built something, or created something, or started that movement, or did something differently, due to the fact they simply didn't do anything with their own life when given all of the resources necessary to do anything they wanted. So, whether you grow up in a family full of riches, or an environment where getting food on the table each evening is a struggle, it is down to your own perception to view your specific circumstance and decide what you wish to do with it.

With Mum, Bobo and Dad in 2017

34. Small Things Matter

In the midst of planning and making big goals and dreams come alive, there are tiny moments, sentences, and things that have such great roles in making all of these things possible. Ever since I had my first opportunity to go on a memorable trip, either in or out of the UK, so since age nine or ten, my mother has persistently asked me to write a journal about my experiences, or write a summary of what I had seen. Because of my extremely playful nature, it was never in my interest to do either of those things, or even pick up a pen, phone or laptop, to jot down some interesting things I had either seen or learnt from my wonders. I remember, vividly, my mother would always tell me both prior to a trip and after I had returned, that I should write a summary. I did occasionally do this for her, but I only used to write one line, or a sentence or two, after going on one of the most amazing trips of my life. I would then immediately go back to playing.

From such a young age I was fortunate to receive exposure to lots of travel. In year 5 I travelled to Italy with my primary school and in year 6 we went to Wales. I visited the Camp Nou stadium in Barcelona before age 13 and had the privilege of travelling to France with my school in year 8. I travelled to so many adventurous places and, essentially, deprived my future self of reading a detailed account of these great personal experiences.

It was only 18 years into my life that I decided to take up my mother's suggestion of journaling. I only decided to start journaling due to the coronavirus pandemic. If it hadn't been for COVID-19, who knows whether I would have even thought about picking up a journal or writing this book. I do not have great motivation for journaling and writing down my experiences of an event, however, I am not too bad at writing. When I was in year 4, my primary school at the time, St John's, entered our class into a creative writing competition along with three other year groups from our school. Each year group was given the chance to write a short fictional story and the children with the best passages were going to get their stories added into a book for publication. With absolutely no memory of what I wrote and what I was writing for, I managed to get my story picked, along with the stories of a few other of my classmates. Our stories were published in a book called 'MINI SAGAS: FICTIONAL FUN' for a young writers' creative writing competition (7 to 11-year-olds) in 2011. At that age, I did not think much of this, nor did I think much of it later as I grew older, unless my parents brought it up. Upon reflection, however, this event really made me wonder whether I might have a gift for writing.

Furthermore, when I write a birthday message, or Mother's or Father's Day message for my family, on occasions, the messages I write have drawn tears from my family's eyes. There was this one time, however, when I decided to write a short review of a sad day for my Banbury Irish teammates, coaches and myself. It was the day we lost 2-0 in our Oxfordshire County Cup final in Kidlington. It was truly a distraught day for all of us, but we had done so much together and achieved so much that season, the loss we received on that day seemed like too much of a blunt cut to our successful reign. It seemed as though there were so many open wounds after the final whistle had been blown – I know that I had quite a few. So, I felt the need to write a short review of what had occurred on the day of the final and share some of my thoughts, at least partially, about the season and our successes so far, including how we managed to get to the final. I posted this short review on my Facebook page, tagging all of my teammates and my coaches. The reaction I received from my coaches, teammates and their families was truly heart-warming. It brought a tear not only to my mother's eye this time, but also to the eye of our head coach, Mr McCallum. It was then, once again, that I received recognition from my parents about my writing and was continuously praised about having a certain way with words and about my ability to write quite well.

Because each of these small things happened at different points in my life, they did not catch my attention too strongly at the time, nor did I ever get my head too caught up about any of these events. However, my mother continuously asking me to write a journal has remained in my memory up until now. It has now even encouraged me to finally start journaling and catch up with everything I missed from all of my previous experiences, to write up and gift to my future self. Having my short story chosen for the writing competition in year 4 had barely any significance to my nine-year-old self at the time, but it sure does have significance in the confidence it gives me today to believe that I am naturally quite a good writer. It gives me the confidence to believe I have what it takes to write and publish a book. Lastly, receiving praise and good feedback from people on a message you have sent, or a small piece of writing you have put together, can once again give you the push you need to believe you have what it takes to achieve something outside of your comfort zone. I was not in the top set for English at school, nor was I seen as a mastermind when it came to writing, but that doesn't matter. You do not have to be the best student in your art class to produce a painting as good as Leonardo da Vinci's famous Mona Lisa. Similarly, you do not have to be scoring the highest marks in your class during your computer science lessons to create a website or app that becomes as big as Microsoft. Therefore, I encourage you to take a look at the smaller yet finer things that occur in your life and embrace them as much as possible, for it may be those smaller things that truly play a big role in planning and achieving your goals.

Reader Exercises:

- As you reflect on the 'small things' that have occurred in your life or have been said to or about you, is there anything you feel you should potentially try out that you have not attempted before?
- Looking at what you currently do in life, are there any factors from past events which contributed, in their own small way, into helping you decide what it is that you do? If so, what are these factors?
- Is there something in life that a relative or friend has constantly told you to try, yet you say no every time? Why not try that same thing out and see what the outcome is?

35. What's in a Name?

Usually, newborn babies are given around three to five names for various reasons. The parents or caregivers of the child may have been inspired by something or someone and so may name their newborn child in celebration of whatever it is that inspired them in the first place. At times, names are chosen because the carers of a child simply like a specific type of name. My name, Neo Loongo Kalungu-Banda, is quite a unique one. People are usually quite interested in the pronunciation of my last name and find my first name extremely cool. My last name is the combination of both my father's side of the family and my mother's side. Before my parents were married, my father was known as Mr Kalungu and my mother was referred to as Miss Banda. When they got married, they agreed that they should take each other's names and this is where the name Kalungu-Banda was born – we are called the KBs for short. Loongo is my late grandfather's middle name from my mother's side. The name Neo was chosen for me by my parents and they were inspired to give me this name because of a very good friend of theirs who also goes by the name of Neo. Mr Neo Dan Moroka is my namesake. My parents decided to name me after Mr Moroka because of the way he treated them as new people in business, as well as the fact that they saw him excelling and doing well in life and they wanted the same for me. They wanted the qualities Mr Moroka had acquired to be installed within me. So, after various conversations with my parents about my name and its origins, my father suggested that I could interview Mr Moroka, who is also one of my godfathers, and ask him a few questions about our name.

Soon, I got in touch with him and organised to interview him online, via a Zoom call, on Tuesday 14th July 2020. Mr Moroka doesn't live in the UK, therefore, with or without the presence of the coronavirus pandemic, the interview still would have taken place online. I began the interview with a brief introduction about the reason I was conducting an interview with him and that the origin of my name was going to be an important part of this book. I then asked Mr Moroka my first question: "Do you know why your parents gave you the name Neo, where it comes from and what inspired them?". Mr Moroka answered, first defining what Neo actually means, being a Tswana name meaning 'gift'. He then went on to mention how his father chose the name for him. It was because he was the first son born to his parents, and his parents felt as if this was a gift to them. At the time, Mr Moroka's father, who is also Mr Moroka, was the only Moroka in the village where Mr Neo Moroka was born, and he was happy he had fathered a son, who he saw as a gift to carry on the Moroka name.

I then went on to ask Mr Moroka the question: "How has your name shaped you?". He began his answer by talking about his career in becoming a farmer. He had a vision of wanting to become a farmer in 1993 and started with farming a cattle post, a place where livestock are kept, which is commonly known in Botswana. He began with trying to drill a borehole, a deep hole that is intended to extract a natural resource, in an attempt to retrieve water. He mentioned how it was truly a struggle. Mr Moroka only managed to actually get some water after drilling his fifth borehole, and mentioned that it was costly. Unfortunately, after five years, that borehole dried up and Mr Moroka was back at square one. In 1998, he attempted to retrieve water once again from drilling boreholes and ended up drilling 29 boreholes in total. Among the 29, seven have water and, among the seven, four are low yielding. However, the other three are very strong so, finally, Mr Moroka now has a lot of water on his farm where he works as a commercial farmer.

The story of how he found his water is quite interesting. During his struggles in searching for water, Mr Moroka sighed to himself that he could not just fail in attempting to retrieve water, he had to succeed. He prayed over it for some time, hoping that God would provide for him soon. One day, he was out with a driller and something in him said there was water in a place where he was looking and he requested the driller begin to drill. He also mentioned that the water in Botswana was very deep compared to the water in other countries in southern Africa. Once the driller got to 125 metres, he said to Mr Moroka, "Mr Moroka, you are just wasting your money. The rock is very hard, it is abrasive, it is not worth it". Mr Moroka replied, "You know what, you go down to 200 metres." At 136 metres he hit the first vein of the borehole water pipe, then at 154 metres he hit the second one. Then, at 180 metres, Mr Moroka stopped him. That borehole sustained him up to the time at which I conducted the interview with him. Mr Moroka is now able to drill good boreholes and he even provides water for other people. He feels that, using his inner instinct and listening to himself is a way that his name has shaped him, and is a gift that he has received.

Mr Moroka also added that he has a high capacity to anticipate questions and that those same questions are ultimately asked. He feels that is a gift in itself. People have also described him as very analytical and he sees this as the way that his name is manifesting itself and how people perceive him. Mr Moroka finished by mentioning how he has mentored several people who have risen to prominence and he feels as if, when he reflects upon these things and looks at his name, it's not about him, but it's a gift for him to add meaning to other people's lives too.

I then changed the question slightly and asked him: "How have you shaped your name?" He replied that people may see his upcoming words as immodest but, when he looks at himself and his name, he sees 'Neo Moroka' as a brand. This is due to his past accomplishments and what he brings to the table as an individual and in his work. Mr Moroka then went on to talk to me about a time when he was negotiating a contract with an employer who asked, "Mr Moroka, why should we pay you so much money?". Mr Moroka politely replied, "You are not just paying me and hiring me, you are paying for Neo Moroka; you are paying for the brand." The employer concurred and soon Mr Moroka was employed, despite the risk of maybe coming across as immodest in his answer. However, this was not his intention nor was it his aim to be seen as arrogant. He just felt this is the way he sees his name and wants it to be portrayed, as Neo Moroka the brand.

Soon it came to my last question for Mr Moroka and I asked him: "What do you wish for people named after you?" He initially replied that, first and foremost, he wished for anyone named after him to really just be a human being. He then went on to give an example about money. Mr Moroka first mentioned that money tends to change people and that those named after him will hopefully excel and make money, but they need to remember that they are human beings like everybody else. In addition, he quoted Robert T. Kiyosaki and said that, 'Money should reveal who a person is, not what a person is.' Mr Moroka finished by stating that people who are named after him have to really look at their own character and behaviours, for if they are to deviate away from this to a darker side, when they earn money, the money would reflect who they are and may even worsen their situation and their behaviours. However, he also mentioned that, if a person's character and behaviour sustains good actions and deeds, the money will only reflect their good nature.

After the interview with Mr Moroka, we had a more leisurely conversation during which I shared with him how people usually describe me as analytical and perceptive. I also shared that I had gained some experience in mentoring during my time in year 12 and, coincidentally, we are both Manchester United fans. Moreover, after getting a broader insight into the meaning of my name and learning more about its origins, I have been inspired by Mr Moroka to excel in all I put my efforts into and make the most of everyday opportunities. I also wish to carry on the 'Neo' brand and take it to places where it can get exposure, so I can enter into different types of work, expanding the worth of my own brand. From my experiences with Mr Moroka, I would earnestly encourage each individual who has the opportunity to discover the meaning of their name and more about its origins, to do so. Whether this is through discussions with family members, or simply by doing a Google search, it could lead you to the discovery of some interesting and inspirational stories too.

36. The Gap

This book was originally supposed to be written by 21st April 2020 and released shortly after this date, as 21st April is my birthday. It was originally intended to just be a manuscript about the people who have lent a helping hand and given me inspiration in my life and it was, in a way, supposed to be a celebration of those people. I initially began writing this book shortly after the first lockdown in the UK on 23rd March 2020. At the time, I thought that I was going to be able write this book within a month and have completed it ready for printing and publishing no later than mid-May 2020. I was so confident that I was going to achieve this, having only actually written up to 2,000 words at the time, that I decided to announce to all of my Snapchat contacts that I was going to have a book about inspirational leaders published by 21st April 2020. I failed to meet my set goal and deadline drastically. I was clearly mistaken about this wild claim and ignorant of the process and time it takes to write and publish a book. I made a rookie mistake. I soon learnt my lesson though and hoped all of my Snapchat contacts who had seen that post did not remember what was written, or had any recollection of me saying I was publishing a book. Take it from my experience, it is not always the best idea to announce to people, let alone all of your contacts or followers, your intended plans, any upcoming projects you're working on and want to release or publish, or even your goals, because you simply don't know what the future holds. After the post I made about my book in March 2020 and my experiences of writing and learning, and knowing more about the process of how a book is published,

I did not make a single post about the book again and tried to keep the project as quiet as I could. I only told close family members and friends and, at times, these conversations were only for ideas.

I did actually end up finishing my writing about the people I initially intended to write about by the end of April. I knew that I did not manage to meet my set deadline, but was happy about the fact that I had just finished writing my first ever book. Or so I thought. After writing about my last inspiration, the wordcount of the book was around 10,000 words, so it seemed like it was going to be a very short book. I was content with this as I did not really have much prior knowledge and experience of authoring a book. Champ and I even thought that the book would be good if it was quite short, as it would be unique and quite different to most ordinary books. In the midst of all of this, I remained extremely excited about the fact I had written my first ever book by the age of 18 and felt very accomplished. By the end of April, I was ready to push forward to publishing it and getting it out there as soon as possible. This was a big thing for me at the time; I wanted to be able to say that I managed to publish a book at 18 years of age, so I was exceptionally keen on working hard, getting the writing done and then releasing it as soon as possible.

I had discussed with my father when the manuscript could go to the editors and where we were to go from there, after I had finished writing about the people who had inspired me in life. My father said how he was going to get in touch with the editors and find out what next steps we would take. During this time, the UK was still in lockdown and it soon came to the time when I decided to carry out 'My Locked-Down Expedition Adventure'. Now that I had finished 'writing the book', I was able to allocate more of my time to other things and my mini expedition was something that I was hoping to get the chance to do throughout lockdown. It was just a matter of deciding when the best time to do it would be. Little did I know, as I took my first steps while I walked in lockdown, I had also taken my first steps into a space that is commonly known as 'The Gap'.

Working in or from 'The Gap' is a concept that is practised in Theory U, a methodology for transforming self, organisation and society. Theory U was developed by Otto Scharmer of the Massachusetts Institute of Technology (MIT) and the Presencing Institute. The late President of South Africa, Nelson Mandela, is said to have operated from 'The Gap' each time he was faced with a crucial moment of decision making, or confronted by unusual circumstances. Mandela was a South African anti-apartheid revolutionary, political leader and philanthropist. He was also the first Black President of South Africa, and is still seen as one the greatest leaders in human history due to the way he dealt with the challenges and setbacks life threw at him. This was especially true of the manner in which he served his 27 years in prison for standing up against the evils of apartheid. One year before Mr Mandela was elected President of South Africa, there was an incident where Mr Mandela dealt with a particular situation using 'The Gap'. Mr Mandela had a fellow leader who was a freedom fighter and was also the leader of the South Africa Communist Party, who went by the name of Mr Chris Hani. Mr Hani was the political son of Mr Mandela and their relationship was far above the surface of politics. On 10th April 1993, Mr Mandela was informed, during a political meeting, that Mr Hani had been murdered by the white regime. When Mr Mandela was told about Chris Hani's murder, he stood still. Some say he was like a statue for more than five minutes. It was as if he was not breathing. Due to the death of Mr Hani, black South Africans were fired up and were ready to fight against their fellow white South Africans. Mr Mandela knew this after hearing the news. He later addressed the nation, stating that violence was not the answer in solving the issue of apartheid that many South Africans were suffering from and that the country needed to unite and rise above it. Mr Mandela also stated that violence, as a whole, needed to stop within the country, immediately. Mr Mandela's speech addressed to the nation is a speech that is said to have saved South Africa from self-destruction.

It was during that moment when Mr Mandela came to a

standstill and almost became a statue, that he got the insight into what language he needed to use in addressing his fellow countrymen and women. Upon hearing about the death of Chris Hani, Mr Mandela went into a place deep within himself before responding to the situation. Instead of reacting instinctively and instantly, as many of us tend to do during stressful times and when receiving shocking news, Mr Mandela allowed his mind to digest the information he had received and he came up with the best solution to attend to the current situation. He went into 'The Gap'. 'The Gap' is essentially a practice whereby, when presented with a stimulus, good or bad, you should allow yourself to enter a period of reflection about the situation in order to tap into another way of knowing. It is the idea of not acting instinctively or rushing into action when big or serious things have happened, and instead allowing a period of reflection to occur. I have had my own experience of entering 'The Gap' and it was actually throughout the process of writing this book.

It was before, after and during my expedition in lockdown that I entered 'The Gap', and this time that I spent there completely changed the narrative of this book. Before I embarked on my expedition, the only thing in my mind was to get my 10,000-word book out. It didn't matter to me that the book was extremely short and was more or less going to be like a brochure, the main goal was to release the book as soon as possible with the goal in mind of being an author by age 18. After my expedition was complete on Monday 18th May, it was a few days after this when a lightbulb switched on in my head. One evening, my mother, father and I were all sitting in our conservatory as the light of the evening began to slowly fade away. We were discussing my book, the things I had decided to write about and what the next steps were going to be. My father questioned me on whether I had included any experiences throughout my life where I have been an inspiration to others. I replied that I hadn't and I was not able to think about many times where I had been an inspiration to others. Then my father, with a grin in his face, sat up in his chair and began to mention some events and periods throughout my life that he thought I had been an inspiration to others. My mother also began to add her own contributions to some of the suggestions my father was making and this was the lightbulb moment.

It was as if I was being taken into an old storage room where I had all of these memories of my life, and I began to see them for what they are and could be, especially in regard to writing about them in my book. I soon asked my parents to pause while they were unleashing all of these new ideas and thoughts and I went to get a pen and paper and began taking notes of all of these ideas they had managed to come up with. It was during this discussion that the book expanded from just being about people who have inspired me, to involving places and events that have inspired me, as well as times when I have been an inspiration to others. I think it was the expedition that I carried out between Friday 15th May to Monday 18th May 2020 that had sparked these ideas that had begun to flow out of my parents' minds – my father's mind especially. I soon realised after this that I was nowhere near finished in writing my book and still had a long way to go until I could even think about sending it to the editors.

My parents gave me ideas and stories for this book that led me to writing 120,000 more words on top of my initial 10,000 words. It almost scares me that I was prepared and ready to release this book when I had only written one small part of it, feeling this was sufficient and good enough to be published. I had the idea of releasing a book by age 18 so engrossed in my mind, that it almost led to me publishing only a small section of what has been written about in this book. If it was not for me unintendedly entering into 'The Gap' and having that time away from writing, I may have ended up publishing only a quarter of what I had to share with the rest of the world, just to be able to say I released a book at a young age.

After telling Champ about what had happened with my parents and the new ideas for the book, which came after my expedition, he was fully on board with the idea. He had even said that writing my first 10,000 words about the people who had inspired me, was only the first part of the work. He said that when my parents came up with more ideas for the book, it was God's way of letting me know that I wasn't done yet and I had only just begun the journey of writing my first ever book. Champ believed that having that time away from the book and being able to connect with nature during my walking expedition was only a break from writing and God had more work for me to complete and share in my book, now that all of these new ideas had come to the surface. Furthermore, if it was not for my experience in 'The Gap', you wouldn't have read about most of the stories told in this book.

From my experiences, 'The Gap' is a space that every single individual should embrace. It is a space where innovation, creativity and great ideas are born. If given the time and practice, time in 'The Gap' can be the difference between a new company becoming locally known and gaining small profits, or developing ideas, marketing strategies and a brand that leads to the same company becoming a multi-million franchise. Time in 'The Gap' can be the difference between an individual choosing a profession that is in their best interest, or a profession they believe is in their best interest but simply turns out to be a career they hate waking up for each morning. 'The Gap' allows you the time and space to make rational decisions about a range of things. It may be that you need to make a crucial decision about your future, your profession, a project that you are working on, or how you react to news you have just been told. In any of these circumstances, and many other circumstances and decisions that are faced on a day-to-day basis, 'The Gap' is likely to be a space that is in your best interest and should be practised with an open mind.

Reader Exercises:

- Have you ever experienced times when you have entered into 'The Gap' and, if so, what was the result of this experience?
- How often do you take the time to enter into 'The Gap' when faced with various situations throughout life, good or bad?
- Are you a person who tends to respond to different situations and news instinctively and quite quickly, or are you someone who takes their time when presented with important information and serious situations? If you usually respond quickly, try taking a slower approach next time and see what is different.

37. My Duke of Edinburgh Awards

When I was a student at BGN in year 9, I decided to put myself forward for the Bronze Duke of Edinburgh Award. For those of you who do not know what the Duke of Edinburgh (DofE) Award is, it is an award in the UK which is awarded to people aged between 14 and 24. It is a voluntary, non-competitive and flexible programme of cultural and adventurous activities. It is awarded by the Duke of Edinburgh, thus its name. There are several different levels to the Duke of Edinburgh Award, and it gets progressively more challenging as you go from bronze to silver to gold. You are required to dedicate time to four different sections in the Bronze Duke of Edinburgh Award. The first is physical: you must endure two hours of exercise per fortnight for up to three months, whether this is walking, cycling, or playing a sport. The second is volunteering: you must dedicate two hours of your time per fortnight to freely volunteer in a place or organisation of your choice, without receiving any income from it, for three months. The third section is skill: you are required to dedicate two hours' practice of a new skill per fortnight, for up to three months. Each individual is also required to choose either of the three sections and do an extra three months of one of them, totalling six months. The last section is an expedition. Participants are required to have at least six hours of planned activity every day on their expedition. There is no set distance that individuals should cover, but out of these six hours, participants are likely to walk a distance of up to 16 kilometres. The expedition lasts for two days and one night, and is spent outside, camping at a campsite.

For my bronze award I did football as my physical activity, as I was playing for Banbury Irish at the time and this was quite easy to fulfil because I would usually play up to two-and-a-half hours of football per week, with one training session and one match played each week. The skill I decided to learn was cooking. For my volunteering, I asked one of my teammates from Banbury Irish whether he could ask his father if I could help coach his younger set of players for my DofE Award. My teammate's father, Garreth Aldous, kindly took me on board for three months. You are also required to have an assessor to whom you report your activities and keep updated, in order to show proof that you have completed your set hours for each section. Once I completed my Bronze Duke of Edinburgh Award, this counted as the first night I had ever camped outside for a whole night. The first time I had attempted this, was with a few friends of mine from my primary school while I was in year 6, it resulted in the six of us heading up to our friend's room who was hosting us for the evening. My Bronze DofE expedition experience is one from which I have great memories and recollection of. It was an experience that allowed me to connect more with nature, especially as phones are not allowed during the expedition. I was also able to connect more with my peers and learn more about them. This was especially true for the girl I had liked since I was in year 8. I had the opportunity to actually talk to her a lot more and find out more about her but, at the time, as well as for the majority of our secondary school days, she simply couldn't see me as as anything more than a friend. As a group of Bronze DofE students, we were fortunate enough to have completed our expedition during the summer months of the school term, so the weather was extremely nice. The expedition was carried out in Banbury and was therefore local to many of us – it was even near to the area that I live. From my experiences of earning my Bronze Duke of Edinburgh Award, I was able to make so many good and laughable memories, that I knew I definitely wanted to continue on and do the silver award.

The following year, when my classmates and I transitioned

into year 10, we were once again given the opportunity to do the DofE Award. If we had previously completed our bronze awards, we were now able to try for our awards. I was sure that I wanted to do the silver Silver Duke of Edinburgh Award and fully intended to hand in my application form. However, due to my lack of urgency with my application, I left it slightly late and ended up handing it in a day after the deadline. After handing it in a day late, the Geography teacher at my school, who was administering the award, said they were not going to accept my application. I pleaded with him and apologised for my lateness, knowing that there were still a few spaces remaining, but he didn't want to hear it. I wasn't allowed to do the Silver DofE Award and missed the opportunity, which was entirely my own fault.

Being late was something that I was known for throughout my time in secondary school. At times I was late to class along with friends of mine, late to registration, late coming out of the changing rooms during PE lessons because I was messing about with my friends, and a lot of the time I was late getting into the car to leave for school each morning with my parents. This bad habit remained with me throughout most of my secondary school years, until towards the end of year 12. Slowly, I reduced the frequency where I was late for things such as my classes, but being late in the morning was a habit that I still struggled to break. Even when my parents gave lifts to my friends Sean and Champhe each morning, they both still managed to get into the car before me and they had to walk to my house where the car was parked, whereas I only had to step out of my front door. This practice of being late came back to bite me during the experience of being rejected for the Silver DofE Award, and therefore became a practice that I no longer wanted to be good at. I highly recommend that others should not be good at being late either. So, after being rejected for the Silver DofE Award, I continued with my studies as I headed towards my final year at BGN.

After writing my exams and entering into sixth form, the opportunity of doing the Gold Duke of Edinburgh Award was announced very early on to the year 12 students. I was slightly unsure as to whether I wanted to part take in the Gold DofE Award, as my hands were already quite full with other things, such as my studies and playing football five times a week. I gave some thought to whether I wanted to partake in the award and asked my teachers for guidance on how much of my time the award would take up. I decided to go ahead with the award when I discovered that I was only required, once again, to do up to two hours of each activity of each section per fortnight, but just for a prolonged period of time. In addition, because I had not completed my Silver DofE Award, I was required to do more hours than those who had completed their Silver DofE Awards already and so had to do my physical activity for up to 12 months, my skill for nine months, and my volunteering for 12 months. This time around I stuck to playing football as my physical activity as I was doing a minimum of three hours of football per week already, which enabled me to reach my required hours of physical activity very early on. For my skill, I wasn't sure what I wanted to do, could do or learn, but, after hearing from one of my classmates who had also signed up for the award and planned to learn the guitar, a lightbulb switched on in my mind. I decided that I was going to learn how to play the piano as I did not know how to play any musical instrument.

Initially, I wanted to have lessons with the music teacher at my school, who is a great pianist, but I soon realised that it wasn't going to be possible as I did not want to pay his high rate of £15 per 30 minutes. It wasn't the fact that money was a problem at the time, it was just that I didn't want such sums of money coming out of my parents' pockets for something that I could have easily taught myself or learned another way. Therefore, I used my initiative and went to find the best pianist in the entire school, Diego Sunga. Diego is the younger brother to one of my classmates who I studied A-level Psychology with and was known as the best pianist in the entire school, having completed his Grade 8 piano by the age of 16. Diego was a year 10 student at the time I requested his free help for piano lessons and he agreed, stating that I wouldn't need to pay him a penny. I was now learning the piano for free, as opposed to paying £15 per 30 minutes, and Diego was now learning more about his own craft as he became my teacher.

For my volunteering, I decided to help Mr Aldous in coaching his (then) U12s Banbury Irish team. There was a slight twist this time around in my volunteering, however, as Mr Aldous had recruited an all-girls team and was managing girls instead of boys. It was my first time ever coaching girls in playing football and I was looking forward to the challenge of the new experience. The expedition also differed slightly from the requirements demanded from the Bronze DofE Award. In the Gold DofE Award expedition, we were required to walk for four days and sleep in tents for three nights. We were also required to carry out the expedition in far more extreme weather conditions, compared to the blazing sun of the summer when we completed the Bronze DofE Award in year 9. The terrain on which we walked also had to be a lot steeper and required us to do much more climbing for a longer period of time too. Participants in the Gold DofE Award are required to have at least eight hours each day of planned activity, while remaining outside. There were 14 of us in total and our expedition was going to be carried out on the western side of the UK, in Wales.

We were first required to do our practice expedition to get some experience of what the real expedition was going to be like. So, in April 2019, 14 of my classmates from my year group and I, as well as our four teachers, headed to the Brecon Beacons in Wales to carry out our trial expedition. We left school very early in the morning, close to 7am, as it can take a minimum of 3 hours to travel to Wales from Banbury. We had done all of our planning of our routes, the distances they would be, and had rationed our food properly between our two groups of seven students each. We were now ready to just walk and get the experience of what the Gold DofE Award had in store for us. Immediately we arrived in the Brecon Beacons we were required to walk on the first day, as the practice expedition was conducted during our Easter break and our teachers and us students wanted to maximise the time that we had at home to relax. The practice expedition lasted from 5th to 8th April and was one hell of an experience. The type of sights we were able to see were simply magical to all 28 of our eyes. The deep quality time we were able to share with one another was truly special, as there were no distractions whatsoever. We had no access to any social media or real internet. The only form of internet and service we had was on the Nokia 'brick' phone that was given to each group in case of emergencies. Put simply, we were out in the wild. The majority of the time it was the 14 of us walking together, in pairs or threes, and that was it. We were walking in mountainous land, following our set routes and maps, trying to get our set kilometres under our belts. We were fortunate that it was spring as the sun did not set as early, so even if we were outdoors and walking for seven to eight hours, we were still able to walk to our designated camping spot for the evening and sleep for the night.

As exciting and as fun as I may have described our expedition to be so far, throughout it there were countless challenges. One of the biggest challenges that I felt I faced, and maybe a few others of my classmates faced too, was when we had to walk up Pen y Fan. Pen y Fan is the highest mountain in South Wales and totals 886 metres in height above sea level. The weather was quite cold that day and the winds were very strong. As we were having to walk upwards and climb Pen y Fan, each metre we climbed up closer towards the summit, the temperature consistently dropped and the strength of the winds continued to become greater. It also began to rain, so we were walking up Pen y Fan in cold, windy and wet weather conditions. This was extreme, even for my teachers who are very outdoorsy people and had many experiences in outdoor activities such as these. The one nice thing about the walk up Pen y Fan was that we were walking where there was a glacier and land full of snow due to the cold temperature. As we continued to get closer and closer to the summit, our path towards it continued to get steeper and steeper. At one point I genuinely felt as if I was walking up a wall while making my way up Pen y Fan. I was starting to feel the lactic acid in my legs and I soon began to regret trying to walk through the just-below-knee-high snow early on. I had seen my PE teacher doing it and thought that it would be very good for the legs. Even as a footballer who had just completed a season of playing football up to five times a week and was pretty fit at the time, I was feeling the effects of walking up Pen y Fan on my body, especially my legs, which helped me get around on the pitch. The visibility was also so poor at the time that, unless we were within a 20-metre range of the summit, we couldn't actually see how far was left of our journey. We eventually came to the end of our difficult triumph when we saw the summit and heard the cheers of some of the people who had managed to reach it first. We were soon walking on ground that was a much easier terrain to handle and could see the Pen y Fan stone in the distance.

Before reaching the stone, a couple of the girls who had managed to make their way up after the boys had reached the summit began to cry, because of how hard the task was and how good they felt at having completed such a difficult task. Even the girl who was the best long-distance runner in our year group across the six years we had been at school and who had represented the school at countless athletics competitions, couldn't help but shed tears. I did not shed tears after completing walking up Pen y Fan, but I did feel that I tapped into another level of resilience. During that walk towards the summit, I truly felt the difficulty of the task that essentially was on my shoulders, having to carry a bag weighing between ten and 20 kilograms, while walking up 886 metres in the conditions that we experienced. The fact that I not once thought about quitting was truly special for me. I believe that I didn't feel as if I wanted to quit or say that I couldn't do it, because I was walking with and seeing people who I knew were probably a lot less physically fit than me, and they were simply plodding onwards towards the summit. This is where I encountered the thought that, if they could do it, I could definitely do it and, fortunately, I did. Resilience was definitely something that my Gold DofE Award practice expedition gave me more of and the experience inspired me to continue to build and grow, as I believe it did for my other classmates. That day, walking up Pen y Fan truly showed me what sort of things I was capable of achieving, and it inspired me to continue to grasp more achievements and feed into my own personal growth. It was an experience that I dearly hold close to me.

After completing our practice expedition for the Gold DofE Award, we were now prepared and ready to take on our real and assessed expedition, which took place once again in Wales, in Snowdonia this time. The expedition was conducted between 7th and 11th October 2019. We were once again required to arrive at school very early in the morning and left on the minibuses by 7am as we had the previous time. I usually sat at the front, next to the driver's seat on the minibus, with a friend of mine called Rylz who was in my group for the entire Gold DofE. We usually did this because we liked to have the full view of our journey and see every area that we crossed, especially once we arrived in Snowdonia. Our PE teacher, Mr Woodham, usually drove our minibus, which was the bus that all the boys decided they wanted to be together on. Mr Woodham was among the most liked teachers in our school, due to the way he was able to connect with the pupils and, especially, sixth formers. He treated us more like adults than school children. Once we arrived in Snowdonia, we were not required to walk on the first day as we had arrived an entire day early to get ready for our four days of walking. So, on the first day, we just arrived in camp, set up our tents and entertained ourselves. There were now only 13 of us, due to the fact that one of our classmates had decided that the Gold DofE expedition may have not been for them after the challenging experiences of our practice expedition. This person was actually from my group and this meant that our group was now down to six people, which didn't actually make much of a difference other than sharing the weight of our food rations.

So, throughout the first day of our expedition, we just chilled out at camp and conversed with one another about what was to come the following days. The weather wasn't too bad on the day that we arrived, as it wasn't raining nor was it extremely cold. The views were also quite wonderful where we had set up camp. Due to the fact that it was autumn in the UK, it was dark by around 7pm so we didn't have anything to do other than sit together inside our tents, switch on our flash lights and chat with each other, or simply go to sleep around 7pm or 8pm after we had eaten our evening meal. Doing this meant that we were fully rested and ready for the following day, as we had plenty of sleep under our belts. We were woken up the following morning by the natural light of the sky, at around 7am. We never left our tents until it was just before 8am and would normally speak with one another about what lay ahead that day, or what we had overcome the previous day. Each morning of our assessed expedition we were required to leave our campsite by 9:30am at the latest and, before this time, we had to wake up, freshen ourselves up, have our breakfast – which was usually just a couple of energy bars or some ready-made porridge – pack away our tents into our bags, slip on our walking boots and get walking. We did this religiously every morning of the four days we spent in Snowdonia.

The assessed expedition didn't feel as tough as the practice expedition, due to the fact that we had practised what it was going to feel and be like. It was definitely tougher than the practice expedition in regard to the weather conditions, as well as the distances we walked and the terrain we had to climb. However, the fact that we had prepared for it meant that it did not feel as challenging overall. Some of the highlights of the Gold DofE assessed expedition definitely included the scenery. On one of the days, I was walking with my group and, at times, I decided to set the pace and was at the front. While I was walking, deep in thought, I decided to look back to see whether I was going too fast for the rest of my group to keep up with. When I turned around, we were at quite a high point on a mountain and my classmate Giovanni was just behind me. The weather was good that day, the sun was shining and it was strangely warm for October weather in Wales. Immediately, I saw Giovanni and the backdrop of the scene that was behind him, and I felt as if I was watching a movie in that split second. I just looked at him as he was walking towards me and it genuinely looked as if I was watching some sort of 1980s Hollywood film scene being shot in the hills of Hollywood themselves, but I was also in the movie myself as I was in the same environment as Giovanni. I quickly told Giovanni about what I had thought and he said that yes, it did feel like we were watching a movie because of the scenery around us. That made sense to me. If I had seen Giovanni behind me while we were walking in our school corridors, it probably wouldn't have looked like a movie. After learning this, I truly wanted to look through the eyes of someone else in my group, so that I could also see how I looked in the movie scene environment, because Giovanni looked pretty damn cool when I turned around to look at him.

Other highlights of our expedition included the bond that I was able to experience with classmates of mine who I was not regularly that close with during school hours. Most of the pupils who completed the Gold DofE at my school were from the same friendship group. The only people who I had some sort of connection and friendship with were Giovanni and Rylz and this was mostly because we were in the same group from the beginning of the Gold DofE Award. Despite this, on both the assessed and practice expeditions, I really got to know and learn a lot more about my other 11 classmates, along with Giovanni and Rylz, especially. I was able to bond well with Rylz because we had shared the same tent for the practice expedition, as well as the assessed expedition. Rylz even taught me how to set up a tent. Giovanni and I managed to build a bond and relationship that was completely full of laughter, jokes and good energy. Anytime that we were walking together, we would always be laughing about something and cracking jokes back and forth with each other. We would joke about me wanting to just 'flag' (continue doing an activity while one is getting tired and losing energy) the entire walk and quickly rush through it, taking as few breaks as possible and walk while taking quick breaths, in and out, as if I was competing in a running race. This was not favoured among the rest of our group, as it was a group of mixed abilities and fitness, and not everyone was able to simply 'flag' five kilometres up a steep hill. We would also joke about hypothetical situations that could have happened to us as we walked, as well as joke about things to do with our school. Giovanni and I laughed so hard on the last night of our expedition, as we stood outside our tents looking up at the star filled sky, that our stomachs ached each time we chuckled or laughed the next day. This was an experience I truly enjoyed, being able to build bonds, friendships and memories with people I had not commonly had the opportunity or time to do this with before. The absence of phones also made this time all the more special and truly helped in spending quality time with one another.

My final highlight of our expedition was when we climbed up Snowdon. Snowdon is the tallest mountain in Wales, reaching up to 1,085 metres in height above sea level. Both groups were required to trek up Snowdon as our most challenging day, covering 17 kilometres in total. The climb to the summit of Snowdon was a much more enduring trek during which we really had to pace ourselves, take breaks when necessary, and look out for one another. The weather was extreme and the conditions far worse than my teachers and our assessor had expected us to face. The winds were even greater than the ones during our practice expedition, the rain was far heavier and fell a lot quicker, and the temperature was slightly lower. While we were walking, we felt warm and were able to keep walking through the extreme conditions because the physical work of having to carry our heavy bags up Snowdon was enough to keep our bodies, organs and muscles warm. Nonetheless, as soon as we stopped for a break for more than 20 seconds, we soon became extremely cold once again due to the fast-moving wind. We simply had to continue walking in order to stay warm, regardless of whether we were tired or our muscles were fatigued. We soon managed to reach the top of Snowdon, but were around 300 metres away from the summit, the peak of Snowdon. While we stood very close to the top of Snowdon, with barely any visibility around us due to the fog and fast-falling rain, we decided, in that moment, that going to the summit may not be safe due to the extreme weather conditions. Also, we had already achieved something by climbing as far as we had. A few of us, myself included, thought that because we had made it as far as we had with less than 500 metres more to reach the summit, we should have just gone for it. However, a few members of our group simply wanted to go down because the weather was far too challenging on the body.

So, as we decided to make our way down from Snowdon, without reaching the summit, the weather began to pick up even more and the temperature dropped too. The rain began to aggressively hit our faces and the wind made it difficult for us to communicate with each other unless we were within a one-metre distance of one another. I was leading the way down Snowdon, as there was only one way down and it didn't require much map reading, which I did not decide to give much practice to across the two expeditions and when we planned our routes. You may also remember from my own personal expedition, during lockdown, that map reading was not one of my natural skills. While walking down Snowdon, at one point, I thought that it was possible that I could have gotten serious hypothermia up there. The rain had soaked every inch of skin on our bodies and had filled our walking boots with water. No matter whether you had the best, most expensive waterproof gear, there was no way it would have survived the rain that was being unleashed from the sky that day. So, everyone was completely soaked from head to toe, we were extremely cold due to the strong winds, our visibility was poor, and it seemed like we were on an unending path as we couldn't see further than 30 metres ahead. I genuinely thought that, if we didn't get to lower ground in good time, something bad could have happened to any of us, especially myself as I was feeling the effects of the wind and my soaking wet clothes, which were only helping in decreasing my body temperature. After this assessment in my mind, I informed the other group members that it was crucial we got down from Snowdon as soon as possible, as on us may have gotten hypothermia.

The pace of the group still felt quite slow, as people were now tired from walking up Snowdon as well as from our previous days of walking. I felt that it was necessary to put matters into my own hands and, for my own safety, it was necessary to begin running down Snowdon. I informed the rest of my group about this decision and they understood why I felt I needed to do this, even though it seemed I was leaving my group behind, which is definitely not what I intended and is definitely not the aim of the Duke of Edinburgh Award. So, I began to run down Snowdon with my large backpack on my back, keeping my eyes open for any bits of path that may have caused to me to slip. I would run and stop for brief moments, just to check that I hadn't gone too far away from my peers and, once I saw them, I would continue jogging down the mountain. At one point I jogged on for a total of five to ten minutes before stopping when my group called my name and said they couldn't see me anymore due to the poor visibility caused by the weather. It was soon after this that we were met by our assessor, who came to check we were doing okay in the extreme weather conditions and, within a few kilometres, we managed to reach an area where the rain was no longer as forceful and where the wind had begun to slow down dramatically. It was the calm at the end of the storm.

Rylz seemed to be extremely hungry after walking down Snowdon, due to the amount of energy we had exerted after walking up and back down the mountain in the conditions we had experienced, as well as to ensure that our body temperatures didn't fall too low. Our assessor and teachers told us that the weather we experienced was not one of the criteria for our Gold DofE Award and it was incredible how we managed to get through it. Once we returned back to camp on the day of conquering Snowdon, we discovered that the other group had managed the great achievement of reaching the summit, all the way to the top. However, once they got there, a classmate of mine called Agata had actually suffered from hypothermia. Agata was only wearing two thin layers along with her waterproof jacket. Due to the weather on the day we conquered Snowdon, her thin layers got drenched and helped in reducing her body temperature. Agata later told me that, as she and her group got closer to the summit, her body temperature was continuously dropping to the point where her body was almost beginning to shut down. In order to reach the peak of Snowdon, Agata had to be helped by our teacher, who had to almost carry half of her body weight. After they came down from the summit, Agata's group had to set up a storm shelter near the café towards the top of Snowdon and the girls who were in Agata's group had to take off the wet clothes on her upper body and provide warm clothes for her out of other group members' bags. During this moment, while the wind and the rain were not making the weather conditions any better for any members of the other group, Agata was not able to speak, nor was she able to move her hands. Fortunately, our teachers and the rest of her group managed to get Agata down before her hypothermia got close to the point where she would have required hospital treatment. She had to jog down Snowdon, as I did, with one of our teachers who carried her bag for her as well as his own. Jogging and vigorous exercise on the way back down Snowdon was necessary in order to get her blood flowing normally once again. She was also given many treats to get her energy levels back up. Thankfully, Agata was fine in the end, but it was quite an experience for her, the rest of her group and our teachers. Agata described walking up and down Snowdon as the most uncomfortable task she had ever endured, especially as she knew that her body temperature was decreasing with each step she took closer to the top of the mountain. She was and still is extremely grateful to the rest of her group and their quick initiative in helping her when she was in need of assistance, and to our teachers who also showed great levels of heroism. Agata's experience and my own experience of Snowdon, and not actually dying or suffering from hypothermia, were things that inspired me once again. My Gold DofE endeavours inspired me to go and test myself at all times, and test what my body and mind are able to go up against, no matter how extreme or cold the task may be.

To conclude, my experiences in completing my Duke of Edinburgh Awards were ones that I learned a handful of skills. Learning to play the piano has been one of the greatest decisions I have made in my life so far. Coaching girls in how to improve as footballers was one of the most fun things that I looked forward to doing every fortnight. Experiencing new ways of life, new activities and new skills, were opportunities that truly enhanced my own personal growth. I have never been able to connect with nature in a more full and complete way than when I went on my DofE expeditions. I even connected with nature in a more physical way, due the fact that during Gold DofE you have no access to toilets and are required to carry a trowel and toilet paper for any time you are in need of the toilet. Once, during my practice expedition, I had a call of nature throughout the evening and needed to go just near a tree a couple of metres from the campsite during our first day. A PE teacher, who was teaching me A-level PE at the time, was walking past the same tree at the same time. As soon as I saw her, I panicked and asked her to look away, warning her that I was currently in the middle of something. She immediately looked in the opposite direction and chuckled as she walked past. I also chuckled and wanted to ensure that I had finished my meeting with nature by the time she was on her way back to camp. It was at moments like this, when I got to experience doing things such as that, that I felt so liberated, and at one with nature.

I got to experience things from my DofE awards that I had never experienced before in my life and I am grateful for every minute I got from these experiences. It is for this reason that I encourage anyone with the opportunity to do the Duke of Edinburgh awards. Most definitely put yourself forward and do it. It doesn't even have to be a Duke of Edinburgh award per se, it can be anything that is truly going to show you new ways of life, take you out of your comfort zone, and build you as a person. From my experiences, when encountering situations like these, it always turns out alright in the end.

Gold DofE group sat outside together in the Brecon Beacons on the last night of the practice expedition in April 2019

My PE teacher Mr Woodham taking a picture while we walked up Pen y Fan in April 2019

38. The Coronavirus Pandemic: Neo's Take

At the start of May 2020, I decided to start reading a book written by Yuval Noah Harari, called 'Sapiens: A Brief History of Humankind'. The book is as the title states and gives a detailed and well written account of part of the history of homo sapiens, as well as the rest of humanity, and how they came into existence. I decided to start reading 'Sapiens' as a way of keeping busy due to the lockdown that was announced in the UK on 23rd March 2020, as a result of the coronavirus pandemic that began in Wuhan, China, in 2019. I also started reading the book because reading was not one of my strengths and was an area I wished to improve upon. I wanted to read an historic book such as 'Sapiens' because, at the time that the coronavirus had managed to reach most continents of the world and begun to cause quite some havoc, I wanted to learn more about all the events that had occurred in the world and upon humans who had lived on the earth before me.

It was after my conversation with my next-door neighbour during the first week of lockdown, as described earlier in this book, that I realised a lot of things had gone on around the world before I arrived, after the second millennium. I felt a great need to learn about these events, either through watching documentaries and TV series, or through research and reading books that gave detailed and reliable accounts of events. 'Sapiens' was a book that had been lying around in the bookshelves of my home for some time. I had seen it by my father's bedside a few years before I decided to pick it up, while he was reading it. On 3rd May 2020, I decided to go downstairs and pick up two books to read simultaneously. 'Sapiens' was the first one due to my eagerness to learn more about the history of the world. I also picked up another, called 'A Rich Dad's Guide to Financial Freedom' by Robert T. Kiyosaki, because my father had wanted me to learn more about the use of money, now that I had a lot of free time on my hands because of the cancellation of my A-level exams. I didn't read the book by Robert Kiyosaki as much as I read the book written by Mr Harari.

I was hundreds of pages into 'Sapiens' far more quickly than I would have expected and discovered so many interesting things about the history of humankind. I learned what some of the first species of humans looked like and where they came from, such as Homo rudolfensis (East Africa), Homo erectus (East Asia) and Homo neanderthalensis (Europe and western Asia). I was shocked to learn that the first species of humanity originated from my native continent, Africa. I was also reminded of the fact that different species of human beings evolved to form us, Homo sapiens. It was so interesting to learn that humans just like you and me lived with another form of the human species, Homo neanderthalensis, at the same time, thousands of years ago. Can you imagine that? Living with another form of human species that would have looked, talked and walked very differently to you, but was still very similar to you, just a different species of your own kind. It would be like another human species evolving in the present day, that was five times the size of the average human being, reaching up to 8.5 metres in height. We would just be insignificant, smaller forms of human beings, that would have to avoid being stepped on by this extremely large form of humans.

Another thing that I learned about human history which was quite a shock to me, was how the food chain worked. Most humans who lived up to one million years ago, used to wait until the lions ate their prey and then wait until the hyenas and jackals ate the leftovers after the lions, and then our ancestors would eat whatever the lions, hyenas and the jackals had left. During those times, humans ate after the lions. This was a complete shock to me, because I could never imagine a world where human beings were not at the top of the food chain. This was because, at the time, things such as efficient communication between humans and fire did not exist. However, humans were still able to sustain themselves on a diet of leftovers from other main predators, who were at the top of the food chain, and would eat much smaller creatures. As time moved on, humans developed and grew in intelligence; we discovered fire and soon worked out how to jump to the top of the food chain from a position in the middle. After this, the lions ate after the humans.

Ever since human beings made their way to the top of the food chain and began to know how to work together as one for what they wanted, it was an upwards and onwards road to world domination as a species. The human species is the most dominant species above all other 8.7 million species in the world, which includes animals, plants, bacteria, and any living organism. Some may say that it was simple evolution that led to the dominance of the human race, others may argue that it was God's will for human beings to have power over the rest of the species of the world. I don't disagree with either of these claims, especially being a strong believer of Christianity. However, I believe that, at different points along the long line of our history as a species, we have crossed the line regarding how much power, dominance and authority we have over the world. It is this misuse of power that I believe led to the outbreak of the coronavirus pandemic.

There is still a debate on the origins of the coronavirus but there is one dominant theory. It has been suggested that the coronavirus originated in a species of bat called horseshoe bats. These bats are said to have transmitted the virus to other wild animals and sea animals that are sold in wet markets and the virus was passed to humans through the handling and potential consumption of these same animals in wet markets in Wuhan, China, in December 2019. This is the theory of many Chinese scientists and virus experts. The virus is believed to have developed in a bat cave. Bats have been vectors for several forms of coronavirus for up to a millennium. Most animals have been found to have many viruses, but they are usually not passed on to human beings because viruses in animals are usually specific to certain species. As bats have been known to carry many types of coronaviruses for many years, the coronavirus was not a virus that was completely new to the world, it was just new to the human species. It was bats that carried the Severe Acute Respiratory Syndrome (SARS) virus in 2002, when an outbreak happened in China as a result of consumption of bats from a wet market by humans. A wet market is a place where many animals, legal and illegal, are caged, mistreated, and killed just before they are consumed by the buyer. Animals that are sold in wet markets are usually kept in quite unhygienic places, which is what allows them to catch and develop different viruses by sharing and swapping their infected fluids with other animals kept in the same conditions, as well as the fact that they are constantly around dirt and bacteria. Wet markets are found quite commonly in different parts of Asia, China especially, with over 40,000 different markets. It is, therefore, clear to see how wet markets can pose a serious health risk.

Moving forward, past some of the worst experiences faced during the global pandemic during 2020 and into January 2021, I was watching breakfast TV on 19th January. I had seen, during the adverts, that a documentary called 'Outbreak: The virus that shook the world' was coming on ITV later at 9pm. I had remembered the time it was going to air as it seemed very intriguing and well put together. I also hoped to watch it with my parents, as we usually watch anything that is educational about the world together. During that time, the coronavirus global pandemic was still going on and the virus was still spreading. The UK was seeing its worst numbers at the time, in regard to daily deaths that were attributed to COVID-19. It may have seemed like a crazy thing to watch at the time while I was still living through the global pandemic and was yet to come out of it. I knew that I was in a much better state at the time, compared to my first reaction to lockdown in March 2020, and

I didn't feel as if I was going to unnecessarily scare myself, but watching such a documentary definitely could have given me a scare. Moreover, later in the evening, I informed my parents that I wanted the three of us to watch only the beginning of a documentary, as it was quite late and because they had also wanted to watch 'EastEnders'. I didn't tell them what I wanted us to watch, because I didn't want to frighten them into not wanting to see what the documentary had to show and say. So, I waited for 9pm to come around.

Two minutes before the start, I asked my dad whether he could change the channel to ITV1. The documentary was just beginning and we were all sitting on the sofa in the living room. I was sitting on the side of the sofa and I remained there, as I didn't think that we were going to watch this documentary for long and I would soon be upstairs again, in my room. As we got more into the documentary about the pandemic, how it began and how it escalated, we couldn't help but remain completely engaged. I soon took a seat in between my parents and got comfortable. The documentary was teaching us so much about the year that we had just experienced, in just one hour and 30 minutes. We were able to see and hear how the coronavirus originated, jumped to human beings and spread throughout the world across four continents. It almost had the atmosphere of a horror movie, considering what the entire world had faced during the year 2020. There were no jump scares, as we had all essentially taken part in this real-life horror movie and knew everything that had happened in it, but it was simply astonishing to see it on a television screen. The documentary summarised the entire start of the COVID-19 pandemic and its implications, right to the point of its broadcast in January 2021.

With 30 minutes left to go, my mother had begun to doze off on my left and my father soon realised that this was not something he wanted us to watch any longer, as we were all soon going to be preparing for sleep. Therefore, we paused it after we had watched one hour of it and had learned so much and so many covered truths. I tried persuading them, saying there were only 30 minutes left for us to watch, but they insisted that we continue watching during the day as opposed to at night and just before bed. I knew that, after this, it was very unlikely that we were going to finish watching the documentary and had even sensed this earlier on, so I pressed the record button and decided I could finish it upstairs on my own.

We hadn't reached present day in the documentary, but I had a hunch that it was going to have some positive sides to it, including the news of the vaccines being produced and rolled out globally. I went upstairs to my room, switched on the television and resumed watching from where I had left off with my parents. I managed to watch the remaining thirty minutes and, after finishing it, just sat in deep thought for a moment, thinking about the past year that humankind had faced and what the current situation of the pandemic was in January 2021. I didn't necessarily feel scared or spooked, more on the side of being educated. I did, however, feel the need to watch an episode of the nature series 'Winterwatch' to give me a sense of peace of mind before I decided to hit the hay for the night. The following morning, my parents and I got into a short discussion about the documentary, as we had throughout it the previous evening, and came up with a few points which sat with me.

We discussed the fact that the Chinese government had known about the coronavirus long before it spread to other parts of the world and had insisted that doctors and news broadcasters keep this information quiet. Many people outside of the Chinese government do not know why the Chinese government decided this was necessary and still do not understand their thought process in doing this. It is thought that the Chinese government like to show the rest of the world that they are a country which is organised and in control and, having a virus outbreak in the country that was spreading quickly would have soiled their highly visualised image as a country. Because the Chinese government decided to keep quiet about the existence and rapid spread of the coronavirus among its population, and that it was killing individuals, events such as the Chinese New Year still went ahead, which was an environment that allowed the virus to spread rapidly. I also later learned, in another documentary, '54 Days: China and the Pandemic', that when the SARS virus came around in 2002, the Chinese government tried to keep quiet about the news that SARS existed and allowed the spread of SARS to occur in China at the time, as well as the rest of the world, not reporting any cases. In fact, the government only decided to announce that SARS existed five months into the epidemic. The only compensation regarding China's atrocious actions and decision making, was that SARS had a significantly lower mortality rate than COVID-19.

Furthermore, Chinese people travelled out of China in January 2020, to countries all across the world, while the Chinese government once again decided to delay the announcement that a deadly virus existed, COVID-19 this time, and that it was transmissible from human to human. I think that the Chinese government's lack of transparency in informing their population and world leaders across the globe, was a big mistake and came at a cost that the rest of the world had to suffer. Because people from China had flown to different countries and regions of the world, the virus was now spreading among the rest of the world too. Being New Year, it was also one of the busiest times of the year. People were excited, spending time with family and friends, and in a lot of close contact with each other. At the time this wasn't a problem at all, as no one knew that the COVID-19 even existed and were clueless to the fact that the person they were standing next to could be carrying the disease and could have been transferring it to them as they spoke.

Events such as Mardi Gras went ahead in America in February, which caused mass gatherings of just under one million Americans over the days that the festival was celebrated, and this was simply a hotspot for the virus to spread among people. However, by then, the Chinese government had announced that coronavirus was a thing and that it was real and killing people, but President Donald Trump did not think it was a threat to the people of America, or so he made it seem. He constantly downplayed the virus and its severity in his speeches and rallies for the 2020 presidential elections, and pretty much made quite a significant number of Americans believe that COVID-19 was either a myth or nothing worse than seasonal flu. It was later revealed that, in early February, the time at which he was downplaying the virus, President Trump had phone calls with other members of the American government and was very aware of the severity of the virus and its highly infectious nature. Despite knowing this information, he still allowed an event such as Mardi Gras, causing mass gatherings of people, to go ahead in the US, after clearly stating during one phone call that coronavirus "is deadly stuff". His reasoning for not telling the people of America about the seriousness of the coronavirus was that he didn't want to cause panic among the country. In January 2021, America surpassed 400,000 deaths attributed to COVID-19 and had been the country with the highest number of deaths up until that point of the pandemic.

While I was watching the documentary about the global pandemic, I had witnessed the President of Brazil, Jair Bolsonaro, also completely downplay the severity of the situation. This came despite Brazil being among the top five countries throughout 2020 with the highest COVID-19-attributed death rate and, in November 2020, he preached to the people of Brazil that it was nothing to worry about, stating that it was overrated, that they were all going to die one day anyway and they shouldn't stop living their lives for the sake of a global pandemic. He even insisted that Brazil needed to stop being a country of 'sissies'. By January 2021, Brazil had over 200,000 deaths attributed to COVID-19 and was the country with the second highest death rate in the world.

The UK government took a very different approach to the rest of the world. They decided to delay lockdown, and actually insisted that the UK was very much ready for COVID-19 after hearing about it from the Chinese government in January 2020.

The Health Secretary at the time, Mr Matt Hancock, had said persistently that the UK was ready to fight the virus, that it had the correct personal protective equipment for its NHS workers, and was prepared for what the coronavirus had to bring. The UK was severely warned by countries who had already suffered the effects of the virus, such as Italy and Spain, that the world needed to take COVID-19 seriously. Despite these early warnings, the Prime Minister of Britain at the time, Boris Johnson, didn't feel the need to lockdown the country, even after seeing everything else that was going on around the world. It is believed that Mr Johnson feared the economy would suffer by locking down the country and he was worried about the education of children from all age groups. Surely the economy was not more important than the lives of British people and I am sure that the closure of schools would not have meant that children stopped learning entirely, but could have quickly converted to online learning and home schooling for a period of time in order to stop the spread of the virus. Cancelling one year of public exams didn't seem like much of a sacrifice in comparison to the potential of losing loved ones. It was for the above-mentioned reasons, as well as the science provided by UK scientists, that Mr Johnson decided to lock down the country a few weeks later than it was recommended and it is said that his lack of urgency could have resulted in the loss of an additional 15,000 British lives. All those lives lost, due to the bad decision making of one person.

When it came to around December of 2020, Mr Johnson decided that it was best for the people of Britain to enjoy a five-day Christmas period where they were able to mix with two other households, and he decided to open up different parts of the country. Britain had just come out of its second lockdown at the beginning of December, which most people barely even described as a lockdown due to its misguided, confusing and fairly relaxed rules. Once the number of COVID-19 cases and deaths began to increase in the UK once again, Mr Johnson put his tiered system into place across the entire country, which was not very effective overall, but which also resulted in many people not being able to enjoy the five days of Christmas, which had now been reduced to three days. Some were still able to enjoy the holiday restriction-lifted spree if they were in a tier that permitted this. Many people were against the three-day Christmas get together and the relaxed rules, feeling that the idea of saving Christmas was overshadowed by the pandemic. Many people had bad feelings about the impact it would have on the pandemic in the UK once the new year began. After the three days of Christmas, most regions and counties of the UK were in the highest tiered system, which reflected restrictions similar to a national lockdown. On 5th January 2021, Mr Johnson decided to place a third national lockdown on the country, due to a surge in the number of coronavirus cases and attributed deaths. Throughout 2020, the UK had the highest number of reported COVID-19 deaths in Europe and, by the end of January 2021, managed to surpass a shaming total of 100,000 deaths attributed to the pandemic.

This has been a lot of bad news, statistics and numbers for a book that is supposed to be based around inspiration, but this is simply a reflection of the sad reality we experienced. We have seen there has been a common theme in what has just been described. That common theme is poor leadership. The President of China at the time, Xi Jinping, and the Chinese government demonstrated poor leadership in the way they decided to handle the news of the coronavirus outbreak. This led to the death of thousands of Chinese people and millions of deaths around the entire world as a result of people from China unknowingly travelling to different regions of the world to spread the virus. President Donald Trump showed poor leadership and an immense level of poor judgement when he decided the best way to handle COVID-19 in America was to act as though it didn't exist and carry on with life as normal. President Jair Bolsonaro failed in leading Brazil through the pandemic by downplaying it, similarly to other world leaders, from the beginning and allowing it to take hold before he could put the necessary measures in place to fight it. Last but not least, Mr Johnson showed his inadequateness in leading the UK and

Britain, in particular, through a global pandemic through his lack of urgency in making big and crucial decisions when they needed to be made as well as his poor judgement in choosing the correct decisions during specific periods of time.

I believe, as many others do and have clearly shown, that the coronavirus pandemic could have been avoided. It could have been avoided in the first instance with a reduction in the slaughtering of live animals in wet markets and a decrease in the usage of wet markets. It could have been avoided if the Chinese government have been more transparent with the rest of the world about what had begun in December 2019 (or possibly sooner) and what it was escalating to. It could have also been dealt with a lot better overall once acknowledged by certain global leaders of some of the most powerful countries in the world, through better judgement, urgency and plain honesty. The pandemic was not dealt with in the correct manner in some parts of the world, but other countries, such as Taiwan, only had up to seven deaths by January 2021. This is attributed to their readiness for the pandemic and taking the necessary measures, early enough, to prevent catastrophe from occurring. Places such as Taiwan have suffered before from previous epidemics and therefore have experience in how to deal with them.

Also, in 2015 and through his TED Talk, Microsoft owner Mr Bill Gates had warned the world that the next war that the human race was going to face wouldn't involve guns or nuclear bombs, it would involve disease. Bill Gates had completed his research and discovered that the world was not ready for the next epidemic that was going to come. He had clearly stated that some healthcare systems in different countries around the world were simply not efficient enough or prepared to face the next disease the human population would encounter. He showed models of what a new deadly virus, transmissible through air, could do to the number of people in the human population. Bill Gates even stated that the Ebola virus, which began in 2013, was a wake-up call to the world that we needed to prepare for the next epidemic or global pandemic. Mr Gates was completely correct in the fact that the world was not ready for the next epidemic and that only a small minority of places with large populations knew what to do. Countries are supposed to regularly have training practices of what they require to fight pandemics that go on around the world. What happened to this training in countries such as China, America, Brazil and the UK? China may have known what do when locking the country down, but they surely did not know how to articulate that there was a dangerous virus on the loose.

When catastrophes such as the COVID-19 pandemic occur, it is down to the people of each nation to hold world leaders and governments accountable. Yes, everyone makes mistakes and world leaders are only human, but it is simply unacceptable to allow such poor judgement and leadership to take place during a global pandemic, resulting in the deaths of millions of people. It is unacceptable to allow the people who made schoolboy errors to get a pat on the back and be told that "it is alright". Lives were lost due to poor leadership and decision-making by these four governments. The leaders of each nation and its government members need to be held accountable for their actions, and their actions most certainly shouldn't go without being noticed, discussed, or processed further. It is because of the previous reasons described that, in future, as a species, we need to seriously consider who we vote for to be in charge of our countries, lead our nations and, ultimately, run the world. It is seriously important to consider which type of personalities and characters you would like to have in charge of your nation. You vote for them, so you decide. The people of America voted for President Donald Trump in the 2016 presidential elections, but I'm guessing they never saw President Trump having to deal with a global pandemic during his presidency. The people of Britain voted for Prime Minister Boris Johnson over Jeremy Corbyn in 2019, but I'm also guessing that those same people only thought that Mr Johnson was going to have to deliver a deal on Brexit for Britain, as opposed to having to deal with a deadly virus that he showed no knowledge or ability to deal with. It is crucial that each presidential election and government election are taken ever so seriously and are considered fully, for you never know when the next global crisis could be upon humanity.

It is due to this coronavirus pandemic that I have been inspired to be more interested in what is going on in the government of my own country, as well as the governments of other countries across the world. The pandemic has shown me that, in times of crisis, even the people at the top can make a common human mistake that can lead to complete catastrophe across the entire world. It has shown me the importance of selecting the most appropriate and best candidates for roles in governments across nations. It has also shown me that, when world leaders are not handling situations correctly or are making decisions that could lead to more destruction, they simply need to be stopped, controlled or, in some cases, even impeached (twice if necessary). People who are among the younger generations of the human race and aim to be future world leaders, need to pay close attention to some of the mistakes leaders of the older generations have made in the present day and have made with respect to the coronavirus pandemic. For no one knows what is around the corner in life and you must ensure that your main priority is to be fully prepared and ready to face it.

39. It's in the DNA

It is often thought and said that when a human offspring displays similar behaviour to that of its parent/s or goes on to do the same career as one of their parents, the cause of that behaviour or life choice is that it is built within their DNA, or it is simply 'In their blood'. Many people often like to say these types of phrases in regard to family inheritance of different skills and attributes, especially gifts. If a talented professional footballer has a son who ends up being an extremely good footballer from a young age, some will say that it is in the son's blood that he is such a talented and able footballer. Those individuals who are born from mothers who are viewed as extremely intelligent may be told that they get their brain and thinking from their mother, or the parent of the child who is deemed the most clever. There have been countless real-life examples that fit concepts such as "It is in the person's DNA" or "It is in their blood".

Take late President George Herbert Walker Bush, who was President of the United States of America between 1989 and 1993. Among his six children, his son George Walker Bush also went onto become President of the US between 2001 and 2009. Now, you can argue that this was destiny or simply luck. If we divert into sport and look at a few examples of skills, traits and career paths being a part of one's DNA, we see some evidence of this from the former professional footballer Patrick Kluivert, a Dutch legend who played for FC Barcelona. One of his three sons, called Justin Kluivert, also became a professional footballer and currently plays for a team in Germany. President of Liberia, George Weah, was a former professional footballer and footballing legend who was awarded the Ballon d'Or Award, which is an annual award regarded as the most prestigious individual award for football players. One of his two sons, Timothy Weah, also went on to become a professional footballer and is currently playing in America. Many sons of basketballers, both former and current, such as the sons of Hall of Famer Shaquille O'Neal and current NBA player LeBron James, follow in their father's footsteps. Shaqir O'Neal and Bronny James are currently basketball prodigies who are likely to be among the picks in the 2022 or 2023 NBA drafts.

From the examples mentioned, you could potentially argue that the reason why some of these people have chosen the career paths they have chosen, is simply because it was written in their DNA at birth. However, many people would argue against this wild claim due to the fact that there is barely any robust scientific evidence surrounding it to help provide any truth to this theory. Despite this, it can still be viewed as a theory and is down to individual interpretation as to whether it is true or not, or at least has some truth to it.

During a WhatsApp call with my aunty Anna, my mother's sister, in January 2021, we were discussing this book that I was still in the process of writing and she passed a theory across my mind. During our call when my Aunty Anna was telling me how proud she was of me for writing a book, she said to me, "You know, writing a book is a family business." I questioned her about what she meant by this. I initially thought that she wanted any profits that the book made shared between the entire family, due to the fact that, without the rest of them and my other family members, there would be no book. She then brought closure to my thoughts when she told me, "It is in the DNA". I asked my aunty to explain further and she went on to mention the fact that my father has written three books, one of which my immediate older sister, Bobo, helped in writing. She then told me that my grandfather, John William Banda, who I am named Loongo after, also wrote an unfinished book before he died. I knew all of this information already, because I had attended two of the book launches my father held when I was slightly younger, but also because, in 2020, I had been a part of a project to help finish my grandfather's book and had the honour of reading and editing it. This all happened during the time I was writing my own book, but it never really played on my mind too much and I never gave it much thought.

Previously, having studied A-level Biology, I knew there was definitely not a genetic link between my father or my grandfather and me in regard to writing ability. However, I did find it quite strange that it was all coming around at the same time. In February 2020, I also decided to start reading my father's first book, 'Leading Like Madiba: Leadership Lessons from Nelson Mandela', 14 years after it had been published in 2006. Since I was not much of reader, it did take until I got into my teens to finally decide to open my own father's book and read the contents inside. For some reason, however, I am happy that I read it at the time I did. It was a few months before my 18th birthday and I was at an age and maturity that enabled me to completely and fully digest the information that was going from my eyes to my brain. I even told Champ at the time that, while I was reading it, I heard my father's voice in my head and felt as if he was talking to me directly each time I opened the book.

Furthermore, little did I know that in March 2020 I was going start my own authoring journey in writing my first ever book. Initially when I began writing, it felt so organic, free, natural and healing. It also felt this way due to the fact that I was writing during the time when lockdown had begun. I would usually write in the early hours of the morning, such as 6am or 7am, and write a one thousand-word chapter in between 30 and 45 minutes. In the early stages of my writing, I was writing extremely fast and my thought process was very rapid in articulating my thoughts through to my fingers and onto a keyboard. In regard to certain thoughts and ideas that I considered on a daily basis, or that just happened to cross my mind, it felt extremely relieving to write them on paper and have them there and out of my system and my head in some form. I would still think about these same stories, events or experiences, I still do today, but, because I had made a memory of them and that memory was kept safe and secure and available to access whenever I wanted, the thought didn't pass my mind as much and I felt like I could move on from that moment in my life and on to the next. I was not completely leaving a certain memory or event in my life behind, but instead not thinking about it too deeply anymore and, in a way, reflecting about a certain period in my life with a different perspective and lots of nostalgia. It was therapeutic in a way and continued to be so.

I had never experienced anything like that at all, not in the manner that I did in my early days of writing. Once I started, I never stopped. I would continue to churn out pages and words about my life and anything that was on my mind. Initially, in the early stages of writing this book – so between March and April – when I first got my hands on the concept of writing and began the practice, I wrote about anything and everything I could and mostly anything that played on my mind that I felt needed to be moved from my head and onto paper. For those of you who have watched or read 'Harry Potter' movies or books, it was almost the same concept whereby Professor Dumbledore picked out different memories from his head with his magic wand and stored them safely for whenever he wanted to revisit them. It felt exactly like this when I wrote and, each time I read over things that I had written previously, it felt like the same concept. So, during the early stages of writing, I just explored the feeling and practice of writing my thoughts down, went crazy with it and got spikes of euphoria and a lot of relief each time I did it. Due to the fact that my typing ability and thought process all happened so quickly, majestically and as one, it felt like I had practiced and mastered this skill for many years prior.

Personally, I do not believe that things such as inheriting skills and intelligence from one's parents are biologically true. People are able to inherit physical characteristics from their parents, such as height and eye colour, but I think that is as much as an individual can biologically inherit from their mother and father. Nevertheless, I do acknowledge the fact that one's environment can have a significant impact on the skills and activities that they come to learn and enjoy, and even their career paths at times. I believe that many of those athletes mentioned earlier have been surrounded by things such as football and basketball since the time they were able to either kick a football or hold a basketball. Being exposed to something from such a young age is almost as good as incorporating a specific genetic code for a specific sport or activity in one's genes. At times, it is all that some athletes know or have known. Some athletes' first memories in life are seeing a ball, tennis racket, or even a paddling pool in the case of professional swimmers.

This concept of certain activities being in one's DNA due to the family history isn't solely tied to sports either. Some musicians have had music in their environment and playing in their ears from the time they came out of their mothers' womb, due to the fact that one of their parents is a musician. Some children who grew up to be artists were given penicils, coloured pens, paint brushes and paper from their artistic parents. In some cases, individuals have only known what it is they grow up to become or do, because their parents did the same thing and exposed them to the same career path or industry while they were still extremely young. However, one doesn't always discover one's true passion and calling in life from a young age, or after being constantly exposed to it from a young age. Some discover it years or decades into their lives and realise that their mother was a teacher, but for 20 years of their life they were always interested in becoming a lawyer and never even gave teaching a thought. After becoming a lawyer didn't work out for them, they may have decided to try out teaching law and soon discovered their true teaching passion through this less direct route. This same thing can happen with a range of activities and career paths in life and is often commonly found in many families. Whether either one or both of your parents happens to be a doctor, musician, consultant, car salesman or a banker, being open minded to at least trying out this activity will always work out to be a win-win situation, in some capacity at least. Your first win may be that you discover that what your parents do is definitely not for you and is something you never want to do and therefore you never have to think about going into that industry of work. The second win is that you discover a unique and new passion that you never thought would have pleased you in the manner that it is able to, and you embark on a new journey with a new hobby. Fortunately, I experienced the latter win of that gamble.

40. Album Mode

'Album mode' is a phrase used among musicians and many people around the world. It is the human form of airplane mode. A person in album mode does not wish to receive calls, texts, or hang out with anyone that much during this period. Their main priority is to finish the music album or music project they are working on and then celebrate afterwards. Many musicians talk about going into album mode and the experiences of being in it. Well-known artist Drake has been known for being in album mode and once, when he was working on his fifth studio album, 'Scorpion', he was challenged to a music battle. Drake responded to the music diss that he received from rapper Pusha T with his track called 'Duppy Freestyle' and stated in one of his verses 'Don't push me when I'm in album mode'. Although album mode was originally the concept of being fully focused and concentrated on a music album, it may also be a task or goal that you have set for yourself and you are doing everything within your power to achieve it. In January 2021, I had my own experience of entering into album mode, but it was actually never my intention to do this.

On Sunday 3rd January 2021, I had just finished attending an online church service with my mum and dad. After the service had finished, we all sat down in our living room as we began to prepare for the coming year, starting with the first full week of the new year which was beginning the following day on Monday 4th. My father was sitting on our long sofa with my mother and asked the both of us, "Is there anything that you need to have achieved by the end of January?" I thought about this question and replied, "Mmmm... there's not really anything that I need to necessarily get done by the end of January, but there are things that I want to achieve this year", referring to getting my book to editors and getting it published. After my reply, my father said, "You know, a year is so long", reminding me of the fact that there is so much time in a year and that it is very easy to simply waste some of this time. I let this sit with me for a minute. He then told my mother and me what he wanted to achieve and get done by the end of the month, and all he actually intended to do was plan something thoroughly that he was working on for the upcoming year.

Once he said this and I heard the idea of planning, I had a high level of realisation in my mind. I had wanted to finish writing and have all work on this book completed in 2021 and have it published, yet I had no plan for this goal. It then dawned on me that I had this huge goal, most probably the biggest goal I have ever set in my life thus far, for which I had done a lot of the hard work already, but I still had many things to do to finally reach the finish line. So, immediately after hearing my father talk about the idea of planning and actually planning a year, month-by-month, I decided to do this myself. So, that day, I set myself the goal to finish working on the book in regard to writing the remaining content, proofreading the content and doing the necessary research by 31st January. Then, on 31st January, I planned to hand the draft of the book to an editor. I had no idea whether I could reach this goal whatsoever, having never even attempted it before but, looking within myself and at my capabilities, I told myself that the least I could do was give it a go.

I wrote this goal down in my calendar and, ever since 3rd January, I just chased it. I informed Gilbert and Champ about the discussion I'd had with my parents. I talked about the realisation that, at the start of the year, while many people love to say that the year is going to be 'their' year and they are going to achieve X, Y and Z, they never actually end up doing half of the things they said they would, or they do not remain consistent in doing these things, because they haven't actually set plans. I was one of those people, in regard to never planning my goals properly. I never used to look at a new year and think about how I could tackle it and do well throughout the calendar year, because I always used to work within the timing of my school terms. So, while most people experience years from January to December, I saw my year beginning from September and finishing in July, when I completed a full academic year of school. I would then have summer and restart the year in September. I just used to work like that because I always based my successes on what I did in a school year, as opposed to an annual year.

My friends took the advice I shared with them on board. However, despite the structured and promising concept of planning, it isn't always the best method for everyone, and each individual has their own way of working. Gilbert, for instance, is a musician. His industry requires a lot of creativity from him and he isn't always creative 24/7 so, at times when he writes lyrics for songs, it is because he has a creative spark and it happens in the moment. Therefore, his line of work is a lot more flexible and doesn't necessarily involve a regimented and routine working style, which is what I was trying to incorporate into my goal. I did argue with Gilbert and stated that I understood this and I suggested that he could have a more structured month and way of managing his time to achieve his goals in music, through making the plan and goal to write four songs by the end of January, for example. That goal would have been targeted and specific and was at least a benchmark for him, as opposed to having an end of month goal along the lines of just going to write as many lyrics as he could in January. That tenuous goal would have been too vague and misguided; Gilbert could have reached the end of January having only written one or two verses. In this regard, you simply have to weigh it all up and figure out which method works for you – whether you find planning easier and more structured, or whether you're more flexible and like to go with the flow with your time and month. I soon came to realise that I was definitely a planning person.

During January 2021, Britain was in lockdown for most of the month, beginning on January 4th. I had a lot more time on my hands than I would have done if I was not under lockdown. Some of my friends who attended university still remained at their homes in our local town, such as Sean, Champ, Gwin and Jekhio, so I was able to see one of them for a walk, as outdoor exercise was allowed with one other person under the lockdown restrictions. I saw Champ here and there whenever I passed by his home and caught up with him standing outside his home, but most of the time I was just at home with my family, as everyone else in Britain most likely was. Due to the fact that I wasn't able to see any of my friends very often, I was just at home with my parents and my sister, Bobo. Time at home wasn't too bad during lockdown, as I had the book to focus on and had all the time that I needed to reach my goal of handing the book to an editor by 31st January. Despite the fact that the country was under lockdown, I still didn't feel the need to use my phone or social media that much, because I generally feel that those things waste my time. I only feel this way when I am not contacting any of my friends, family or members of the mandem and when these people are also not contacting me. My phone is just there in order for me to scroll through my contacts' Snapchat stories, WhatsApp statuses and my Facebook News Feed, and for me that wasn't of much use to my life and still isn't.

I realised that my friends and I barely talked on a day-to-day basis, because that is simply the style of relationship we have with each other. We aren't a group that messages each other every single day, nor do we message the group chat all the time; we actually only talk every so often and that can mean maybe two to three weeks without contact. Most of us like having this type of relationship, however, because it allows us to get on with our lives and do the things we want to do with our time. Whenever we do get in touch with each other and check up on how one another is doing, it is as if we never stopped talking in the first place and a week or two of our life is easily summarised and articulated to each other, either through a Facetime call or through voice notes. Having this knowledge,

I felt at the time I was only using my phone when I was bored and wanted to keep entertained.

I already knew that social media isn't the best place to allow your brain to spend time and energy and I have covered my thoughts about social media in previous chapters. So, on 7th January, I decided I would undergo a week of detoxing from social media platforms Snapchat and Facebook. I informed the 'Innovators' group chat that I am in with Gilbert and Champ and told them that if they wanted to contact me or ask me for any advice about anything they were doing or planning, they would need to use our WhatsApp group chat as opposed to our Snapchat group chat because I was going to be going on a social media 'fast' from Snapchat. So, I deleted the apps on the morning of 7th January and continued living my life. I didn't feel the need to delete WhatsApp because I have my family group chat on there, along with my contacts, and the information that I am exposed to via WhatsApp is a lot more limited than apps such as Snapchat and Facebook.

Initially, in the first week of my social media detox, I realised that I had a lot more time on my hands because I wouldn't turn to my phone during my break while completing my Psychology lectures. Instead, I would go downstairs and see how my parents were doing, or pop my head into my sister's room to see what she was up to. I also realised how dependent I was, to some extent, on apps such as Snapchat to keep me preoccupied at times whenever I was just chilling. Even though I really did not use social media as much as the average person, I realised that I missed it at times, especially if my other household members were busy. I felt a certain loneliness and craved some social interaction, which I felt I would receive if I saw what my friends were up to on their Snapchat stories. Just that one week of not having social media showed me how I was still not fully independent of it and I wasn't happy about this at all.

After the week had passed, I reflected on it and realised the advantages of not having social media. The pros were that I was so much more productive and I was able to live in each and every single moment, whether that be while I was eating food, going for a walk, spending time with family, or watching television. I also soon began to care less about what my friends and other people were up to because I was no longer being exposed to this and I was happy about that. I care for my friends and wish to check they are doing well, but I was still able to do this through sending them iMessages or WhatsApp texts. However, I didn't feel the need to see what they got up to with their time, all of the time, which allowed more of my focus to be centred towards myself and my goals for the month. I felt that the advantages of not having social media were so great that I wanted to attempt an entire month without it sometime; I was thinking maybe in February. After having this thought, I realised that potentially, I could be heading back to Leicester and that if I was at university it would be a lot harder not to have social media because events and gatherings would be going on with my flatmates and other friends of mine and it simply wouldn't work. I then realised, having still not reinstalled Snapchat and Facebook on my phone, that I could do my one-month detox from social media there and then, especially due to the fact that I only had three weeks remaining. Therefore, I did so and continued to allow the 'fast' to continue until 4th February.

During this period, I still continued to balance my university work with the work on my book. I was fortunate in that, for the first 18 days of January, I had not begun semester two of the academic year and only had to sit three open book exams in the week beginning 11th January. I wasn't sure whether I could balance the two, especially as this was the first time I had sat university exams and it was my first semester as a university student, but I attempted it. For that week, I completely prioritised my studies over the book and only worked on the book when I had finished my set hours each day of revising for each of my exams. I would still be writing content for the book, however, even during my exam week. Due to the fact that my exam was open book, I was at ease with revising and wasn't too worried about dedicating too much time to the book. After

I completed my final exam on Friday 15th January, I ended up sending all three exams on that same day, by 11pm, and looked forward to a weekend of rest from studying. After I finished my exams and entered into the remaining two weeks of January, I realised that, throughout January, I had gone into a space and mindset I had never experienced before.

Champ left for university on 17th January, Sean and Gwin had left a lot earlier and I didn't see Jekhio at all throughout January. My friends went back to their universities because some felt they would study better at university than at home, and others were simply tired of being at home. I knew that I would not be heading back to university and had to remain at home to push my book project. I was in great comfort being in my home and around my family and I knew, from the start of my Christmas holidays, that no matter what happened in regard to lockdown or no lockdown, I was going to remain at home until the end of January to work on my book and cover some real distance in the process. With the help of my parents, my father especially, I knew that the only way I could achieve what I wanted and achieve my designated goal was to remain home and get the work done with their help and assistance whenever necessary. With most of my friends gone and no social media to distract me, I was officially in album mode. I didn't know this at the time, but I soon came to realise it as the days passed.

After I began my semester two of university, I still had a lot of time on my hands because my university was being very lenient with the workload they provided for students on my course during the first week of term. I didn't even feel as if I had properly returned to university yet, it was more of an introductory week. Once I realised this, I again capitalised on my time and dedicated hours to my book and continued to make ground. As 31st January approached, I continuously planned in my head and on paper whether I had enough days left to get my intended 'to do' list completed and reach my set goal. During this time, I was doing it all. I was writing content for the book whenever an idea sparked in my head or was suggested, I was proofreading content that I had written months ago and, in the last week of January I began to do the last stage of my January programme – my research.

Throughout this time, new ideas were literally coming into my mind as I was preparing to send a draft off to my book editor. I managed to meet my editor, Jules, via a Zoom call on 21st January and this was truly a special moment for me. It felt as if I was transitioning into the next stages and processes of the book, the editing and printing stages. My father even introduced me to the person who edited this book for me stating, "Here is the author!" Once I heard this, I began to actually digest the fact that, when I finished writing and publishing this book, I would become and be known as an author. It felt crazy to hear this in my head as I had never said it out loud, or heard anyone ever say that to me until my father did during the Zoom call. Meanwhile, as I continued trying to achieve my deadline, I went into a place and an environment that my physical and spiritual being had never experienced before. In the last week of January, beginning on the 25th, I went through an evolutionary process. I realised what I had done, been doing and managed to achieve so far that month. I soon realised that each day I lived felt like 48 hours as opposed to 24 hours, due to the fact that I was doing as much in one day that, a couple months ago, I would have probably only been able to do across two days.

I realised, throughout January 2021, that I had seen the most darkest mornings I had ever seen before during winter, in one single month. I was doing hours of work that were unknown to me before I started writing this book. I was in album mode. My sole intention was to finish my work in order to hand it to my editor by 31st January, as I had stated during the Zoom call that this was my intended goal. Nothing else mattered. Not my phone, not social media, not the news. Nothing else mattered more to me during that period and those remaining seven days of January, in particular, than delivering on my promise to myself in handing the book to the editor by the end of the month. I was in a deep state of focus. However, I still lived a normal life, saw my family, my degree, and went for walks with them. I also happened to increase the amount of exercise I was doing throughout January, as I had so much free time on my hands. My world genuinely only revolved around my mental and physical health, my family, my psychology degree and my book. My world was as simple as that and made it all the more easier to produce efficient productivity on my book. I would maybe call Champ once or twice and that was to simply inform him of what was going on in my mind and my life and the changes I was going through. Most of the time, I would be so excited on a Facetime call to him because of what was happening to me, and would almost be shouting while talking with him. I realised that on some level, I was evolving.

My days consisted of waking up at 7am, working out for an hour or so, showering, and then sitting at my desk to complete my school work or, if an idea came to mind, I would have to pause my lecture to write down the idea or contents needed and then return to my lecture. I also realised, during my time in album mode, that I enjoyed my university work a lot more, due to the fact that, whenever I was working on the book, I was doing what I loved and what I was passionate about and it was an activity that didn't feel like work at all. Then, once I started my university work, it acted as a break from my focus on the book and allowed me to think in a different way and learn something different. Before, when I was in sixth form, I would need at least a two-hour break after a full day at school before I returned to studying. While at university, I could write for up to three hours, take a 30-minute break, watch my pre-recorded lectures for that week and begin to take notes. It was almost as if writing had become a hobby by then. I had a call with Champ on Saturday 30th January for any last ideas he had for me in regard to the book and, after I told him about the month I had experienced, I said to him, "I am literally in album mode." He replied, "Yeah, literally". It was a shock to me that I had undergone such a state and period in my life. In one month, I managed to achieve what would have probably taken me three months without the act of planning and goal setting.

At points during my time in album mode, I would open my

laptop screen and look at the pages and thousands of words I had managed to churn out and think, Wow, what have you done? At times, it almost felt automatic and as though it had happened so quickly and in such a short period of time. It was almost as if I stepped out of my house to go for a walk one day and ended up returning the same day, having walked 100 miles. Then only at the end of walking 100 miles is where I felt that I had decided to sit down, rest my legs and look at the path I had paved for myself.

In the end, I didn't actually hand my book to my editor by 31st January. I missed my deadline by 30 minutes and emailed it to them by 3am on 1st February. This wasn't the best of decisions because I hadn't fully completed my research and still required information and confirmation about certain stories and events from people who have been mentioned in the book. When I went to sleep that night, I didn't feel the relief that I thought I was going to feel when I handed my work to my editor. Instead, I woke up a few hours later in the early hours of 1st February, immediately informed my editor that the draft I had just sent them was not the latest version and then ended up working on the remaining minor details that still needed filling in and confirming. I was then ready, by the evening of 1st February, to hand in my first proper draft of this book after working on it throughout the day. I felt that setting my extremely aspirational goal and only missing it by a fraction was the most important part of January 2021. The idea of rushing in order to send my work to my editor as quickly as possible wasn't the aim. The whole concept of 31st January got to my head slightly and is what caused me to press the send button in the early hours of 1st February, knowing that I was sending an incomplete version of my work. The aim of setting my aspirational goal was simply to work as hard as I possibly could and realise my capabilities when given the opportunity, time and space. If I reached the goal, great. If not, I was going to learn that I needed to set slightly less ambitious goals.

January 2021 showed me another side of myself that I had not seen before, even during times in my life when I have really showed high levels of discipline and a strong work ethic, January 2021 was different. It showed me a relentless, hungry and crazily ambitious side of myself that I had never before witnessed, especially in that form. Album mode of January 2021 set the tone and benchmark for the whole of 2021. It made me think about the possibilities of doing an album mode month for every month in a year.

I saw the possibilities in my own ability and mind. It is because of these reasons and the eye-opening experience I encountered in January 2021, that I encourage each individual to attempt their own form of album mode. It doesn't have to be as draconian, such as deleting all social media apps for an entire month. It may only be for three days out of seven each week, it is entirely up to you. I just believe that, if you have a task or a project that you are working on and either want to get it complete by a certain deadline or reach a certain milestone, going into a state of album mode for a period of time that you are comfortable with, can help you to achieve a goal that you may originally have thought would take you years, in a matter of months. Elon Musk once said, "Stop being patient and start asking yourself, how do I accomplish my ten-year plan in six months? You will probably fail but you will be a lot further ahead of the person who simply accepted it was going to take ten years".

Reader Exercises:

- Have you attempted trying to achieve a goal of yours in a much shorter time frame than you originally expected yourself to complete that goal?
- Have you ever entered into your own form of album mode in order to achieve a goal? What was your experience of this and how effective did you find it in attempting to reach your set goal?
- Are there times when you have performed way above your own expectations of yourself? What factors led to this enhancement in performance and how can those

same factors contribute in helping you to obtain that level of performance again?

End of Section Reader Exercises:

- What events in your life have inspired you and how do you use these events to inspire you to achieve other things in life?
- Do you take the time to reflect upon different moments throughout your life and think about how they have had an influence on your life today?

41. Reflections from Neo: It's Not About Me

In the beginning, this book started off being about me. It was all about whether Neo could write a book and whether Neo could publish a book at 18 years old. Even though I was writing about inspirational people and leaders who have influenced my life, the main aim of my writing was to become noticed and established as a young author, and to have this book placed under my achievements. Over time, however, this changed. During my early days of writing in March 2020, whenever I would write about the inspirational people who have been mentioned, my aim was to inspire the reader as they devoured each and every single word that I wrote, especially when it came to my concluding statements about those inspirational people and how you could apply their philosophies and actions to your own life. After getting the ideas from my father to write about times where I have been an inspiration to others, as well as other places being of inspiration to me, the book continuously made its own path and began to stray further away from this concept of being about me and being about a young author publishing a book in my teens. It began to be more about the reader and people within society. I began to realise, as I read over my words, that the information, stories and events I was writing about actually had the potential to inspire people. It was after this that I realised the book was no longer just about me, it was also about the people I was writing for and trying to inspire with my writing. It was my way of contributing to humanity. I saw my own knowledge, understanding and interpretations of the world as potentially being useful to others, and felt the need to share it.

As I reflected, in the early months of 2021, I realised that the world, earth and humans are just one big system. This system includes life, food, water, accommodation, social interaction and many more things that occur in life. In this system there are millions of species, both living organisms and non-living organisms, animals and our own species, Homo sapiens. I realised that, as humans, we are all connected in some form and all work within the same system. For example, if the binmen and women in society were not around, who would take our rubbish to landfill and enable us to live in clean homes? There would be rubbish everywhere and we would be living in a very dirty world. If we did not have teachers in our schools and universities, most of us would think and behave no differently to our ancestors who lived many years ago. If there were no architects or construction workers to build our homes, then where would we all live – especially with the exponential increase in our population as a species? I realised, during my reflections, that each individual on earth has a role to play in this thing we call life. Each individual must contribute to humanity, whether they wish to or not.

Most of the time, people don't even know they are contributing to humanity on a daily basis. One contributes to humanity when representing one's school at an athletics event – the contribution is helping their school become successful in that competition. One contributes to humanity when advising the younger generations of the correct ways to live, passing on lessons about how to avoid mistakes they have made in their own life. One simply contributes to humanity by smiling at another person in the street and that same person who receives the smile goes on to have a good day and feel good about themselves and their life due to that one smile they received. People contribute to humanity and the world on a large or small scale, it is down to an individual to decide how much they want to contribute to the human family and the world.

Some of the people mentioned in this book have contributed to both my own life and to the rest of the world on an enormous scale. The reason I have chosen to write about some of the people I have mentioned in this book, is because their contributions have been so influential to millions of people, that I could only be inspired by their actions. The musicians, athletes and actors discussed in this book have brought immense entertainment to many individuals across the world, and have inspired millions just through their actions and views on life. Some of the people mentioned have served countries for close to a decade and have done it with exceptional excellence. In the case of Barak Obama, for example, I do not know what more a person can do to contribute to the world than lead the most powerful country on earth and do it with complete decency and humility. It is for this reason that I felt the need to share some of my own thoughts and views about these individuals, what they have contributed to humanity, and how many others around the world can also do the same through learning from these people – alongside some of my own little life stories.

I do hope that you have managed to gain new insights about life, the world and, most importantly, about yourself in taking the time to read this book. Lastly, I hope the stories, events, places and people mentioned can inspire you to make the contributions you wish to make to the world.

Afterword

Neo Kalungu-Banda is a remarkable young man. At this fascinating moment in our history – navigating a global pandemic, emerging out of lockdown, assimilating the trenchant criticisms of our society from Black Lives Matter a young, black man reflects on life and offers us insights to, people, places and events that have inspired him.

Surprising, unexpected, precocious, revealing, opinionated, insightful, prophetic maybe, wise even these are the thoughts of a young man making sense of his world. This is a man who from his very earliest age 'ran before he walked', and who thought nothing of playing with Leo Blair's toys when his mum took him to Number 10, Downing Street as a toddler. As he says, "Don't be afraid to take actions that seem as if you are running before you are able to walk if you truly believe you are capable of doing so. For you never know, it may be you who ends up taking the first steps that lead to great things to come."

What Neo sees, what Neo thinks, what Neo feels are important and noteworthy. Seeing the world through Neo's eyes, noting what he observes, registering what he thinks, getting a flavour for his 'lived experience' is important. If we are to rebuild our social capital after years of letting it erode, we, especially we older, privileged 'old guard', need to listen and listen well to this voice of a new generation, a voice of an alternative view.

We need to listen to Neo, listen to his generation, listen to the voices of those he represents. He himself has a small intimate group of young men, his "mandem... a slang word that originated from Caribbean English and is used popularly among most millennials around the world. It is defined as a gang or a group of male friends." If BLM means anything, it means this life matters, this person's views need to be heard, this story is significant.

The book, INSPIRED, sets out another, virtual mandem, some well known public figures – Stormzy, Will Smith, Michael Jordan, LeBron James – and some, important figures in Neo's life – his father, his hairdresser, his Year 9 science teacher.

And, just to break the exclusivity of the 'gang' – his mum, Aggie is an honorary mandem.

Neo is the product of his remarkable parents, Martin and Aggie. They certainly have inspired him to commit himself to what I can only say is a piece of prodigious productivity in writing this book. As he observes, "When I saw my parents work relentlessly and keep busy as they did and continue to do, it only inspired me to do the same. Being in that type of environment and around such people only inspires you to act in a similar way and start doing things yourself." And, as he himself reports, "Writing a book is [part of the] family business" in that he is following in his grandfather's footsteps, and his father's.

"What's in a name?" asks Neo, reflecting on why he bears the unusual name, Neo. Like many, I'm guessing my associations with the name leap immediately to the most famous Neo around, Keanu Reeves in the film 'The Matrix' – a film that predates our Neo by a few months. That Neo was confronted with a choice in the film, "Do you take the Red Pill or the Blue Pill?" Ah, that's the question! The pill of knowledge or the pill of blissful ignorance? Our Neo has chosen to be a psychologist – so, that's the Red Pill for him (same as his namesake in the film!). He's training to become an expert in human psychology, training to make people's lives better through the application of his craft, training to confront all those 'Agent Smith' clones out there who want to force-feed everyone with mind-numbing blue pills. Our Neo is not named after that Neo, he's named after his godfather, Mr Neo Moroka.

And his godfather tells him that Neo in the language of Tswana means 'gift'. His godfather also told him to think of himself as a 'brand' – when he looks at himself and his name, he sees 'Neo Moroka' as a brand. This is due to his past accomplishments and what he brings to the table as an individual and in his work. In this book, we see the 'gift' he is, and we are witnessing the birth of the bBrand, 'Neo Kalungu-Banda'.

COVID-19 and lockdowns are an indelible part of Neo's experience. Brand Neo took shape in the crucible of a global pandemic. But Brand Neo has deeper-rooted elements too, not least his firm Catholic faith. At the beginning of the first UK lockdown, Neo set himself a set of tasks, tasks that reflected his unwillingness to just languish. One of the tasks he set himself was to read Yuval Harari's 'Sapiens: A Brief History of Humankind'. As Neo writes, "I wanted to read a historic book such as 'Sapiens' because, at the time the coronavirus had managed to reach most continents of the world and began to cause quite some havoc, I wanted to learn more about all the events that occurred in the world and upon humans who lived on earth before I came." Yuval Harari, in his subsequent book, 'Homo Deus: A Brief History of Tomorrow', writes:

> *Since new twenty-first-century technologies are likely to make such fictions only more potent, understanding our future requires understanding how stories about Christ, France and Apple have gained so much power. Humans think they make history, but history actually revolves around the web of stories. The basic abilities of individual humans have not changed much since the Stone Age. But the web of stories has grown from strength to strength, thereby pushing history from the Stone Age to the Silicon Age.*

'The web of stories has grown', indeed is growing as Neo shares his story in this book. In 'Sapiens' Yuval Harari says, "Telling effective stories is not easy. The difficulty lies not in telling the story, but in convincing everyone else to believe it." Neo is trying to convince us...

Barak Obama is one of the people who has inspired Neo. Neo affirms Obama's "thoughts on masculinity. He shared his views on what it means to be a man and stated that being a man means you are reliable, respectful, hardworking and compassionate." Neo draws lessons from Obama, he writes:

> *As an individual, if you are able to adopt and display half of the humility and care for people which President Obama has displayed throughout his life, I am sure it will lead to crowds of people always wanting to be around you and in the same presence as you. Being able to use your voice and influence in a way in which leads to good and real change in the world, will only lead to you being recognised as a good leader. Lastly, having the confidence, courage and ambition to go and achieve something as big as becoming the President or Prime Minister of a country, let alone the first black leader of a nation, will only lead to an even bigger and greater legacy in your name.*

"Having the confidence, courage and ambition," says Neo, in writing this book he is certainly demonstrating all three traits. Brand Neo is being formed as he shares his observations, insights and recommendations. Eighteen years ago, another young black man set out his thoughts on lineage and legacy, Obama, speaking at the Democratic Convention in Boston in 2004 said:

> *I stand here today, grateful for the diversity of my heritage, aware that my parents' dreams live on in my two precious daughters. I stand here knowing that my story is part of the larger American story, that I owe a debt to all of those who came before me, and that in no other country on Earth is my story even possible....It's the hope of slaves sitting around a fire singing freedom songs. The hope of*

immigrants setting out for distant shores. The hope of a young naval lieutenant bravely patrolling the Mekong Delta. The hope of a mill worker's son who dares to defy the odds. The hope of a skinny kid with a funny name who believes that America has a place for him too.

Obama won because he told an optimistic story of 'a skinny kid with a funny name'. Neo may not be that skinny, but like his great cloud of witnesses, his mandem, he holds a hope. And we would all do well to fan that hope, to welcome the vision he sets out. We live in a more cynical age, but those of us who witnessed it will recall how Obama caught the imagination of a sufficient number of voters to ensure success (famously summed up by his 'Yes – we can' phrase). At the time of the primaries, we remember it being said that the possibility of the USA having its first African-American President was built upon those who had gone before. As Jay-Z said:

Rosa Parks sat so Martin Luther King could walk. Martin Luther King walked so Obama could run. Obama's running so we all can fly.

This happened, then this happened, then this happened. Why? "So we could all fly"! Neo wants us to fly.

Nick Isbister

Dr Nick Isbister is an Executive Coach and Organisational Development Consultant. He's been in business for over 25 years. He is the founder of Listening Partnership Ltd., a business that exists to harness the power of story in leadership, executive coaching and organisational development.

He's the co-author of The Story so Far: Introduction to Transformational Narrative Coaching, Story-making Leadership: A Guide *and* Organisational Stories & Leadership Sensemaking: A Guide.*References.*

References

Prologue

https://www.oxfordlearnersdictionaries.com/definition/english/inspiration#:~:text=inspiration-,noun,in%20art%2C%20music%20or%20literature

https://www.oxfordlearnersdictionaries.com/definition/english/motivation?q=motivation

CP: Neo's Take

- Yuval Noah Harari, Sapiens: A Brief History of Humankind (Vintage: 2015)
- https://www.nationalgeographic.org/encyclopedia/biodiversity/ (species no.)
- 'Outbreak: The virus that shook the world' – Documentary
- '54 Days: China and the Pandemic' – Documentary

Will Smith

- https://www.eonline.com/uk/news/732375/the-fresh-prince-feud-a-history-of-original-aunt-viv-janet-hubert-s-25-year-old-beef-with-will-smith
- https://www.the-sun.com/uncategorized/1836715/will-smith-janet-hubert-fresh-prince-red-table/#:~:text=In%20an%20interview%20with%20an,dog%20me%20in%20the%20press.
- https://www.youtube.com/watch?v=y_WoOYybCro

Africa

- https://www.sheldrickwildlifetrust.org/about/mission-history

The Pitch

- https://en.wikipedia.org/wiki/Jay-Jay_Okocha

Drake

- https://www.insider.com/drake-life-career-timeline-2018-10#he-started-writing-song-lyrics-as-a-teenager-4
- https://www.youtube.com/watch?v=Jp_yMsBHRzY&t=3092s
- https://www.youtube.com/watch?v=jQ9-JhcsDAQ&list=PLxuaaONzLc3ecLllZs4nToCl1kPQXaFv1&index=4

- https://en.wikipedia.org/wiki/List_of_most-streamed_artists_on_Spotify
- https://www.billboard.com/articles/business/chart-beat/8464292/drake-scorpion-first-album-1-billion-global-streams-one-week/
- https://languages.oup.com/google-dictionary-en/
- https://en.wikipedia.org/wiki/Giphy
- https://en.wikipedia.org/wiki/Hotline_Bling
- https://www.billboard.com/articles/news/awards/9570382/drake-billboard-artist-of-the-decade-2021-billboard-music-awards/

Michael Jordan
- The last dance Netflix series
- https://en.wikipedia.org/wiki/NBA_draft

President Obama
- https://www.youtube.com/watch?v=w28OqqTrCbA
- https://en.wikipedia.org/wiki/Barack_Obama
- https://www.nytimes.com/1990/02/06/us/first-black-elected-to-head-harvard-s-law-review.html

LeBron James
- https://en.wikipedia.org/wiki/Cleveland_sports_curse
- https://en.wikipedia.org/wiki/LeBron_James

Run Before you Walk
- https://www.webmd.com/parenting/baby/features/stages-of-development#2

Social Media
- https://www.businessofapps.com/data/most-popular-apps/

Shakespeare for schools production
- https://www.shakespeareschools.org/about-us/mission-values-ethos

Starting University
- 'https://en.wikipedia.org/wiki/GCE_Advanced_Level_(United_Kingdom)
- https://en.wikipedia.org/wiki/General_Certificate_of_Secondary_Education

Lourdes
- https://en.wikipedia.org/wiki/Bernadette_Soubirous
- https://www.usg.edu/galileo/skills/unit07/internet07_02.phtml

My DofE awards

- https://www.pkc.gov.uk/article/17414/What-is-involved-in-The-Duke-of-Edinburgh-s-Award-#:~:text=The%20Duke%20of%20Edinburgh's%20Award%20is%20a%20voluntary%2C%20non%2Dcompetitive,whatever%20their%20background%20or%20ability.
- https://members.scouts.org.uk/documents/AdultSupport/doe/fs120304.pdf

It's In the DNA

- https://en.wikipedia.org/wiki/George_H._W._Bush
- https://en.wikipedia.org/wiki/George_W._Bush
- https://en.wikipedia.org/wiki/Ballon_d'Or
- https://nbadraftroom.com/p/lebron-james-jr/
- https://nbadraftroom.com/p/shaqir-oneal/

Album Mode

- https://www.urbandictionary.com/define.php?term=Album%20Mode
- https://www.pinterest.co.uk/pin/767230486510928739/

The Mandem

- https://www.cyberdefinitions.com/definitions/MANDEM.html#:~:text=MANDEM%20is%20a%20slang%20word,in%20North%20London%20(which%20was

Perception Is Key

- https://www.google.com/search?q=perception+definition&rlz=1C5CHFA_enGB918GB918&oq=preception+def&aqs=chrome.1.69i57j0i10i433j0i10l6.3913j1j7&sourceid=chrome&ie=UTF-8
- https://www.alexander-levittfunerals.com/download/13534/BuddhistFuneralT.pdf
- https://en.wikipedia.org/wiki/Rebirth_(Buddhism)#:~:text=The%20Buddha%20and%20Rebirths,had%20been%20in%20each%20life.
- https://www.linkedin.com/pulse/20140512234002-23063390-motivation-inspiration#:~:text=So%2C%20inspiration%20is%20something%20that,be%20bothered%20getting%20things%20done.

My Upbringing

- HUSTLE HARDER, HUSTLE SMARTER – Book by Curtis Jackson (50 Cent)
- https://nypost.com/2017/06/24/how-diddy-went-from-drug-dealer-to-raps-gatsby/
- https://en.wikipedia.org/wiki/Jay-Z#:~:text=According%20to%20his%20interviews%20and,patterns%20on%20the%20kitchen%20table.

Acknowledgments

To God, thank you for holding my hand along this journey, guiding me and giving me the time, capacity, patience and all the necessary skills to write this book.

To my family, Bobo, Agnes and Martin, thank you all so much for giving your time and energy to help come up with ideas for this book and be the backbone and support I very much needed during the entire process of writing and publishing this book. Thank you all also for giving your time to read the manuscript and help me develop it.

To my editor, Jules Foreman, thank you for helping me bring this project to life and giving it its structure, flow and storyline. You have been so helpful to me when it has come to ideas and any guidance needed on 'INSPIRED'. I am forever grateful for your contributions and help.

To my brother, Gilbert, thank you for wildly telling me to write a book while we were on facetime and writing part of this book.

To my brother, Champ, thank you for writing a piece of this book and for being my right hand whenever I needed you. Thank you for helping me come up with ideas for this book, on request, and for the good energy and encouragement you gave to this project and to me each time that we spoke.

To my brothers and coach, Sean, Warren, Javah and Graham, thank you for writing part of this book.

To all the influential and inspiring people I wrote about in this book, thank you for your admiring work and huge contributions to humanity.

To all those who have contributed to this book, I am

extremely grateful for your openness, kindness and willingness to be a part of this project. A big thank you does go out to Kalusha Bwalya and Nick Isbister, in particular.

BV - #0036 - 120422 - C24 - 229/152/18 - PB - 9781914002083 - Gloss Lamination